LIFE IS LUCK

Lessons From a Paperboy and How to Improve Your Luck

John Morgan

FOUNDER, MORGAN & MORGAN

Published by Maison Vero
1619 Providence Road South, Suite 220-254
Marvin, North Carolina 28173

Inquiries may be directed to: Maison Vero, 1619 Providence Road South, Suite 220-254, Marvin, NC 28173, or info@graymilleragency.com.

For information about special discounts for bulk purchases, please call (949) 333-4872 or email info@graymilleragency.com.

Maison Vero is a partner brand of The Gray + Miller Agency, a speaking, literary, and talent consortium.

For more information on the talent represented by The Gray + Miller Agency, or to bring any of our thought leaders to your organization or live event, please visit our website at graymilleragency.com

Cover Design: Zach Sharples
Book Design: Mike Elwell

Manufactured in the United States of America

Paperback 978-1-969508-35-6   E-book 978-1-969508-36-3
Hardcover 978-1-969508-34-9

TABLE OF
CONTENTS

FOREWORD

In 2019, when my father was placed in the intensive care unit, my sister and I stayed at his bedside to hold onto every last minute with him.

A nurse came by the room and told us he had a visitor—and in walked John Morgan.

As the hospital staff panicked, tripping over themselves at the thought he was there for legal reasons, I reassured them, "Don't worry—he's a family friend." But that description felt far too simple for John. I consider him, his wife, and their children part of my extended family. He has been my boss, mentor, and friend for twenty seven years—but that hospital visit was unexpected.

He stood over my father and spoke to him as if he were conscious. He joked with him, congratulated him on outliving the average life expectancy, and told him it spoke volumes that he was surrounded by his children. Then he promised he would always watch over me.

The next day, my father passed away. I know he had peace that he could let go.

If you have been blessed to know John and have heard all his stories, you know you will never meet someone more entertaining. He is animated and diverse and the most unpredictable person I know. You leave every conversation you have with him feeling happy, filled with zingers you'll use daily, especially in business.

As I walk through the attractions I oversee, I hear his voice: "If it's a foreseeable accident, it's a winnable lawsuit." Now that's motivating!

I once asked John when he first knew he had the fire in his belly — he told me it was when he was seven years old! There was a contest to sell the most greeting cards — the winner was rewarded with a bike.

A Kentucky boy who grew up poor and wanted more… who wanted to win. How would an ambitious kid make more money back then? A newspaper route.

One day, as we were talking about his life as a paperboy with his brothers, he recalled a time when his father took their earnings while they were sleeping — and John woke up as it was happening. I asked him what he did. He said, "Nothing. What can you do? We just had to sell more."

My heart ached. Who does that to their children? But then I realized that these moments — whether good or bad — shaped him. His response was simple: work harder, do better.

Through many circumstances that no one would call luck, John built a dynasty. His brother's accident motivated him to become a lawyer, and his belief that knowledge is power propelled him to build the largest law firm in the country.

We once had someone sue us, and just a few months later, that same person was sending John's firm business. Even in the worst circumstances, something good emerged because of the way he responded. As Charles R. Swindoll once said, "Life is 10 percent what happens to you and 90 percent how you react to it." John reacts skillfully!

So what is John's response?

Absolute honesty, even if you don't want to hear it. Listen to others, because you never want to be the smartest person in the room. Don't throw stones, because we have all fallen short. Show compassion, because you never know when you'll need it.

But most importantly, fill your life with love, laughter, and unwavering loyalty.

And through these…

Life is LUCK!

Janine Vaccarello
Chief Operating Officer, *WonderWorks* and *Alcatraz East*

INTRODUCTION

Once upon a time, a long time ago, I was a paperboy in Lexington, Kentucky. As an older man now, I have often looked back at those days with my paper route and wondered what it all may have meant for my future. The longer I have been around, the more convinced I am that we all have genetic seeds planted at birth that make us who we are. In the case of the paperboy or papergirl, I believe it was an entrepreneurial seed.

The reason I have been fascinated for so long by what I call the "paperboy" or "papergirl" phenomenon is that those who had a paper route in many cases proved to be the next generation of great entrepreneurs and capitalists.

The interesting thing about the paper route and all that went with it is the tremendous responsibility young boys and girls had at such an early age. A paper route goes on every single day. Bad weather, bad dogs, or bad people—it never allows even one day's rest. If someone calls and says they didn't receive the paper, the paperboy or papergirl are immediately back on their bicycle delivering a second paper, even though the first paper may have just been stolen or damaged.

What is interesting about the paper route is the type of child who decides to own that route. In my case, we had to buy our paper routes. My grandmother went with me to the Second National Bank in Lexington, and cosigned on a very modest loan. But that loan hung over my head like the Sword of Damocles. I was hell-bent on getting that note stomped out sooner rather than later. Having debt at eleven years old is a daunting responsibility. But that responsibility brought with it great lessons that would aid me and other paperboys and papergirls into our adult lives.

As I have thought about the paperboy in my life, it has also caused me to think long and hard about how much luck plays into everything we do. One left turn, instead of one right turn, could and does make our lives totally different. Luck, both good and bad, plays an outside weight on our ultimate success. I believe luck may be responsible for 99 percent of all we do and all we achieve.

When I was in law school, one day I felt like I needed to clear my head. While I am Catholic and attend Sunday Mass, I wasn't much for daily Mass. However, that day, I decided to go to an afternoon Mass at St. Augustine's, close to the campus of the University of Florida.

Those daily Masses were not the long ordeals found on Sunday. Instead, they were a time for quiet reflection. The particular day I decided to go to afternoon Mass turned out to be one of the most fortunate days of my life. When I went into the church, it was sparsely attended. Maybe twenty people at best.

I sat in the rear of the church praying, thinking, and listening. When it came time for Communion, I stood up to get in line, and in front of me, I saw a young woman who caught my eye. After she had received Communion, she turned to walk back to her pew, and I then saw her face for the first time. I was smitten. Just plain old Wow!

I decided to do something that was very much out of my comfort zone, something I had never done before. I walked up to a total stranger at church and introduced myself. It took a lot of balls for me to do this.

When I met her, I was pleasantly surprised at the reception I received. Her personality seemed to match what I had hoped for. I asked her for her phone number and if it would be okay for me to call her sometime. She said "yes."

As it turned out, this beautiful young woman had recently graduated from the University of Florida Law School and was currently teaching legal writing to law students like me. So not only was she beautiful, but she was also very smart. She would soon be moving to Orlando to begin her legal career at a law firm called Akerman Senterfitt.

The young woman I met that day turned out to be my wife—the mother of my four children—and today we share six grandchildren and counting.

The reason I bring this story up is because I have thought about it a thousand times. What if I had not gone to Mass that afternoon? How different would my life have been had I not met Ultima that afternoon?

That makes me think about how many left turns, right turns, U-turns, or no turns have dictated the fate of my life. I have wondered whom I would have met and how much different that life would have been for me. I can't even imagine this life without my wife and our family. Yet one knee-jerk decision to walk down the street and go to Mass to clear my head and pray resulted in this life I have enjoyed.

Life is Luck

As I have thought about that chance encounter with my then-future spouse, it has also caused me to wonder about all of the other chance meetings, decisions, and just coincidental introductions that resulted in changing my life.

I have come to the conclusion that luck can be extremely helpful but at the same time severely destructive. Luck and chance play an outsized role in most everything we do. But when I discuss luck, especially with very successful people, they often want to hear none of it. We all want to be self-made, as if we did it all on our own. In this book, I plan to examine how luck plays such a vital role in life, business, politics, sports, and love.

The truth of the matter is, from the moment we are born until the day we die, there are so many variables presented to all of us, it's almost impossible to figure out who will be successful and who will not.

Just the odds of being born are next to impossible. And then once we are born, variables such as what country we are born in, who our parents are, what our race, religion, and sex are, play a disproportionate role in who and what we become.

Many people are born in one city and die in that city. That may be good and that may be bad. "Army brats" move many times during their lifetime. For many of these military kids, moving frequently was the greatest gift of all time, and for others, they had intense trauma from repeatedly getting settled only to be uprooted again. The key thing about these variables is that most of them, especially in our early years, are totally out of our control.

Whenever I say to people, "Life is luck," some are immediately offended and not receptive. The reason I believe this is true is because we desperately want to say we did this all on our own—that we are self-made men and women. The desire to succeed on our own is overwhelming.

In life, you will sometimes hear people talk about their tough childhoods; but the problem is, you knew some of those people during childhood, and it did not seem tough at all. Lots of us have the desire for our story to be that we walked to school five miles in the snow uphill each way. The narrative that we "had it bad" makes us feel much better about our success after overcoming such difficulties and obstacles. Many of us want to be more than we are, and most of us think we are more than we are. That's why when I interject the word *luck* into people's life narrative, they recoil.

But think about this. In the jungle today, a lion will be born and a sloth will be born. Neither the baby lion nor the baby sloth had anything to do with where they were born or what they are. Nature or God made that determination.

Obviously, it is safe to say most of us would rather be the lion than the sloth. It is also safe to say the lion is going to have a much better life in the jungle than the sloth. The day the lion is born, he is king of the jungle. The day a sloth is born, it is simply a sloth forever. Basically, a sloth goes up into a tree, sleeps all day, comes down, eats, defecates, and goes back up into the tree. A far different life than the king of the jungle.

The fact is the lion had absolutely nothing to do with its good luck and fortune. It simply happened. Likewise, the lazy sloth had nothing to do with the genesis of its birth or what it was. But one thing is certain: the sloth is one of the laziest animals in the animal kingdom.

Unlike lions and sloths, who have no concept of luck, good or bad, we are human with human consciousness and intellect. So we can at least recognize what we don't have any control over and what we do. Even when it's often in our nature not to do so.

Some mules have it in their nature to be very hardworking. A mule can plow a field for eight hours if it wants to. On the other hand, some mules are the most stubborn animals in the world. Good luck getting the bit and bridle around their heads, much less hooking them up to a plow.

Two mules, two different personalities, and two different lives on this earth. The hardworking mule will remain on the farm forever, until it can plow no more. The grateful farmer usually puts the old mules in a side yard where they enjoy their remaining days eating and drinking. On the other hand, the lazy mule may be found in a glue bottle in a drugstore. Farmers don't tolerate lazy, stubborn mules.

One of the interesting things I will discuss in detail are the things we can do to improve our chances of success and how we can take advantage of luck by having what I call a "return on luck"—ROL. Some people get lucky but fail to take advantage of that luck. And that is a gigantic mistake. When luck comes your way, it is important that you ride that train as long and as far as it will go.

Many of us have been in the casino watching people play craps. When the craps player is on a roll, there is nothing more electric in a casino. People gather around. They start cheering. Money starts flowing. And before that craps player is through, people are cheering for him like he is Tom Brady in the Super Bowl.

When you get on a hot streak, you need to stay on a hot streak, because those hot streaks don't come that often. I've always found it interesting that as we watch the guy at the craps table or Blackjack table, we are cheering as if they are actually doing something, when in fact, they are doing nothing. They have very little control over their success, yet we cheer them like it's Rafael Nadal in the French Open. I have actually seen people pick the winner up, put them on their shoulders, and carry them out of the casino as if they were the MVP of the NBA finals.

And the winner of that night walks around as if he is an athletic specimen who really had a lot to do with their winnings. The truth of the matter is he had very little to do with it. Now look, if you don't know the rules or what the book tells you to do in Vegas, you, of course, are going to have bad luck. If you decide to hit on 16, you are just asking for trouble.

But by and large, even if you know all the rules and what the book says to do, it is luck that carries 99 percent of your success. However, at the end of that night when that winner goes up to his room, he goes in as a champion who has really done something on the floor below. This book will examine many areas of our life and the success that comes with it. I will examine ways to improve luck, get a better return on luck, and most importantly, how to avoid bad luck.

Avoiding bad luck can almost be as important as attaining good luck. One bad deal, one bad trade, one bad idea can ruin you forever. Especially if you are a person who comes from a "burn the boats" mentality.

One of the areas I will explore is how luck can give us false confidence. That confidence can embolden us to go forward and create gigantic mistakes, because we think that we are more than we are and, in many cases, after lots of luck, actually believe we are geniuses. In that chapter, I will explore how luck can bring arrogance into your business life, and that arrogance can result in the most devastating losses you will ever suffer.

And finally, before I begin, I will also talk about the luck that never came your way, and thank God it didn't. Garth Brooks co-wrote and sang a song called "Unanswered Prayers." The song talks about a time when he longed for a certain woman to be the love of his life. However, that prayer was unanswered, and instead, another person became the love of his life. The person he prayed for would have been a disaster, and the person he hadn't even met or dreamed of became the person of his dreams. In the song he sings, "Sometimes I thank God for unanswered prayers." Those unanswered prayers, that bad luck, turns out to be the best luck.

I hope as we take this journey together you will have insights and ideas you've never thought about. In all the time I've been around, I've never read anything that talks in depth about what I will be talking about in these next chapters. But as my life has unfolded over all these years, I believe more than ever that luck and all that goes with it — good, bad, and unanswered prayers — are key. But what is most crucial is that we recognize luck for what it is — that we take advantage of luck when the opportunity arises, and we make sure our luck doesn't make us arrogant and that our own arrogance does not destroy us.

So let's roll the dice, go to chapter 1, and see how luck plays a role in your life and in your future.

BEING BORN

Of all the things in life, the most luck-dependent is the simple feat of being born. While it seems like an easy proposition, it is actually mathematically far more probable that you will never be born than that you would be born. Let me explain.

Scientists say that the odds of you being born are at least one in 400 trillion. Maybe even one in 400 quadrillion. One in 400 trillion is astonishing. It's like winning the life lottery over trillions of other different players. There is no question that if you are born, you are an extremely lucky person, along with every other human being. Considering the multitude of factors, the chance of you being a person is basically zero.

Male or Female

Once you get over the shock of how improbable it was that you and most of your family were ever born, let's talk about another factor that has had advantages and disadvantages. For most of history, being born a man has been far more fortuitous than being born a woman. Even today in countries all over the world, women are treated worse than second-class citizens. Many governments that are theocracies have a real way of keeping women down. It is abusive at best and torturous at worst.

You can go continent to continent and country to country and still see today the discrimination and mistreatment of women on a global scale. Women are not allowed to go to school, drive, or hold public office in certain societies. In the United States, a seemingly progressive country, women have suffered a long history of discrimination. It wasn't that long ago that suffragists were marching in the streets of America demanding the right to vote. Women were not considered eligible to vote for many years, and for what reasons I am unsure. But voting was just the tip of the iceberg. Also equal pay, promotions, respect, and equal opportunities have long been denied to many women in America.

The odds of being born a girl or boy are roughly fifty-fifty. All of this is pure chance. The roll of the dice.

For women, this unlucky draw has meant less pay, less upward mobility, and fewer chances to lead companies or be in high levels of decision making in the corporate world. Pay discrepancy alone is stunning.

While pay between men and women has had a wide gulf forever, even though we are now well into the twenty-first century, men still earn much more than women. The enduring grip of the gender pay gap is still with us. In 2022, the Pew Research Center found that American women typically earned eighty-two cents for every dollar earned by men. To make sure that gap is not lost on you, that means that women earned 17 percent less than men in 2022. In 2023, *Forbes* reported that when comparing women and men with the exact same job title, seniority level, and hours worked, a gender gap of 11 percent still exists in terms of take-home pay. It would seem that the concept of equal pay for equal work has not made its way to America. The difference between the earnings of men and women has barely narrowed in the U.S. in the past two decades. To make us feel better, it should be noted that South Korea has the largest gender pay gap in the world at 31.5 percent. To make us feel worse, Belgium has one of the smallest gaps at 3.4 percent. No country has yet achieved full gender-pay parity. The top nine countries—Iceland, Norway, Finland, New Zealand, Sweden, Germany, Nicaragua, Namibia, and Lithuania—have closed at least 80 percent of their gap.

It should be noted that the Equal Pay Act of 1963, which was formed pursuant to the Fair Labor Standards Act of 1938 and administered and enforced by the Equal Employment Opportunity Commission, prohibits sex-based wage discrimination between men and women in the same establishment who perform jobs that require substantially equal skill, effort, and responsibility. However, even though this is the law, that is not what happens.

There is also something known as the "pink tax." The pink tax refers to products marketed specifically toward women being more expensive than those marketed toward men. This phenomenon is often attributed to gender-based price discrimination; however, research shows that the primary cause is women sorting into goods with higher marginal costs.

So now we know that the simple act of being born is darn near impossible, and we also know that being born a man instead of a woman gives men much more financial stability and the chance for advancement. In 2023, women leaders reached a new milestone. They now lead more than 10 percent of Fortune 500 companies, including one company in the top ten. While these numbers are woefully low, it is remarkable when we consider the history of women achieving top leadership roles in business. When we get to the highest levels of business in America, women have traditionally and regularly been left out of those top positions.

What is most interesting about these statistics is that studies have shown that teams led by women tend to outperform those led by men. And companies with a higher proportion of women in leadership positions are more profitable. Because so few women were seen in senior leadership positions, there is a lack of data on how they would behave in such positions. An interesting statistic put out by the Personal Finance Club reports that the thirty-two companies on the Fortune 500 that have women as CEOs have significantly outperformed the companies run by men. Over the past ten years, the difference in returns is 384 percent from female-led companies versus 261 percent from male-led companies. A few notable companies with women CEOs at the time of this writing are GM, UPS, Citigroup, and CVS. Despite these glaring statistics and all the progress made, it is a fact that being born a girl instead of a boy has serious financial drawbacks and makes it much more likely you will not reach the highest levels of business in America. In light of the data, it makes no sense. However, the "old boys' club" is alive and well in the U.S. and around the world.

Country of Birth

Once we have been lucky enough to be born, and once our sex has been determined, there is one more significant lucky variable we need to talk about. That variable is the country you are born in. For the 8 billion people walking the earth, many were born into countries that give most of their people little hope, little opportunity, and little to be happy about. It doesn't take long for you to take a globe and spin it and look at the continents and the countries. Try doing that sometime, then look at all of the countries you would never, in a million years, want to be born in. For many, being born in that country is an awful fate. Imagine being born today in North Korea, Iraq, Afghanistan, China, or Russia. Shall I go on?

A while back, I was visiting China with my friends, Grant Hill and Jim Messina. Our tour guide, Lucy, was wonderful. But in having private conversations with her, it was obvious her life was horrible. Standing in Tiananmen Square, I asked her how many people had been killed during the uprising. She looked like she had seen a ghost, covered her head, and said, "No, no, no. Be careful." I had no idea what she was talking about, but I shut my mouth.

Later, when we were having lunch out in the country, I asked her why she reacted that way. She informed us that some of the tourists were actually police, and talking about the uprising in Tiananmen Square could result in serious punishment for her. Her fear was palpable.

That visit to China made me appreciate being born in the U.S. I have now been many places around the world. I can state with certainty that there is almost no place where I would rather be born in and live.

Europe has some neat countries and some great history, but as an American, I'd miss ice and air conditioning.

The entire trip to China for me was very depressing because of the desperation that hung over this vast and powerful country.

Where we are born will, in large part, define our lives, and the happiness and joy that will come with that life—simply by being born in a specific place at a specific time. And none of us had anything to do with being born or where we were born. It was all just pure luck.

By almost all accounts, the U.S. is the richest country in the world. According to Investopedia, it makes up 23.93 percent of the total global economy. According to data from *Forbes*, the U.S. has the highest number of billionaires in the world, with a total of 724. This is followed by China with 698, and India with 237.

Africa is the poorest continent on Earth. The competition is not particularly close. Economic insecurity, political instability, corruption, civil wars, and terrorist insurrections have left millions of Africans living in abject poverty.

When we look at the most impoverished countries in the world, the top five are from Sub-Saharan Africa. Countries such as Somalia, South Sudan, Sierra Leone, Malawi, and Central African Republic make up some of the poorest pockets in the world. Being born there is certainly the opposite of winning the lottery when it comes to lifestyle and upward mobility.

But, of course, happiness is not totally defined by wealth or even economic security. Something must be going well in the Nordic countries, because Denmark came in at No. 2 and was followed next by Iceland in a happiness rating.

According to Frank Martela, a Finnish philosopher and psychology researcher, many of the reasons the Finnish people are so happy is because they don't compare themselves to their neighbors, don't overlook the benefits of nature, and don't break the community circle of trust. Martela told CNBC News, "Focus on what makes you happy and less on looking successful. The first step to true happiness is to set your own standards, instead of comparing yourself to others."

This happiness report and its findings reminded me of a quote I have used to steady myself throughout my life.

"Comparison is the thief of joy."

No truer words were ever said. Much of our unhappiness in life comes from focusing on what we don't have and what others do have, rather than being grateful for our blessings (also known as luck).

When taken altogether — that you are born at all, what sex you are, where you are born — there is a lot to be digested.

All these chances came to you without any effort of your own. We simply landed where we are. Once we land, that only begins our long journey, which will be full of left and right turns and coin tosses that will determine whether we win or whether we lose.

CHAPTER 2

WHO'S YOUR DADDY?

Parents Matter

Once we have navigated being born, the country we are born in, and our sex designation, the next big moment is whom we are lucky enough to have as our parents—or the alternative, whom we are unlucky enough to have as parents.

I live much of the year in Florida, where schools designate ranking by letter grades A, B, C, D, and F. I'm not exactly sure about how the designation comes to be, but when I see the schools and read the grades, they seem to be accurate.

As the father of four children, I have had the distinct pleasure of supervising homework, overseeing school projects, and attending the many extracurricular activities concerning my children's schooling. I can say without reservation that the most stressful times of my life revolved around my children's grades, their test scores for college and graduate school, and where they ultimately went to college. It is far more stressful than anything my wife and I did for ourselves.

I still have post-traumatic stress disorder from the nights trying to get my fourth-grade child to memorize their ten spelling words for the next day's test. Unfortunately for my children, math and science were not my strong suit. If I had not had Chuck Morgan sitting next to me in algebra in the tenth grade, and if I did not have great eyesight, I think I would still be sitting in tenth-grade algebra. There became a time where I was of little help to my children in certain studies. Luckily for my children, their mother was a National Merit Scholar and Phi Beta Kappa. I often think what would have happened to my poor children's educational options had their mother not been there to do science, math, and many other complicated subjects with them.

Literacy and Parenting

Just to demonstrate how parents can play such an important role in the education of their children, we need look no further than some key statistics. First, the average American adult reads at the seventh- to eighth-grade level, according to The Literacy Project. Furthermore, nearly 130 million American adults read below a sixth-grade level. That number represents more than half of the U.S. population, according to the Department of Education.

Americans' literacy rates vary; four in five adults (79 percent) have English literacy skills sufficient to "complete tasks that require comparing and contrasting information, paraphrasing, or making low-level inferences," according to the Program for the International Assessment of Adult Competencies. This is equivalent to scoring at a Level 2 literacy rate or above. At the same time, one in five adults (22 percent) in the U.S. has difficulty completing these same tasks. Nearly a quarter of Americans have low literacy skills.

The Education Department found that the national average literacy score is 264. Minnesota and New Hampshire have the highest literacy scores of any state at 279. On the other hand, Louisiana, Mississippi, and New Mexico have the lowest average scores at 252.

With math, it's not much better. Seventy percent of American adults could perform elementary-level math tasks that were "explicit or visual with relatively few distractors," like whole numbers, percents, fractions, and interpreting simple tables and graphs. But nearly 30 percent performed at the lowest two levels, meaning they were comfortable only with very basic arithmetic, counting, sorting, and similar tasks.

Many parents in the U.S. are ill-equipped to help their children with basic homework centered around math, reading, and science. With every passing grade, it becomes more and more difficult for parents with this level of reading and math skills to be any help at all. I confess here that once my children got into certain math and science classes in middle school and high school, I was little or no help. Even parents who are not smart or have not learned these skills still want their children to excel. Thus, the explosion of learning and tutoring centers.

I've observed that schools ranked with an A-grade seem to have parents and PTA organizations that are A-parents and A-organizations. Likewise, the schools that receive an F also tend to have F-parents. What makes an A-parent and what makes an F-parent?

In my estimation, it all comes down to parental oversight, concern, and understanding of how important school and education are to their children's future. There are many children, kindergarten through twelfth grade, who routinely have no parental supervision whatsoever when it comes to schoolwork. The lack of supervision is because the parents don't care or they can't help (or both), which is a very unlucky circumstance for that child.

With our children, we were constantly monitoring tests, grades, report cards, and conduct. I was paying more attention to my children's grades than I was to my own business. Think of the advantage my children had compared to kids in the same class who had parents who didn't care, or who couldn't help if they wanted to and who didn't have the money for private tutors. The child's parent, simply put, is a game changer.

Now the roll of the dice for whom your parents are is simply that: the roll of the dice. None of us have any control over who our parents are, but how the dice turn up has a dramatic impact on who we are, what we are, and how successful we may become.

On a personal level, I can share that I had two parents who had little oversight over the five of us. We had two alcoholic parents, our mother ultimately deserted us, and neither was paying attention to our studies. This is where luck can also play a key role. Even though we had this parental deficit, somehow the five of us were able to muddle our way through on our own accord and with our own internal ambitions and drive. When people who knew our family learned what became of us, they were absolutely shocked. I went on to law school, two brothers became dentists, our sister became a clinical psychologist, and my brother, Tim—who was paralyzed in a diving accident at the age of eighteen—worked in my law firm as his career. It makes no sense that we dodged the bad-parent bullet, but we did. I'm not here to say that parents can solely be responsible for their children's success and education, but I will suggest that it is much better to have active and caring parents.

One of the factors in my childhood was watching my father. He drank too much and was fired often. When I would walk up to the house and see his car in the driveway in the middle of the afternoon, I would get a sinking feeling because I knew he had been fired again. It was the worst feeling in the world because I knew that chaos would ensue.

Usually, my dad would be sitting at the kitchen table, in his stocking feet, with the want ads spread out in front of him. He would say something to us that rang in our ears for the rest of our lives: "Whatever you do, be a professional—nobody can fire you." It defined us. My dad's bad luck—being an alcoholic and being fired—turned into good luck for me, my brothers, and my sister.

Location. Location. Location

When my father finally lost all the jobs he could get in Kentucky, we moved to Florida. I was devastated. I had to leave my grandmother, who was my only source of stability, and all of my friends. I cried all the way to the airport for my first plane ride to our new home.

We moved into a much worse house in a shoddy neighborhood. Devastation does not begin to explain how I felt. Looking back, however, there turned out to be a silver lining. Where we moved to—Winter Park—turned out to have some of the best schools in the state and in the country. I went to Maitland Junior High School and Winter Park High School, and I got a tremendous education. I was then able to attend the University of Florida and continue my education. The bad luck of being forced to leave my family and friends in Lexington turned out to be incredibly good luck by placing me in schools that allowed me to learn and thrive. Many times in my life, I have looked back at my friends and family in Kentucky and then at my life today. I have often wondered what would have become of me had I not been forced to move to Florida.

The move changed everything for me, my three brothers, and my sister. The bad luck of my dad's alcoholism and loss of jobs turned out to be the best luck for my siblings and me, as we were placed in a city with world-class schools.

Parents Who Choose to Be Parents

I once read a book titled *Freakonomics* by Steven Levitt and Stephen Dubner. It is a fascinating book with a lot of takes on probabilities and events. For example, *Roe v. Wade* was decided in 1973. During the next years, the children born in 1973 grew up and became adults. Eighteen years later, in roughly 1991, the crime rate in America started plummeting and continued to plummet for years.

What had happened, according to the authors of *Freakonomics*, was that the law allowed women who did not want to have a child to have an abortion instead. Consequently, a significant number of unwanted children were never born, and thus never had the opportunity to be raised in homes that were sometimes crack dens at best and hellholes at worst. These unwanted children, who would not have been properly supervised, never had the opportunity to commit the crimes that may have come from a terrible childhood.

It was jarring to read this statistic. But it made perfect sense. Wanted children are loved, nurtured, and taught. Unwanted children are not supervised, are not taught and, in most cases, raise themselves. Terrible homes are breeding grounds for future criminals. With legal abortions, many of these unwanted children were never born and never had the opportunity to be bad.

I know it sounds harsh when put that way, but the numbers don't lie. My wife, for ten years, was the lawyer for Florida's Right to Life. She did that work pro bono. I, on the other hand, am pro-choice and believe in a woman's right to control her own body. The two of us have disagreed over the issue of abortion and a woman's right to choose. But one thing we don't disagree about is the crime that results from unwanted children being unsupervised. It is interesting that the pro-life supporters do so little to provide safety nets for these unwanted children. But the numbers don't lie, and the crime rate fell precipitously.

In 2022, the U.S. Supreme Court overturned *Roe v. Wade* with the *Dobbs v. Jackson Women's Health Organization* decision. I would like you to remember that decision in eighteen years, in 2040, and the years preceding that year. My prediction is that the crime rate will once again begin to rise dramatically in America.

This theory regarding the effect of legalized abortion on crime (often referred to as the Donohue-Levitt hypothesis) is controversial. Proponents of abortion argue that the availability of abortion resulted in fewer births of children at the highest risk of committing crime. The authors of a study published in 2001, "The Impact of Legalized Abortion on Crime," by Steven Levitt of the University of Chicago and John Donohue of Yale University, cited their research in earlier studies and argued that children who are unwanted, or whose parents cannot support them, are likelier to become criminals.

Critics have argued that the Donohue-Levitt methodologies are flawed and that their study does not prove any statistically significant relationship between abortion and later crime rates.

Dubner and Levitt have fended off criticism since they published *Freakonomics*. Who is right and who is wrong? Who knows? It sure makes sense to me. An unwanted child, left to their own devices, is much more at risk than a wanted child. However, my brothers, sister, and I were raised like wolves, and everything worked out.

Good Parents Pay Attention

I think one thing we all can agree on is that good parents have a better chance of having good kids, because good parents pay attention. Kids unsupervised and unwatched have a greater chance of developing bad habits and getting into trouble.

When I was a little boy, I used to see other people's parents and wished that I had a similar home life. Meals were on time. Vacations were taken. Discipline was administered. Homework was a must. I remember going into these homes and seeing these moms and dads, and wondering what that must feel like and how much I wished I were there. On the other hand, the way I was built and programmed made me very driven and hell-bent on being successful.

When I was ten years old, I went to the dentist. I had a toothache on a top-right molar. While sitting in the dental chair, I heard the dentist tell my dad that there were two ways to fix my tooth. He said he could do a root canal or pull it. My father asked how much it would cost for the root canal—$50. He then asked how much it would cost to have the tooth pulled,—$5. Immediately, I heard my dad say, "I guess we have to pull the tooth."

I was dumbstruck. I did not want to lose a permanent tooth. I knew what that meant. But five minutes later, my tooth was gone, and gauze was sticking out of the side of my mouth. I knew then and there that I was going to have to take care of myself.

When I got into the car, I took the cotton out and it felt like the dentist had pulled three teeth. I couldn't believe it. When I walked into the house, I saw my siblings looking at me and they sure felt sorry for me. But I felt sorrier for myself.

However, that bad luck turned out to be some of the greatest luck in my life. I resolved that day, and I remember it like it was yesterday, that I would never rely on anyone but myself for things I needed. Within a few weeks, I was out looking at paper routes and ultimately bought a big route from the Mobley twins. From that day forward, I always had a box filled with money. My green tackle box that I kept my paper-route earnings in was stuffed to the brim. Never was I going to rely on my mom or dad for something as vital as a tooth. That paper route gave me a work ethic and taught me so many valuable lessons that have stayed with me for all of my life. In the next chapter, I will talk about the paperboy and papergirl, and how I believe a seed is planted in some of us that gives us a great head start in life. That seed becomes the blueprint for a successful life because of the lessons learned as a paperboy.

So now we are born. We have been assigned our country and sex. And now luck has handed us our parents. We didn't choose them, and they didn't necessarily choose us. But one thing is for certain: we are with them, usually, for the long haul. And those parents will play an outsized role in our futures and our success. It is all based on pure luck and chance.

CHAPTER 3

THE PAPERBOY

This book is in large part made possible by my years, long ago, as a paperboy. The paperboy is the genesis of this book. Before I was a paperboy, I was a young hustler. I worked for the Cheerful Card Company, selling Christmas cards when I was seven. I shoveled snow, mowed grass, and raked leaves, depending on the season. Having and making money was an obsession of mine. As life went on, I often wondered why I had been so obsessed with monetary success.

My circumstances taught me at an early age that I would need to make my own way. My mother started drinking heavily when I was around eight, and she ultimately left the family. Unfortunately, my dad had trouble holding jobs due to his own issues with alcoholism.

So there we were, five children basically on our own. I often felt like we were raising ourselves. I have never felt sorry for myself or thought I got a raw deal. Just the opposite. At every stage in my life, including the early years, I had an absolute ball. When I look back, objectively, and see me and my siblings, I shudder. But at the time, it was our normal, and we made the best out of it.

Whether I would have ever owned a paper route without my early experiences I don't know. The money I had made up until that point was sporadic—mowing, raking, shoveling snow, and selling Christmas cards. But the day I had a permanent tooth pulled, I knew I was on my own. I made the decision then and there that in case of emergencies in the future, I was going to have a say in my destiny.

When I Started My Route

I bought the route and thus began my entrepreneurial career. I was a businessman, and I was ready to expand my business. I'd had lemonade stands, sold candy and gum at school, mowed lawns and shoveled sidewalks, but this was a permanent solution. This was a real business that operated every single day, and with it came enormous responsibilities.

The interesting thing about the paper route in the past is that children throughout America were largely responsible for bringing adults their news. Whether it be through a route or standing on a street corner, the paperboy or papergirl played a vital role in bringing news to America.

As I have watched newspapers crumble with the advent of the Internet, the loss of physical papers has meant the loss of paperboys and papergirls.

Then, somehow, somewhere, adults started delivering papers, and the paperboy was no more. When I would see adults delivering papers, I used to wonder why they were doing it and not working at a full-time job. With a big enough route, we could make pretty good money. At the peak, my route netted my brother, Mike, and me around $300 a month, which we shared. At the time, this was a small fortune in Lexington. I always had a roll of cash and was ready to buy a round for my friends at the local Dairy Queen.

One of the reasons I think there may have been a decline in home deliveries is because there is no paperboy. When a young person comes to your door and asks if you're willing to buy a magazine, a newspaper, or Girl Scout cookies, it's hard to say no to that young entrepreneur. All of us are impressed when we see a young person out there getting on with life. It charges our own batteries.

I firmly believe that if paperboys and papergirls still had routes, newspaper circulation would be much higher. I know for a fact that I buy lots of Girl Scout cookies, even though I don't want or need any of them. When that little face is standing in my doorway asking me to buy cookies, I can't refuse. I believe it would be the same for newspapers today. We like the idea of helping people build their own dreams.

As time has gone on, newspapers delivered to the house have become almost nonexistent. Even today, this former paperboy reads all his newspapers on a tablet. I held out for *The New York Times* Sunday edition, but I finally decided that was too much hassle and the ink ran on my hands.

Newspapers Launched My Entrepreneurial Life

As my life progressed, I became a serial entrepreneur. There was something about business and making money that consumed me. I read get-rich books, self-help books, and books on great entrepreneurs and leaders. I couldn't get enough. From time to time, I would think about my days as a paperboy and what all that meant in my evolution as a businessman and an entrepreneur.

In life, I met successful people, and they would tell me their stories. I was fascinated with people who started with nothing and created businesses with real value. I loved those stories. They gave me hope, inspiration, and drive.

Many times, when these folks would finish their stories, I would ask a simple question: "Were you ever a paperboy?" Almost every time I asked, the person looked at me strangely, and answered, "Yes, I was. Why?"

After a while, I would tell them. For years, as I studied successful people, I began to believe that success had a lot to do with predetermined luck. That predetermined luck was an entrepreneurial seed that had been with those people since they were children.

We would have the greatest conversations about our respective routes and all that went with it. Former paperboys and papergirls love talking about their routes. The stories and adventures are irresistible. Mostly, though, we are proud that at that age, we were responsible enough to handle such a hard job. Rain, sleet, and snow — seven days a week — we were on the job.

Many times, after these conversations with former paperboys and papergirls, I would receive an email following up on our discussions and sharing more about our days with our routes. Many years later, I feel that my hypothesis that certain people are born with certain business genes is more likely true than not, and that those business genes are some of the luckiest luck anyone could possess. That seed, coupled with the seed of drive, is hard to beat.

- Warren Buffett was a paperboy. His father was a successful stockbroker and U.S. congressman from Nebraska. Buffett didn't become a paperboy because his family didn't have money; he became a paperboy because he had a desire to control his destiny. I believe that most paperboys and papergirls grew up with a strong desire to control their own destinies. Even though the route was unforgiving and constant, it was worth it for control and security.

- Martin Luther King Jr. was a paperboy for *The Atlanta Journal-Constitution*. What better preparation for the long years ahead — the struggles, the fights, and the battles. While King's childhood experiences didn't lead him to entrepreneurship, they did lead him to leadership, passion, and hard work.

- Tom Cruise was a paperboy. On top of being one of the great actors of all time, Cruise is a serial entrepreneur. He controls his movies and his destiny. Just being the No. 1 box-office attraction in the world was not enough for Cruise. Control was what was most important.

- The supermodel Kathy Ireland was a papergirl. She was, and still is, one of the most beautiful women and models in the world. I remember the first time I saw her in *Sports Illustrated*. She was perfect. But underneath that beautiful exterior lived a burning interior with a lot of get-up-and-go. After modeling, Ireland built successful careers in fashion and cosmetics, and now has a staggering net worth.

- Bob Hope, the great entertainer, was a paperboy. Being out there on the paper route gave him lots of moments and lots of laughs. It had to be a great training ground for him.

- Joe Biden was a paperboy. What better way to prepare him for the long and arduous journey of becoming a U.S. senator at age twenty-nine, and the president of the United States in his late seventies?

- Walt Disney, one of my heroes, was a paperboy. When I first found that out, I was not surprised at all. Walt had many gifts at birth. He was a creative genius and an artist who knew how to tell a great story. Then he wanted his stories to come alive, so he did the impossible. He built theme parks where guests could ride his fantasies and movies. If you read the story of Walt and Roy Disney, you will understand that building those theme parks was a tremendous undertaking. Walt was the dreamer and Roy was the realist. Roy was consistently trying to rein Walt in, to no avail. The former paperboy was hell-bent on doing the impossible and making his vision real. No doubt his years as a paperboy prepared him for ups and downs, and to have the ability to persevere when others might quit.

When you start going through the annals of great American success stories, in many cases, you will find a paperboy or papergirl leading that company. The lessons learned out on the paper route were very transferable in business and in any successful life. As a paperboy, I had to sell the customer. I had to perform top-notch service every day with a friendly face. I had to collect their money, then pay the bank, or whoever loaned me the money. I was running a very sophisticated business, for a child. But every successful paperboy and papergirl was born under a lucky star. The young child who kept their route had the ability and drive to be a paperboy or papergirl, and learned the skills to build a great business and a successful life.

I never had an implant placed where my permanent tooth was removed. Over time, my crooked front teeth pulled back because of the space, and I never had braces. Many of my teeth aren't perfect, but it's hard to tell.

When I finally had the money to have that tooth replaced with an implant, I decided against it, because not a day goes by that I am not aware of that gap in my teeth. No, I don't like it. Yes, I wish it weren't there. I really wish I'd had my paper route at that time so I could have paid the $50 for that root canal.

As much as that missing tooth has bothered me all these years, I wouldn't change it for the world. Every time my tongue drags across that empty space, I'm reminded about that day long ago. That gap in my teeth is a constant reminder of what it feels like to be hopeless, powerless, and helpless. It is the most discouraging place in the world. I never want to be there again. I think it helps me with compassion; and mostly, it helps me to never forget and to keep my drive alive.

One of the unluckiest days in my life as a child was when I lost my permanent tooth because my dad didn't have the money to fix it. And one of the luckiest days in my life was the day I lost my permanent tooth because my dad didn't have enough money to fix it.

We can turn bad luck into good luck and use it to find the drive to bring it forward into the rest of our lives. That good luck we make for ourselves is worth all the bad luck it took to get us there.

As this book continues, I'm going to have some famous paperboys share with you their experiences with their own paper routes, how it influenced who they were, and how it made them who they are.

CHAPTER 4

RUPERT MURDOCH AND MARK CUBAN

Over the years, I have become more and more convinced that luck plays the most important role in our success and in life in general, yet I have been surprised at the reaction of others when I suggest this proposition. When I tell people that I believe luck was responsible for 99 percent of everything that has happened to me, I am often met with a blank stare. Sometimes they cross their arms. Sometimes they shake their heads no. And sometimes they just tell me flat out, "I disagree." It has been fascinating to me the varied reactions I receive. People who are successful in life want nothing to do with the proposition that their life and their success are the result of only luck. This is particularly so for the uber-successful. These people are hell-bent on claiming their success as theirs and theirs alone.

People want to be self-made—to have done it on their own and not be beholden to anyone. I have seen trust-fund kids grow up and wrestle with their own impressions of themselves, thinking and knowing they didn't accomplish their success on their own. They inherited their position and their wealth. For many of these people, it is a terrible burden. Everyone wants to have done more, and certainly more on their own.

The Murdoch Family and Succession

I found it fascinating to follow the travails of the Murdoch family. Their family's saga was fictionalized in a very real series called *Succession* on HBO. The Murdochs are a fascinating story and a look into the psyche of the very rich who want to have accomplished something in their own right.

What many people don't realize is that Rupert Murdoch was part of the lucky-sperm club. His father left him a good-sized media company. To his great credit and drive, he took what daddy gave him and supercharged it, becoming a worldwide media behemoth. His holdings ranged from Australia to the United Kingdom and then to the U.S. He became one of the most important people in the world based on his control of the media.

Rupert had six children. Three of his children, Lachlan, Elisabeth, and James, were seemingly vying for not only his approval but to be selected as "the one." It was a fascinating struggle to witness. It was the ultimate game of succession that pitted three siblings against each other, each of whom thought they were the most capable. In the end, it was a psychological study in human behavior, especially for the richest and luckiest among us.

There were many twists and turns throughout the Murdoch internal power struggle. The first problem was that Rupert never really wanted to let go in the first place, yet set up this *Game of Thrones-style* game for three of his own six children to play. As the game raged on for years, each child was given positions of power and an opportunity to distinguish themselves. There were highs and lows for each of them.

All three of the children are fabulously wealthy; $2 billion each. But $2 billion was not enough. No amount of money was. What was important was the ultimate approval from their father and a way to tell themselves that they were worthy and capable. Nobody wants to be the rich kid who was handed everything and did nothing in life.

At one point during the power struggle, James, the more liberal brother, got pissed off and sailed away on his yacht for two years. The one good thing about being that rich is you get to sulk in luxury. He was pissed off at daddy, but not pissed off enough to give him back his $2 billion and go do it on his own.

At the end of the day, Rupert ended up selling off most of the assets he had accumulated to Disney in a deal where he clearly outfoxed the Mouse. He kept other minor holdings and told his son, Lachlan, that he won the contest. As I was watching the contest from afar, I always felt that his daughter, Elisabeth, was the most capable and the most serious of the three. She made the least ruckus and went off to do her own thing on her terms.

The entire Murdoch intrafamily power struggle is fascinating. It shows the desire we all have: to be accomplished and successful in our own right. No one likes the idea of being just a lucky person who inherited everything. Therefore, when I talk to people and tell them I believe that 99 percent of everything that has happened to me has been luck, so many disagree. That concept takes away from their accomplishments. So they push back and tell me that luck did not determine my success, but my work ethic did. When I remind them that some people are simply born to work and some people are not, they don't accept that notion. They believe that any person can *will* themselves to work. But I believe they are wrong.

Sloths. Lions. and Luck

As I mentioned earlier, each month in the jungle, a sloth is born and a lion is born. Each month, one animal is born with the laziest genes in the entire jungle, and one animal is born as king. All they did was be born. But the genetic makeup of these animals determines, in many ways, what success will look like for them.

Let me explain it this way. Have you ever been so tired that you have trouble staying awake while you're driving? That you find yourself nodding off and worrying about crashing? And when you finally make it home, remember how tired you were and how unable you were even to hold your eyelids open for a moment? That is how a sloth feels twenty-four hours a day. Likewise, that same feeling of lethargy is with many of our fellow men and women. They simply don't have the gas in their genetic tank to get up and go. They can't.

The most successful among us don't believe that for a second, because they have never felt it and can't imagine it. The most successful among us not only want success, but they want more and more success. It seems that everyone wants to be a billionaire. The more I'm around, the more I hear that this guy, or that gal, is a billionaire. The truth is there are fewer than 2,600 billionaires in the entire world. Yet, the quest to be a billionaire, especially from the ultra successful, is never-ending.

So when I tell people that I believe their life has been determined primarily by luck, they push back hard. It is something they don't want to accept, because in their mind, it takes away from all of their accomplishments and from everything they have done. And by the way, they are proud of all of their accomplishments. They believe that 100 percent of it came as a result of their intelligence, work ethic, and determination. That luck had little, or nothing, to do with their particular success.

It is all an interesting denial to me. You can go through everyone's life, starting from the beginning until now, and see huge differences of luck breaking their way that set the stage for more future days of good fortune. So many left turns and so many right turns and so many coin tosses got us to where we are today. All of us. And for those of us who made it claim we did it all on our own! No help from the federal government, even though many people went to public school, and went on to public universities with government loans. No help from mentors, even though they taught us and showed us the way. No help from one random action or event that changed our lives forever. For a moment, put this book down and look in your own rearview mirror. Think of those moments in your life where one or two events were the catalyst and cornerstone for building the life you have today.

What is also interesting is that the people who have not done well, and who have not been successful, fully embrace the concept of luck. One hundred percent. They believe in luck, but they believe they were cursed with *bad* luck. And when they look out across the country and see success stories and people thriving and people getting rich, they believe that good luck — not them — is responsible. They believe in the concept of luck. They just believe they were screwed.

I believe that this thought process is why America is so angry at the present moment. Both sides. MAGA Republicans. Black Lives Matter Democrats. And everything and everyone in between who is suffering. They believe they got the short end of the stick. They believe they were dealt a hand of bad luck. In no way do they take responsibility for what's happened; they just know where they are and where they're going. Forty percent of Americans don't have $400 in the bank in case of an emergency. Think about that for a moment. One emergency, and your life stops on a dime.

So there we are. The most successful among us did it all on their own, and for those who struggle at the bottom, this caste system called life placed them in this position of despair because the deck was stacked against them from the get-go.

When I began to write this book, I knew I would have many skeptics, especially among the most successful, but I believe they are wrong. I know what happened in my own life. As I have deconstructed it, all the way back to the beginning and to the present, all I see are incredible lucky breaks that led to further lucky breaks, which led to unimaginable riches. The way I have dealt with the fact that luck has played an outsized role in my life is simple. I don't try to convince myself, or to kid myself, that I did all of this on my own. I just realized that genetics, coin tosses, and being in the right place at the right time contributed to all I have. And once I came to that conclusion, I just focused on being eternally grateful and try to pray every night in thanksgiving.

Mark Cuban's Luck

One of the luckiest guys in the world is Mark Cuban. First of all, who has more fun than Mark Cuban? His story is an interesting one. Cuban was clearly born with a great advantage — the entrepreneurial gene. But his entrepreneurial gene was created on steroids. When you Google him and read his story, you will see clearly that, as a little boy, he was out there hustling and moving and shaking. He was built to work and work hard.

I had the pleasure of meeting Cuban at a dinner I co-hosted for President Obama. He was awesome. Before the night was over, he had taken control of the bar and was actually bartending the event. His personality was off the chart. Just a super person.

It was amazing to meet Cuban and see him in action. I was not surprised at his success from that dinner experience in Orlando years ago.

The Mark Cuban story is very important for many reasons. Unlike most billionaires, Cuban does not delude himself into thinking he did it all and could do it again. He has an estimated net worth of $6.2 billion. Cuban's quote goes like this: "Anybody who has a 'B' next to their name, and they tell you they could do it all again, they're lying their ass off." He concluded by saying, "You've got to have luck. You gotta have timing." It was so refreshing to read that statement from a guy who the world sees as totally self-made.

Cuban cautioned that he wasn't saying he wouldn't do well for himself; he expressed confidence that in the hypothetical scenario of starting over again, he could rebuild enough wealth to lead a comfortable life. But he points out that becoming a billionaire isn't just dependent on your sales talent or ability to craft a great business idea. Cuban knows that luck played an outsized role in his success.

Timing was very important to him. He started a software company called MicroSolutions in 1982. It was just as the digital revolution was coming to be, and he sold it to CompuServe for $6 million in 1990.

Later in 1999, when he sold his audio-streaming service Broadcast.com to Yahoo for $5.7 billion in stock, he quickly sold most of his shares, just before the dot-com bubble collapsed.

Had Cuban held on to his Yahoo stock, simply put, he would not be the person we know today. He has reportedly said the sale of the stock was intentional and by design: "In the 1980s, I watched PC companies just blow up, just go straight up, and then come straight down. I was like, it's going to happen again."

His intuition and study of the past made him sell his stock. There are thousands of other stories where people held their stock and rode it all the way down to zero. One of the toughest things in life to do is to put yourself in a position to be lucky, then make the most of it at the right moment.

The Luck Factor

According to Richard Wiseman, the author of *The Luck Factor* and a psychology professor at the University of Hertfordshire, there are character traits common in very lucky people:

1. Listening to their intuition

2. Practicing optimism

3. Being resilient

4. Leaping at new opportunities

"It is easy for people to exhaust the opportunities in their life. Keep on talking to the same people in the same way. Keep taking the same route to and from work. Keep going to the same places on vacation," Wiseman wrote in a ten-year study published in 2003. "But new or even random experiences introduce the potential for new opportunities."

He seems to be saying that lucky people get out and about and network like crazy while unlucky people sit stuck in one place with no chance for new opportunity. Cuban echoed that same concept in a *GQ* interview.

> *"I was really lucky in that. I was a tech guy who understood networking when the Internet stock market blew up, and I was an entrepreneur who was willing to invest his own money to try to take this new thing called the Internet and see if we could put it in audio and then video over it."*

Cuban added,

> *"If I would have been born three years earlier, three years later, we would probably not be having this conversation."*

Cuban acknowledges what many highly successful people do not: luck was the determinative factor in his success and not just himself—that many variables had occurred all the way from being born until he reached his pinnacle. I believe that his humility is why so many of us admire him. Just as I admire Cuban, I look at that poor fellow, James Dolan, who controls Madison Square Garden, and I watch in horror at the fortune he inherited that he has basically squandered. Dolan is the boy who was born on third base and thought he hit a triple. Cuban hit a grand slam to win the World Series and simply says, "I got lucky."

I'll take Cuban and his humility any day.

CHAPTER 5

MARRIAGE

The War of the Roses

There are many decisions we make in our lives. There is probably none as consequential and full of risk as marriage. The person we marry will have an outsized role in everything we do in the future. The one thing we know, statistically, is that marriage is a crapshoot.

Let's start with a few facts and figures about marriage in the U.S.

According to the American Psychological Association, approximately 40 to 50 percent of first marriages end in divorce. The success rate is basically a coin toss. The divorce rate for second marriages is even higher, with approximately 60 to 67 percent ending in divorce.

Statistics show that the average length of first marriages when couples divorce is eight years. There are so many reasons for divorce, including infidelity, abuse, addiction, mental-health issues, and many more. Most divorces happen between year three and year seven of marriage. Four percent of couples divorce after seven years of marriage. That may be the reason we hear so much about the "seven-year itch." It seems that if you can make it ten years, you are almost home free.

Divorce for Men and Women

Nearly 70 percent of divorces are initiated by women. Another fun fact to go along with this is that over 50 percent of divorced women never want to remarry, while only about 30 percent of men express that same sentiment. It appears that the men have done a number on the women.

When I was a little boy, I once asked my grandmother, who was widowed, why she never married again. She told me, "I've seen all of my friends marry these old birds, and I just decided I would rather be alone than wishing I was alone." What must happen is once some of these people escape marriage, they vow never to do it again.

Divorce rates are higher for Black women than for White women, and they are generally lowest among Asian and foreign-born Hispanic women. The average age for a couple entering their first divorce is thirty years old, and 60 percent of divorces involve spouses between the ages of twenty-five and thirty-nine.

Age and Divorce

Some of this data may indicate that people rushed into marriage because it seemed the thing to do and that other friends were getting married. The rush to marriage in my opinion is the most probable cause of divorces.

For people who wait until the ages of twenty-five to twenty-nine to get married, their risk of divorce goes down to 14 percent. It drops down to 10 percent if you wait until age thirty to thirty-four to get married. In recent years, we have seen that people are getting married at an older age, and millennials are getting married later in life — in their thirties.

Having a good marriage is a very lucky turn of events. The interesting thing about luck is that there are all sorts of things we do and don't do during our life that can make us luckier or brings us bad luck. When it comes to marriage, the statistics seem to point out that marrying early gives you a good chance of having a bad marriage. Waiting longer increases your chances of a good marriage.

In all aspects of life, not just marriage, there are things we can do to increase our chances of success. The problem is, we are impatient, and we think our situations are different. This probability of good luck applies not just in marriage but across the board.

When I've had friends who got divorced, I often asked a very simple question: "When did you know you had made a mistake?" The most common answer I get is, "Right before I walked down the aisle."

Imagine them standing in the back of the church filled with their friends and their soon-to-be spouse's friends, thinking to themself, "I don't want to do this." You know the thought has been raging through their mind for weeks, months, or maybe over a year, but for some reason, they walk right off the ledge. They know in their heart of hearts it's a bad decision, but they make it anyway.

The second answer I get is, "The first year of marriage." Think of how long many of these people stayed in terrible situations until they mustered the courage or the ability to divorce.

Whom we marry is important for so many reasons. We will be co-parenting with this person, and that effort will have a direct impact on our children's future and who and what they become. We also rely on our spouses for support and encouragement. If you don't have a nurturer, or cheerleader, it can be an awfully lonely life. If your spouse doesn't value or respect you, it is demoralizing.

Which Marriages Work?

What has always been interesting to me is that while 40 to 50 percent of all marriages end in divorce, I've wondered how many marriages stay in place, yet the people in the marriage are miserable. There are many reasons people may stay married but may not be happy. Money. Children. Guilt. Religion.

Once upon a time, the life expectancy for most people in America was sixty-five years. That is why Social Security was originally set at age sixty-two. As we know, modern medicine has now increased life expectancy by almost twenty years. That has resulted in many so-called "gray divorces"—older people just saying enough is enough.

Older people getting divorced often puzzled me. My thought was, what took them so long? We know that life can be busy, especially with children and college-age children. Evidently, once all that distraction is over and it's just Ma and Pa Kettle sitting around the house, either Ma or Pa can't take much more of it and divorce in their sixties, seventies and, yes, even eighties.

It must have been particularly interesting when drugs such as Viagra came along. Maybe the wife had felt that at least that part of her marital duties were over. Lo and behold, a new drug gave her old husband a new lease on life. I wonder how many women were happy with the new drug? I've often thought that Viagra may be the catalyst for many of these so-called "gray divorces."

Another interesting statistic is that more than one in every twenty married Americans has taken three or more trips to the altar. The old adage is that the third time is the charm. But as Lee Corso, the ESPN analyst and one of my neighbors in Florida, would say: "Not so fast."

Third marriages have the highest divorce rate—73 percent. The probability of divorce increases with each new marriage.

When I have talked to people about their marriages and divorces, I have observed a basic rule of thumb. I tell them that a young person can rush into marriage, and that rush to the altar was a mistake. Everyone is entitled to one mistake. The second marriage is usually called "the rebound"—people looking for a successful marriage and hoping they can get it right this time. And then finally, there are these people who get married for the third time and then divorce.

What I tell people who have been married three times and divorced three times is that after marriage number three, when we want to address the root problem in all of these marriages, you have to look in the mirror, because after three marriages, *you are the problem!*

We know that up to 50 percent of marriages end in divorce. Divorce researcher and author Dana Adam Shapiro concluded that of the remaining 50 percent, one third are unhappy, one third are "meh" or "bearable," and one third are happy. So roughly around 17 percent of all married couples are happy. That was a depressing finding.

Marriage and Monogamy

It also makes one wonder if human beings are in fact monogamous. Very few animals in the animal kingdom are monogamous. Do yourself a favor and one day Google "monogamous animals." You will find there are very few, and some are surprising:

- Bald eagles
- Wolves
- Beavers
- Black vultures
- Coyotes
- Swans
- Barn owls
- Foxes
- Atlantic puffins

There are a few more, but not many.

To me these animals are fascinating; not because they're monogamous, but because most other animals are not monogamous. So, I've wondered, are human beings naturally monogamous? If human beings are not genetically monogamous, it could well explain high levels of infidelity and then the associated divorce rate. The most commonly accepted data on infidelity is that around 15 to 20 percent of marriages experience infidelity. Twenty percent of married men and 13 percent of married women have admitted to having sex with someone other than their spouse; however, infidelity rates among women are on the rise—having increased by 40 percent in the last twenty years.

The professions with the highest rate of infidelity are sales and healthcare, and the lowest rates are accountancy, banking, and finance.

When you boil all this down, it is startling. Almost 50 percent of married people get divorced. Every time they get married subsequently, there is a much greater chance they will get divorced again. And at the end of all of this, out of all married couples at any given time, only 17 percent are really happy. Happiness is what gives all of us a good life.

I have four children. Three boys and one girl. I have given them all advice on marriage, and it's fairly simple. It's important that they marry someone they respect and share common values with, and make each other better. There are many questions to ask before asking someone to marry you. The final question I advise them to ask themselves is, "Is this the person I want to be the mother or father of my child?" There can be no more important question than that. At the end of it all, for most of us, life's purpose is family and all that goes with it. There are those among us who have been scarred, or simply do not want the trouble and responsibility of a family, and I think those people are doing their prospective spouses and children a great disservice.

Marriage is one of the most important decisions we make, and this chapter has shown how fraught it is with risk. So how do we improve our luck when it comes to marriage? The statistics are clear. The longer you wait to get married, and the more mature you are when entering into this union, the better chance you have of a successful marriage. Once you get past that seven-year itch and make it to ten years, you are almost certain to stay married for life. Researchers believe that married people are happier than unmarried people.

Divorce comes with financial reversal, emotional distress, and often traumatized children caught in the middle. There is a way to improve your luck in marriage, and that is simply to wait a little longer and keep your commitment once you are married. Marriage requires the same or more of the ongoing commitment and effort any successful partnership does. Prioritize your marriage, and it will reap big dividends. There is no question that marriage and who our life partner is, significantly impacts our overall happiness.

To all those who are thinking about getting married, just remember these words: wait, and look before you leap.

CHAPTER 6

IQ AND APTITUDE

As a fetus slowly develops over nine months in the womb, all of the DNA and genetic makeup are already in place, dictating much of the baby's future. Both IQ and aptitude are largely determined by genetics. IQ stands for intelligence quotient and, in short, is the measure of a person's reasoning ability. Just as many people are blessed with height and athletic ability, many are born with a high IQ, or a great aptitude for a certain set of skills.

IQ scores vary from very, very high to very, very low. One hundred thirty and above is considered very superior; 122 to 129 is superior; 110 to 119 is high average; and 90 to 109 is average.

Most people have an average IQ of between 85 and 115. Only 2 percent of the population score above 130. A person who tests at 130 and beyond is considered a genius. An IQ test is supposed to gauge how well someone can use information and logic to answer questions or make predictions.

It's important to note that a high IQ or a low IQ is not the sole predictor of whether a person will have a high-quality and successful life or not. A high IQ does give a person some tremendous advantages over others, but it does not determine one's ultimate success.

People With High IQs

To illustrate how a high IQ could be very helpful in one's ultimate success, it is interesting to know that Elon Musk, the richest man in the world at the present time, has an IQ of 155, which is quite high.

But Elon Musk doesn't win the ultimate prize for IQ tests. Bill Gates, the CEO and founder of Microsoft, scored 160. Bill Clinton, a U.S. president and Rhodes Scholar, has an IQ of 137. Amazingly Bobby Fischer, the great chess grandmaster, had an IQ of 187.

It would be impossible to leave the topic of high IQ scores without focusing on Stephen Hawking. It is generally believed that Hawking had an IQ of around 160, which is considered to be in genius range. Likewise, Albert Einstein, who was celebrated for his knowledge and contribution to physics is believed to have an estimated score of around 160; however, there is no history of Einstein ever taking an IQ test. When asked about his IQ, Hawking was quoted as saying, "People who boast about their IQ are losers."

The upshot of all this is that when you go through history and examine people such as Cleopatra or Wolfgang Mozart, you will discover that they had estimated incredibly high IQs, most likely genius levels. There is no question that a high IQ gives a person an incredible leg up in academia, especially in math and science. If you Google successful people and their IQs, you will notice that most are 130 or above, even though only 2 percent of the population ever reach 130. When you reach levels beyond 130, you are getting into the rarest of rare, but you are usually encountering some of the most brilliant minds ever to walk on the planet.

Throughout history, it is safe to say that some of the greatest minds ever had IQs that rose to genius level. And here's the thing: those people did nothing to earn their high IQs. They were simply conceived, and after that, genetics took over. It was incredible luck. In my research, almost every person that I felt had an IQ of 130 or above actually did. Now, of course, history is littered with geniuses who actually went mad. There seems to be a direct relationship between genius and insanity. But there is no doubt that many have been given a gift of incredible intelligence, which, if used properly, can bring them great success, and more importantly, lead to great inventions that change the world—usually for the better, but sometimes for the worse.

Robert Oppenheimer, the father of the atomic bomb, had an IQ of 135. However, he spent much of his life regretting his invention and its impact on mankind and humanity. A high IQ in the hands of the wrong person, or worse, an evil person, could one day result in apocalyptic results.

IQ and Families

Being born with a high IQ certainly not does not guarantee success. There are many geniuses homeless in America. From time to time, I like to stop and visit with homeless people, and I am constantly amazed at some of their intelligence and personalities. There are undoubtedly technical geniuses who live on the streets who, for whatever reason, never put it together.

A high IQ is luck. A high IQ with parents who are not nurturing, supportive, or interested can result in that luck being wasted away.

As I mentioned earlier, a bad or uninvolved parent can ruin a perfectly capable child, even a child with a genius IQ. We still must study and work to reach our potential. If a child has parents who don't foster their work ethic and aren't focused on grades and conduct, all of that genetic good luck is for naught. Another interesting point when studying IQ is that the average difference in IQ between siblings is twelve to thirteen points. The average difference between two randomly selected people is approximately seventeen points. So some measurable amount of IQ is genetic.

There have been a number of studies showing that a firstborn child will be smarter than their other siblings. However, some researchers believe this is because the parents of the firstborn spend more time and attention with that child, and it has nothing to do with innate intelligence.

This fact only validates the importance of parents' involvement in the academic growth of their children. Oldest children tend to become the richest and most successful, and it could be thanks to their parents. Our success in life may be influenced by birth order, according to the economist Sandra E. Black. And that would make sense. The first child gets incredible attention. As each child comes along, parents are busier, there are more children, and fatigue sets in.

As life begins, each child is born with a certain IQ. For 2 percent of these children, they are geniuses. Part of the lucky-sperm club. But it is no guarantee of success or fortune. It is simply something they are born with that gives them an inherent advantage over others.

Bill Gates and His Childhood

Bill Gates was a very awkward child. When you read about his life, you learn his mother understood his antisocial behavior. She spent hours with him trying to improve his social skills and awkwardness. She also introduced him to tennis, which he plays to this day and excels in. Mama Gates understood that she had a very special child, but she also knew that he had some very special needs. She recognized what she needed to do to help him be more socially acceptable. Bill was born with a 160 IQ, but his real luck was having the mother that he had.

Many factors came together to make Bill into the billionaire philanthropist he is today — including how his parents, Mary and William Gates, raised him. They weren't afraid to be a little unconventional when it came to raising Bill. He has revealed three aspects of his childhood that helped shape him into who he is today:

1. THEY STRESSED THE IMPORTANCE OF COMMUNITY.

    The Gates family made a point of being involved in community work and philanthropy, making sure their kids participated too. Mary was a firm believer in an idea from Luke 12:48: "To whom much has been given, of him much will be required." Bill Gates Sr. once told *Forbes*, "From the beginning, she instilled it as an important value in our family." As life has gone on, it's clear that Gates got this message.

2. THEY GAVE HIM A SIGNIFICANT AMOUNT OF INDEPENDENCE.

The Gates family enrolled Bill in a private school known to give their students unusual amounts of freedom. It was at this school that Bill discovered computers.

By the time Bill was thirteen, his parents allowed him to visit the University of Washington at night to use their computers. They also allowed him to leave home for periods of time, like to go to Olympia, where he was a page at the state legislature, and to Washington, D.C., to work as a congressional page. In his senior year of high school, he took a break to work as a programmer at a power plant in southern Washington. And all of this occurred before he dropped out of Harvard University to move to New Mexico and found Microsoft.

His parents were concerned, but ultimately, they supported their son, who eventually moved the company closer to home in Seattle.

Like Bill, this world has other billionaires with high IQs who dropped out, knowing that college was a waste of time.

3. THEY WOULDN'T LET HIM GIVE UP JUST BECAUSE HE DIDN'T EXCEL AT SOMETHING.

It's easy to let your child drop out of activities when they don't excel, but that's not what Bill's parents did. They made sure he continued to participate in swimming, soccer, football, and playing the trombone—even if he wasn't the most gifted in those areas. His parents understood it was important that he learned he didn't have to be good at everything, and that failure was perfectly normal and acceptable.

"At the time, I thought it was kind of pointless," Bill Gates said of the activities in an interview with *Fortune*, "but it ended up really exposing me to leadership opportunities and showing me that I wasn't good at a lot of things, instead of sticking to things that I was comfortable with. It was fantastic, and now some of those activities I cherish. They had to stick to it because I pushed back a lot, but it was fantastic advice."

Bill's parents are a great example of double luck. He was born with an incredible IQ and to parents who knew how to nurture it and push it. Double luck is better than pure luck.

IQ and Aptitude

The first cousin of IQ is aptitude. Aptitude is simply a natural ability to do something. It has more to do with innate traits you were born with than what you might have been influenced by. Musical or athletic talents are good examples of aptitudes. Most people recognize that some things are easy for them but other things feel harder. IQ tests measure statistically how intelligent a person is, while an aptitude test measures how well that person can apply their intelligence to different scenarios. Thus, my reason for calling them cousins.

IQ is often considered to be related to aptitude. In American business, aptitude tests are a shortcut in determining whether a person is a good fit for your company or not. Thousands are administered a day. People's careers are started or ended simply by taking an aptitude test. They are incredibly accurate, and certain tests also determine what your aptitude is, but not only if you're giving false answers. The sophisticated tests that determine if the applicant is lying ferrets those results out. These tests determine an individual's skill or propensity to succeed in a given activity. Aptitude tests assume that individuals have inherent strengths and weaknesses, and if they have a natural inclination toward success or failure in specific areas based on their innate characteristics.

There are many great aptitude tests that are tremendous roadmaps to a person's likely success. We have all probably taken the Myers-Briggs test once or twice in our life, or the Princeton Review Career Quiz. These tests give employers a great insight as to the likely success of the candidate. Of course, no tests are perfect or final. But these aptitude tests are a great way to separate the wheat from the chaff — to eliminate especially those who probably have no chance of succeeding and also identify those who could be coached to do better and be successful.

So once a person is born, their IQ and aptitude are going to be key drivers in their ultimate life's work. Just as strong and hands-on parents can improve the child's grades and abilities, a bad set of parents can let a great talent go to waste by not applying their God-given skills to life.

My IQ and My Childhood

I have no clue what my IQ is. Every time I have sat down to take one of these tests, my mind starts to hurt and I can't finish. I have taken that to mean I do not have a high IQ. Since I've never finished, I don't know how low my IQ may actually be. That may be a blessing.

As I've mentioned, both of my parents were alcoholics, and there was no focus at home on our grades or report cards. We rarely did our homework, and if we did, it was on the way to school. When I think back on those days, I shudder. Basically, I was mucking along and just getting along. Math and science were like hieroglyphics to me. They made no sense at all.

Once, my wife and I were in Las Vegas and went to see George Carlin at the Bali Hotel. During his monologue, he remarked, "I'm so glad I took geometry in high school. A day doesn't go by that I don't do a proof or two." When he said it, I thought he was talking to me. All of those days in math and science classes, I used to say to myself, "What am I doing here?" I knew that I did not have the aptitude for math or science. I knew that no matter how much time I put in, it was going to be impossible. Yet, I had to keep going to graduate. To this day, I have bad dreams about some of those tests. As my life has gone on, I have thought about the lack of parenting I received as a child and have wondered, "Was I smart and not encouraged, or was I just average and not challenged?" I have determined for myself that I have an average intelligence but incredible street smarts. Street smarts are very different than book smarts. There are different kinds of smarts throughout the world.

It has been my belief that street smarts are what got me to where I am today, not book smarts. I finally got decent in math when I started putting dollar signs next to the numbers. I became an idiot savant with that math.

During my childhood, I started out at Christ the King, a Catholic school in Lexington, Kentucky. After fifth grade, we changed schools — I believe because my parents didn't have money for the tuition — and we moved to a public school. Once I got to the public school, I was given a reading test. Although I was entering the sixth grade, my reading test indicated that I read at a fourth-grade level, and I was sent to the fourth-grade class.

Humiliation does not begin to describe my feelings at the time. My brother, Mike, was in fifth grade, and his reading test and score allowed him there. So I had a brother one year younger than me and I was in a reading class one grade under him. It was a very rough patch for me. It was bad luck hitting me square in the face and humiliating me for everyone to see.

When this happened, I decided I was going to take this bad luck and change it. Fortunately, my homeroom teacher, Miss Brewer, knew I was distraught and embarrassed, and wanted to help me.

Back in the day, there was a reading system called SRA (published by Science Research Associates). Each time you completed a certain color, you'd move to the next color and more advanced reading. Miss Brewer and I began in earnest to try to dig me out of my deep hole.

I lived in her classroom after school. I was devouring those SRA reading materials like a madman. I actually enjoyed the process. Additionally, I began my lifelong love of books. Miss Brewer told me I should always have a book by my bed, and I have ever since.

Back in those days, I read books about athletes and U.S. presidents. I couldn't get enough. By the time I was nearing to the end of my sixth-grade year, my reading level had improved. I was actually reading at my grade level, and I got to leave the classroom with the smaller desks and the younger children. All thanks to Miss Brewer for loving me and believing in me.

Because I spent so much time with Miss Brewer, I spent a lot of time talking to her about everything. I learned she had been a beauty queen at the University of Kentucky. Even though she was a beauty queen, she never married. I had a tremendous crush on Miss Brewer and one day had the nerve to ask her why she had never married. She told me something that turned out to be very lucky for me. She told me that many boys did not ask her out because she was a beauty queen and because she was beautiful, and because they must have thought she would say no.

Later in life, as I began to develop my own interest in women, I thought about Miss Brewer not being asked out because she was so beautiful. My wife is one of the most beautiful women I have ever seen in my life, and I'm certain my experience talking to Miss Brewer taught me to take a chance when I asked her out.

So the bad luck I had by being put into fourth-grade reading turned out to be good luck. It introduced me to Miss Brewer, who introduced me to SRA and mentored me back to reading at my own age level, but more importantly, gave me the life lesson to have the courage to ask someone out that I may not have ever done. Throughout this book, we will see times of bad luck turning into good luck.

IQ and aptitude are two factors that give us incredible luck—luck that often translates into unimaginable riches. I would love to take the richest people in the world, those who didn't inherit their money, and test all of their IQs to see where they land. My prediction would be lots of 130s and above. IQ, aptitude, and parents who were are able to help them wring the most out of their gifts have the best chance of real luck in life. And some of us are lucky enough to have a Miss Brewer in our lives—a mentor who made all the difference.

CHAPTER 7

TENACITY

Tenacious is mostly a very positive term. When someone is called tenacious, they're probably the type of person who never gives up and never stops trying. They are someone who does whatever it takes to accomplish a goal.

Unlike IQ and aptitude, my research does not seem to lend any credence to the fact that tenacity has any direct genetic link. However, in my life I have many times identified those who are tenacious, even at an early age.

Tenacity in Kids' Sports

My wife and I have four children. Three boys and a girl. Consequently, many of our days were spent on sports fields, basketball courts, soccer fields, and at their schools. Along the way, I took my turn coaching my children. I never wanted to coach too much because I always felt that the helicopter parent was a dangerous parent. On the other hand, I didn't think it was fair that I not contribute by coaching, at least a little.

As a coach and a spectator, I had the pleasure of seeing tenacity at a very early age. There are kids who have IT, and there are kids who don't. And you can see it as clear as day.

One of the early signs I witnessed was when my child or other children would be obsessed with a ball. They simply could not put it down. They never got tired of kicking it, throwing it, or chasing it. They were built like Labrador Retrievers.

When I saw children like this, I often wondered where life would take them. In judging their tenacity at an early age, I felt I had a pretty good handle on what those kids might be like later in life. Kids who love the ball usually grow up still loving the ball and become great athletes. Stories and early videos tell that better than I can.

During practices and games, there were kids who cared and kids who couldn't care less. The kids who identified with tenacity hated to lose and would do anything not to lose. Some even cried when they lost. Anytime I saw a kid crying after losing a game, I wanted them on my team. I like kids who care. Show me a good loser, and I'll show you a loser.

Tenacity is more than just endurance, though endurance is a critical part of tenacity. It is endurance combined with the absolute certainty that what we're looking for is going to transpire. Tenacity is more than just hanging on. I believe it is also being afraid to fall off. Fear of failure is something that haunts many of us our entire lives and drives us like nothing else. Tenacity is the tool we use to fight off failure.

I've never figured out what is more powerful: the fear of failure, or the glory of winning. Years ago, as a little boy, I loved watching *ABC's The Wide World of Sports*. Each show would begin with athletes doing different sporting events. The host, Jim McKay, used to introduce the show by saying, "The thrill of victory, and the agony of defeat."

Those words resonated with me as a child and still resonate today. One of the clips from the show had a ski jumper tumbling head over heels down the slope, visualizing for us "the agony of defeat." And what is definitely true is that the thrill of victory is so much greater than the agony of defeat.

Tenacity in Life

Tenacity is vital in sports, but tenacity is also vital for success in life. Many times you hear that someone has "grit." Grit is the cousin of tenacity, and it just means that we have to dig in that much harder to achieve. Grit is tenacity on steroids.

Those who have a tenacious side to them are most likely to have very specific goals and be extremely driven. Failure is not an option to folks with true grit. Failure is a lesson on the way to success. Many people get knocked down and never get back up. Failure takes it out of them, sometimes in the first round. For the tenacious person, failure is just one bump in the road to the ultimate prize of success.

As I have thought about those kids in sports and in school, I have often wondered, "Were they just lucky enough to be born tenacious, or was their doggedness, persistence, and courage learned and developed along the way?" Research doesn't seem to have an answer, nor does science. But my gut tells me these people are born with something special.

Years ago, I read a book by Pat Riley, the great basketball coach. The book was titled *The Winner Within*. It was a fabulous read. My takeaway from the book was that some people are born with something special, and that specialness allows them to be the winners within. There is no way to be a consistent winner in life without tenacity and grit. It is a major differentiator.

I would love for a university or a group of scholars to look into the entire concept. Go back and look at adults who had this tenacious drive as children, and see if it translated to their success later in life. I have a great friend who is one of the most successful lawyers in all of America, Brian Panish. To this day, he is still obsessed with his little league statistics. His proudest accomplishment is his batting average the year he played on the same team as the Kansas City Chiefs coach, Andy Reid. Panish is quick to point out at any given time that he had a higher batting average than Reid. And he tells Reid this anytime he has a chance.

That batting average obviously meant a great deal to Panish. He is obsessed with it to this day, as well as his football career in high school and at California State University, Fresno. Panish grew up to be one of the most relentless lawyers in America. If someone is represented by him, they are probably going to receive a tenfold result by hiring him. He simply hates to lose. That fear and loathing of losing is hallmark in the tenacious person. Losing is simply unacceptable.

It can be easy to confuse tenacity with stubbornness. However, there are key differences. Stubbornness is driven by not wanting to change your mind or position on something. Tenacity is driven by your determination to achieve a goal, and unwillingness to give it up until you do.

You may wonder if tenacity is a compliment. My answer is yes, it is. Tenacity is persistent determination. It's considered a good character trait, since a tenacious person will achieve a goal they set, despite any difficulties.

I would bet a lot of money that the most successful people in life and in business are tenacious. You have probably heard the phrase "Patience is a virtue." It is also true that tenacity *and* perseverance are virtues.

Tenacity, Resilience, and Grit

The differences between tenacity, perseverance, and grit are nuanced.

- TENACITY is the mental strength to resist opposition. It's the quality of staying determined.
- RESILIENCE is sticking to a project, task, or deadline, even when the going gets tough. It requires figuring out adjustments to get the job done.
- GRIT complements the traits of resilience and tenacity, adding guts, courage, initiative, and intention.

Tenacity and *resilience* apply to everyday tasks. Grit extends perseverance to not only enduring setbacks and failures, but doing so long enough to reach a distant but important goal.

Two critical components of grit are *passion* and *perseverance*.

- PASSION comes from your interest in your job or task and from a sense of purpose — it happens when you have conviction that your work is meaningful.

- PERSEVERANCE is resilience in the face of adversity, a kind of single-minded determination that characterizes the grittiest individuals.

One common thread of those with tenacity is they have specific and defined goals that they are hell-bent on achieving. Without these goals, they can never reach victory and success. The pole vaulter can never go higher unless he continues to raise the bar, changing his goals along the way. It was the same for the four-minute mile — a seemingly impossible feat years ago but is now broken on a regular basis. Those records were broken by tenacious athletes who had very specific goals. This same concept works similarly in life and in business.

Enhancing Your Luck

In certain situations, it's darn near impossible to enhance luck — like a toss of the coin. There is very little you can do in a coin toss to enhance luck, other than to cheat.

However, in life, there are situations where you can enhance your luck. The easiest place to explain it is on a Blackjack table. It is very foolish to ever hit your cards when you have 16. The odds of busting are too great. That situation allows a person to enhance their chances of winning by not hitting their cards.

Similarly, if you are dealt two aces, the book says you split those aces. The reason being is you have a better chance of hitting 21 that way and, in some cases, having two blackjacks.

The cards we are dealt and shown in life oftentimes give us the opportunity to be luckier, because we know what the smart play is. It is true that people hit on 16 and make 21. It is also true that some people don't split aces and still win that particular hand. Every blind squirrel finds a nut every once in a while. The smart squirrel uses information from the past to make informed decisions in the future, which enhances the chance of finding more nuts.

In the upcoming chapters, I will demonstrate some of the ways you can improve your chances with luck by making calculated and informed decisions. For instance, a tenacious person who is laser-focused on their goals will increase their probability of success.

Working Smart

Tenacity is not just about working hard; it's also about working smart. Most people who are born with tenacity develop a clear goal and a plan of action. These people also have the ability to adapt when things don't go according to that plan. At the end of the day, tenacity requires a combination of determination and flexibility.

A tenacious person generally has defined goals. These specific goals give the person a leg up on luck. A tenacious person with goals has a tremendous advantage when it comes to enhancing luck… hope is not a plan. A plan has goals that are strictly set and off-ramps that are available when those objectives fail, with a Plan B or even a Plan C, if necessary, to achieve the desired result.

Once goals are set, it is very hard to dissuade a tenacious person. It's very hard to make them throw in the towel or throw their hands up in surrender. Because goals and desires are generally hidden behind layers of obstacles and walls, tenacity is a must-have for success.

Louis Pasteur, the famous scientist, spoke for tenacious people everywhere when he said, "Let me tell you the secret that has led me to my goal. My strength lies solely in my tenacity."

The cornerstone of tenacity is the firm conviction that not only is your goal achievable, but that YOU will achieve it. It has been said that tenacious people set their goals in 3D. They see it, feel it, and smell it. It is so vivid to them that they are totally convinced it is all within their reach. In their world of imagination, it's a done deal.

Tenacity and Goals

Tenacious people aren't stubborn. If stubbornness can be attributed to them, it's about their goals and not their methods—only their goals are set in stone. As for how they achieve their goals, they are flexible. They are willing to take different paths, regroup, rethink, even start over to ultimately achieve their goals.

Not having goals is much like going to an airport with no ticket, no luggage, and no idea of where you're going. Essentially, you are allowing your destiny to be determined by chance rather than yourself. My grandmother used to say, "It looks like it wasn't planned. It looks like it just happened."

A person with goals has a life that seems planned. The person with no goals has a life and career that just happens.

One of the ways to set a goal is known as the SMART technique:

1. SPECIFIC. Be clear about what you want to achieve.

2. MEASURABLE. Make sure your goals can be measured so you know if you're winning or losing.

3. ATTAINABLE. Your goal should be reached within the time frame you have chosen. The goal should have a specific starting and ending point.

4. REALISTIC. The goal needs to be something within your reach and can be done in a way that is relevant to your life's purpose.

5. TIME-BOUND. Set a timeline to keep yourself posted so you finish at the time you set.

One final thought about goals. Study after study shows that people who write down their goals are three times more likely to succeed than those who just had goals in their head. It is very important to write down your goals. Then you have to think about what you really want and the steps you need to take to get there. Written goals make it easier to stay on task and periodically check your timeline to see if you are going to finish in the time you projected.

The tenacious person with a set of defined goals is very likely to be more successful than a person without defined goals. Setting goals, whether you have a history of being tenacious or not, will benefit you.

Tenacity is what gives us drive. The opposite of driven is indifference. And whether it's on the little league field or the Pop Warner field, there are kids who are driven and kids who are indifferent. We can see it in practice, and we see it in games. These children grow up to be adults. One of the reasons I am so fascinated by the paperboy and papergirl is that those kids were clearly driven at an early age, and grew up to be exactly who we thought they might be. The same goes for the kid on the baseball field who tries his heart out on every play and cries when they lose.

People and animals are born with drive, tenacity, and grit. They are also born lazy, unmotivated, and uninterested. I believe that those lucky enough to be born with the tenacious gene have a huge head start in life and are most likely to be the ones most successful.

One thing to remember though: Even if you were born with those genes, you will enhance your life and luck by focusing on specific goals, putting them in writing and spot-checking them from time to time.

A lion is tenacious. A sloth is lazy.

CHAPTER 8

DYSLEXIA, THE SUPERPOWER

Just like a child born with certain genetic advantages, IQ, aptitude, drive, and ambition, many children are born with genetic hindrances, or at least seemingly hindrances. Dyslexia is a very common condition usually discovered in children around the ages of five and six. A child with an affected parent has a 40 to 60 percent risk of developing dyslexia. This risk is increased when other family members are also affected.

It is commonly thought that dyslexia is genetic, and research has suggested that a number of inherited genes may predispose someone to develop this brain disorder. On the other hand, other risk factors include low birth weight, being born prematurely, and being exposed to substances during gestation that can affect brain development.

That is a stunning 20 percent of the population in America who develop dyslexia. Interestingly, most people with dyslexia are, at least, average or above average IQ. So the good news is that dyslexia is not related to intelligence at all.

There are some serious misunderstandings about dyslexia. When my brother, Tim, was a child, he had difficulty in school. He had difficulty with reading and with math. He was diagnosed early on with learning disabilities, and although I never remember any professional diagnosis, it came to be understood in our family that Tim had dyslexia. The way it was explained to us is that when he read, he read backward. I remember hearing that for the first time and thinking, "How will he ever make it through life?" The good news for Tim and for dyslexics everywhere is, that is simply not what happens.

Dyslexia can't be "cured." It is a lifelong affliction. But with the right support, many dyslexic people can become highly successful students and adults. It is common for people with dyslexia to have trouble reading at a good pace and without mistakes. They have a hard time with reading comprehension, spelling, and writing. But these challenges aren't a problem of intelligence. It primarily affects the skills involved in accurate and fluent word reading and spelling. Some of the difficulties are phonological awareness, verbal memory, and verbal-processing speed.

Phonological dyslexia is characterized by difficulties breaking words down into syllables and into the individual sounds. The smallest sound in a language that carries meaning is referred to as the phoneme. Phonemes are what distinguish words such as "cat" versus "cut," and "dog" versus "log." Children with dyslexia often have poor phonological awareness, which is often seen as the cause of poor reading abilities. But it does not mean they are reading backward. It is not a visual problem but a weakness in phonological processing. There are four main types of dyslexia:

1. Phonological dyslexia.

2. Surface dyslexia, which is marked by the difficulty in recognizing whole words.

3. Rapid naming deficit, which makes a person have difficulty naming a letter, number, color, or object quickly and automatically. It slows the processing speed down.

4. Double-deficit dyslexia, which affects both the phonological process and naming speed. The majority of the weakest readers fall under this category.

The good news is that most dyslexic people can learn to read well with proper support. Spelling, however, appears to be a difficulty that persists throughout life. It is not understood why this is the case, just that it is known that dyslexia impacts phonological processing and memory. "Cat" becomes "cot," and "now" becomes "own." It is insidious and difficult.

Naming speed, particularly letter naming, is one of the best early predictors of reading difficulties. Therefore, it is often used as part of the screening measures for young children. Slow naming speed results in problems with developing reading fluency. It also makes timed tests very difficult because of the processing involved.

While dyslexia appears to be linked to certain genes that affect how the brain processes reading and language, it is not a deal killer and actually has superpowers that are either genetically inherited or developed as the child learns to cope with their dyslexia.

Speaking as the brother of someone who was believed to be dyslexic, it is like a riddle wrapped in a puzzle—very hard to get your arms and mind around the concept. It is safe to say that on its face, dyslexia is bad luck for those afflicted, as their studies and learning will be difficult and slow. On the other hand, as I have studied dyslexia, it also has been imparted to me that dyslexia may, in fact, give many of the people afflicted a superpower that the rest of us don't have—that their bad luck may in fact be good luck.

The Power to Adapt

The most amazing thing about human beings is they learn to adapt. Those who are blind and deaf seem to adapt to their reality and perform amazing feats. Likewise, those who are dyslexic are forced at an early age to come up with positive coping strategies to offset their deficits. They work harder or smarter. Being organized is paramount, and having a positive attitude toward new challenges is extremely helpful.

Over time, language-processing skills improve simply by participating in life—listening to teachers, parents, peers, and music. And as processing improves, so does phonemic awareness and other foundational reading and learning skills. In short, the child with dyslexia starts off with a great disadvantage in reading and math because of the disability. However, with coping skills and just living life, they learn to overcome the disability and actually do great things. They find a new way, a better way, and in many cases, a superpower. They replace old ways of learning, communicating, and succeeding with their own ways, which are many times more creative and more effective.

One thing for certain is that one of the primary strategies for overcoming dyslexia is working harder and smarter and being highly organized. Dyslexic people learn that this is their way to get ahead. Now here comes some good news and some of the superpowers that accompany dyslexia. Because people with dyslexia tend to have difficulty processing language, they tend to be naturally more inclined toward visual and spatial thinking. Wherever possible, a great dyslexic trick is to organize information using diagrams, graphs, maps, charts, pictures, etc. Many dyslexic students will find it helpful to translate information they read into some kind of visual representation and to review new concepts by simply drawing them.

They also use highlighters and annotations in the margins of text to help keep track of important information and essential concepts, and for cutting down on rereading. The advent of audiobooks has been a great equalizer for the dyslexic. It allows them to learn without getting caught up in the mechanics of reading. As time goes on, these audiobooks will be used more and more for younger children.

Many people with dyslexia find that font choice affects their reading speed. A 2013 study found that, in general, sans serif, monospace, and roman fonts are easier to read than serif, proportional, and italic fonts for people with dyslexia. Font color can also affect ease of reading. And finally, reading aloud is another trick used to keep you focused on whatever you're reading, and can be useful to prevent skipping over words. All of this to say that there are ways to work around dyslexia, and as they go through life, all these adaptations and maneuvers will allow dyslexics to reach their full potential.

My brother, Tim, who struggled mightily in school, was an eloquent writer and communicator by the time he reached middle adulthood. He worked with me at my law firm for almost twenty-five years, and I was able to watch his progress in real time. Early on, I used to get memos from him that made me cringe and understand what he was dealing with. However, as the years went by, the memos became clearer and eventually outstanding. Tim had learned how to adapt and to unlock his potential. Remember, dyslexia has nothing to do with IQ, drive, ambition, or aptitude. It is simply a learning disorder.

Influential Thinkers With Dyslexia

Now for the very good news. Some very influential thinkers and successful people in history were dyslexic.

It is commonly thought that Albert Einstein was dyslexic because, like many people with dyslexia, Einstein was a late talker. He didn't speak comfortably until he was six years old. In fact, that period of his early life is so well known that delayed speech in kids is sometimes called the Einstein Syndrome.

He struggled with reading aloud and with word retrieval. He struggled to express his thoughts and ideas, and also struggled with foreign languages. Einstein had a very difficult time in elementary school. His classes, like many, relied heavily on memorization and rote learning. He did very well when he switched to a new school that encouraged creative thinking and learning.

People with learning differences are forced to think outside the box. Einstein was no exception. His ability to think creatively meant he came up with ideas other scientists had never imagined. Remember $E = mc^2$!

Einstein excelled in visual imagination and spatial reasoning. He attributed his conception of his special theory of relativity to a thought experiment in which he envisioned himself riding on a streetcar traveling at the speed of light.

He also frequently described his thought process as being nonverbal: "Words of the language, as they are written or spoken, do not seem to play any role in my mechanism of thought," he wrote to mathematician Jacques Hadamard in 1945.

He further wrote to his friend and psychologist Max Wertheimer, "Thoughts did not come in any verbal formulation. I very rarely think in words at all. A thought comes, and I may try to express it in words afterwards," and finally, "Writing is difficult, and I communicate this way very badly," which was reported by physicist Robert Shankland in *Conversations with Albert Einstein.*

Simply put, this genius, who won two Nobel Prizes and changed the world in so many ways, thought differently than the rest of us. And that thought turned out to be the musings and studies of a genius. The way of the world was to memorize words and math and regurgitate them. Einstein, like other successful dyslexics, found a better and more useful way—even a way that should have been taught instead of the rote learning the rest of us were subjected to.

And Einstein is not alone. Steven Spielberg, the renowned Academy Award-winning director, was not diagnosed with dyslexia until he was sixty. Richard Branson struggled in school and dropped out at sixteen, a decision that ultimately led to the creation of Virgin Records. Pablo Picasso was dyslexic. He stated, "I paint objects as I think of them, not as I see them."

The list goes on and on: Leonardo da Vinci, Anthony Hopkins, John Lennon, Jay Leno, and Jennifer Aniston. Because there are so many dyslexics in this world, many have had to find their own way, which turned out to benefit mankind in immeasurable ways. Just for fun, Google "famous dyslexic individuals in the world," and your jaw will drop.

At the end of the day, what I believe is that this bad luck of dyslexia, in the end, can turn out to be the best luck. This new way of thinking was more creative, more vibrant, and allowed these individuals to break boundaries that the rest of us never would have dared to attempt because we were locked into the old ways of thinking. Because they were forced to learn and to cope differently, it is my belief that it was a better way. Because this bad luck turned into great luck, these individuals have been given superpowers that allow them to do what the rest of us may not be able to do, because we have never dared to dream, or to think, like they do. That might be dyslexia, or any other kind of so-called disability that sharpens an individual in ways few other things can. But in the end, it serves to turn bad luck into the best of luck.

CHAPTER 9

GIVE AND TAKE

Selfishness Versus Kindness

I've often wondered if selfishness is a genetic or a learned behavior. There does not seem to be much support for selfishness being in the same category as IQ, aptitude, and drive. More likely, it's something we develop over time.

We have all seen the child in the sandbox who is not satisfied with their own toys but wants everyone's toys, even though they can't play with all of them at the same time. When we see that kid, we think, "greedy kid."

Many of these children grow up and continue with this behavior. There is a difference between being selfish and being self-centered. Self-centeredness is similar to selfishness, but the two concepts are different in very important ways:

- Selfish people often knowingly behave in ways that hurt other people so that they can benefit at that person's expense. Selfish people are so preoccupied and focused on themselves that it may be impossible to even have a second thought about how their behavior affects others.

- Self-centered people are simply overly focused on themselves. The *Merriam-Webster Dictionary* defines self-centered as "preoccupied with oneself and one's affairs." Self-centered people could have remorse once they realize that their actions hurt others.

Selfish people don't give a rat's ass about others' feelings. They are totally preoccupied with getting their own way.

Signs of selfish people include:

1. Having no regard for how their behavior impacts others.

2. Feeling entitled. Getting what they want is paramount. Others' feelings don't matter.

3. Having little empathy or regard for the suffering of other people.

4. One hundred percent of the time is focused on their own self-interest and never on meeting the needs of others.

5. Lack of remorse for hurting others.

6. Constantly manipulating to get their own way.

7. Being unkind, or their kindness comes with a price.

8. Using others to get what they want and to get their own way.

9. Not giving back to others, ever.

Whether a selfish person can love a romantic partner is a heavily debated question. In many ways, it depends on their willingness to change, grow, and prioritize their partner's well-being. However, we can never forget the adage "leopards don't change their spots." My advice is to stay away from selfish people and not risk divorce or hurt down the road.

On the other hand, there are so many people in this world who are kind, wonderful, and giving. You know the people in your life whom I'm referring to. You also know the people in your life you would describe as selfish and, more importantly, everyone in your circle would describe them the same way. We all see what we see.

Recently my five-year-old grandson, Henry, was playing *Monopoly* with my wife. My wife was low on money and almost ready to lose the game. When she informed Henry that it looked like she was finished,

Henry took one of his hundred dollar bills and slid it across the *Monopoly* board so that my wife would not be bankrupt.

Henry said, "That's what best friends do for each other." Henry's love for his grandmother and selfless ways warmed my heart and my wife's heart.

The Givers and Takers in Our Lives

As we have all progressed through life, we have met many of these givers and takers. All of us have friends and colleagues we socialize with outside the office, either for pleasure or for business. There are certain people that never, ever, pick up the tab. We often joke that these people have "alligator arms."

Once, a group of my friends was on a fishing trip in The Bahamas. Our host had a boat and a house, and all of us bought gas, beer, and dinners to make up for his hospitality and to thank him. However, there was one person on the trip who never offered to buy a drop of gas or a round of beer. None of us talked about it at the time. We all just privately noted it.

As you know, filling up a tank of gas for a boat is not cheap. Dinners and drinks in The Bahamas are also not cheap. But on our final night there, as we were driving home after diner, the one person in our group who had the alligator arms announced that he would like to pull into the ice cream store and buy us all a treat. I wish you could have seen our faces as he offered to buy us some ice cream cones. The looks to each other said it all. We had all been thinking the same thing the whole time. Each of us announced that we did not want any ice cream but thanked him for the offer.

Later the next day, as each of us had been simmering internally about his cheapness and selfish ways, we openly dissected his conduct during the trip. He was never invited back to The Bahamas, or any other place for that matter. He was one of life's takers.

Adam Grant

I love to give friends and colleagues books that have impacted my life in a meaningful way and that have given me direction, understanding, and enlightenment for life. One of those books is *Give and Take* by Adam Grant. What I would tell you about Grant is that he is a world-class thinker and thinks in ways that are obvious after the fact, but not as obvious to us before the fact. If you do nothing else, read his books, listen to his podcast, and follow him when you can. He is much like the other great thinker, Malcolm Gladwell, whose books, thoughts, and podcast I also highly recommend.

Grant's book *Give and Take* is instructive in so many ways. Grant categorizes people into three types: givers, matchers, and takers. Givers proactively help others; matchers have a "you scratch my back, I'll scratch yours" attitude; and takers are the suck-ups and backstabbers of the world. One thing is certain—if I gave you the names of friends and colleagues, you would quickly be able to place them in each one of those three categories, based on your interactions with them over the years. It's not hard to do.

In the book, Grant presents a research-backed view of what makes some people successful and others less so. At the end of the day, Grant shows us how reciprocity and success are linked, and that helping others ultimately drives our own success.

When studying the three styles of reciprocity, you may be surprised at who has the most success in the workplace. It's the givers. While some givers are exploited to the point that they burn out, others can achieve extraordinary success across a wide range of industries, more so than matchers and takers. Grant's conclusion is that takers tend to be domineering, using strong language to persuade others, while at the same time flattering powerful people to get ahead.

Why are they so selfish? They see the world as competitive, a place to get ahead. To the taker, life is a ruthless game where they take everything they want, only helping others if the personal benefit to doing so outweighs the cost.

Taking and Giving

A great example of a taker is Kenneth Lay, who was CEO of the energy firm Enron. He took out colossal loans from the company and then sold $70 million in stocks in a well-timed effort to take care himself before the company went bankrupt, leaving 20,000 people unemployed. Lay was convicted and later died on a ranch in Colorado surrounded by his family.

When Michael Jordan played, he advocated increasing the share of team revenues given to the players, but when he became a team owner, he argued for the opposite. His philosophy: "To be successful, you have to be selfish."

Takers see the world as one big pie. They believe there is only a limited amount of pie, and it is up to them to take the biggest piece. They are self-centered and focused only on the benefits they can get from others.

One of the hallmarks of givers is that they prioritize contributing value *to* others, not claiming value *from* others. The giver has a pure and good heart. Now it might seem that when you look at these three—takers, matchers, and givers—you might think the giver is going to be the least successful because he is not as ruthless or as competitive as the other two. The good news is that the opposite turns out to be true. There is much empirical data that points to the giver as the most successful in the long term. The taker is exactly who they are, and the matcher is a quid pro quo person. You help me, I'll help you. It is fascinating that the more giving person who doesn't seem as competitive or ruthless, wins the game of life and business by being a good human being.

One thing that is certain about givers and the benefit of reciprocity is the strengthening of relationships. By giving to someone else, givers show that they value others, care about others, and that having others in their lives is meaningful. When we believe that the person on the other side of the table cares about us, there is an entirely different relationship that develops. This is contrary to the taker, who is constantly looking for an edge. We trust givers. We don't trust takers. We see matchers simply for who they are.

Givers understand that success is not zero-sum. Their goal is not only for them to succeed but for the people around them as well. Givers are quick to share credit and to help others out, even when they may not benefit personally from the effort. They look for ways to increase value and reward for others.

Collaboration favors the giver and the giver favors collaboration. Givers usually see things from all sorts of different perspectives, which makes them more agreeable than most. By contributing help whenever they can, they establish a norm of giving and free-flowing ideas within their teams. In short, people trust them. It is also important to note that self-interest and a concern for others are not mutually exclusive. Successful givers are able to balance their own ambitions with others' goals and interests.

Successful givers are not selfless. Instead, they maintain a high level of self-interest and ambition while also concerning themselves with others' needs. Givers ultimately engage in strategic giving to avoid being taken advantage of, and work to establish a norm of giving in groups.

Givers are not necessarily doormats. They adjust their style when needed. When confronted with takers, they become matchers, while still maintaining their integrity; however, when in a group setting, givers give more, and do so publicly, helping to establish a culture of giving within their organization.

One of the interesting points about takers that Grant makes is that they have an incredibly broad network. This is, in part, because when they burn one bridge, they have to find new people to exploit in order to keep the network going. Matchers generally have a much narrower network. They only deal with people who will reciprocate in kind. As a result, they end up restricting their universe of opportunities. Givers have a much broader network of colleagues and customers than matchers, but in very different ways. A giver meets someone and asks,

"How can I add value to this person's life, and what could I possibly contribute that might benefit this person?" By doing so, they generate a tremendous amount of goodwill that remains dormant until they need it, or until a set of circumstances makes it relevant.

Everything Is About Tomorrow

I have often told my family that if I could inscribe anything on my tombstone, it would be this: *Nothing is about today, everything is about tomorrow.* This is how I have attempted to lead my life. When I buy a drink for someone in a bar, I am not looking for that person to buy me a drink in kind. First of all, I hate the people with alligator arms so much that I want to make sure I'm not one of them. Second of all, it just feels wrong to me to be waiting on someone else to buy me a drink. Finally, I have found in life that in these moments—whether it is a simple act of buying a drink or helping a neighbor—the return on those actions is enormous.

Once, I had an investigator in my Jacksonville office call me to tell me we had signed up a case where a little boy was killed in a crosswalk by a commercial vehicle. My investigator asked the woman what made her call me. Evidently, years before on Christmas Eve, I had taken one of my children to Bob Evans for breakfast. At the end of the breakfast, I left a $100 bill as her tip. She repeated this story to my investigator, who then repeated it to me.

On that particular day, there was nothing I wanted in return, and I never expected to see her again. It was Christmas Eve, she was working, and $100 meant a lot more to her than it meant to me. I walked out the door thinking nothing of it.

At the end of it all, we ultimately settled that case for $10 million. My fee was millions of dollars. My return on that tip is almost hard to calculate. A hundred dollars yielded me millions of dollars, but I never expected to receive a dime. After we resolved her case, this same woman has probably referred me ten cases over the years.

What I find interesting about this story is that I learned about her choosing my firm because my investigator asked her why. But think of the times you have given and received something later, yet you're not even sure or know about the reciprocation. When you go through life giving and not taking, the odds are, those people will show gratitude for your kindness and selflessness. The giver becomes the receiver. Ironically, in life and in business, the giver is the one who receives the most, because they are given it in return.

Takers tend to be very careful at impression management and ingratiation when they're dealing with someone superior or more influential. But they have trouble keeping up that façade in every interaction. It is often their coworkers or subordinates who see them for who they really are. For those of you old enough to have watched *Leave It to Beaver* or watched it in reruns, you may be familiar with the most famous ass-kisser in the history of television: Eddie Haskell. Eddie was a sneak and a fink who was constantly kissing Beaver's mother's and father's ass, while at the same time being devious. Eddie was the prototypical taker. One of the things I constantly look for in people is how they treat waitstaff, people working in the yard, or people working around the house. The person who is rude to the waitstaff, landscaper, or housekeeper is a person who no longer has a place in my world. It is an automatic turnoff and an automatic hard no on this person being part of my orbit.

Givers don't believe that giving credit for others' contributions takes away from their own contributions. Share the credit, share the glory. This makes it a lot easier to keep people on board in a team over time. It basically means that if you're a leader or manager, people will follow you if you rotate to a different organization or a different job. That's very powerful but often hard to do.

Jonas Salk, who invented the vaccine for polio, was not a person who gave much credit, if any, to those in the lab who helped him discover the vaccine. His conduct actually caused the team to fracture and splinter. Salk never made a discovery that was nearly as influential again. This was one of the costs of appearing as a taker in a collaboration:

slighting other people who might deserve credit. If you give credit for contributions, that does not take away from your own contribution. The real takeaway from all this is the giver collaborates, praises, and gives credit. Consequently, people trust them and will follow them to the end of the earth.

The Success of the Giver

At the end of Grant's book and research, the evidence is rather clear. In life, the giver is more successful than the taker or the matcher. While we may have worried about the giver becoming a doormat, over time the giver is seen as a person of compassion and positivity. The giver is someone people want to follow.

One of the ways I believe that we can enhance our luck is to take on more of the role of the giver. This may seem impossible, especially for adults who are set in their ways. As I said earlier, it's hard for leopards to change their spots. In Alcoholics Anonymous, one of the famous quotes is "Fake it till you make it." If you are a taker or a matcher, my advice is simple — start there, and watch your fortunes change dramatically. Your sense of peace and serenity will be enhanced as well. Is better to give than receive. It is also more profitable and fulfilling.

CHAPTER 10

AMBITION

So far, we have talked about genetic endowments that are in place, even before the baby leaves the womb. Such things as IQ, aptitude, dyslexia, and perhaps in some cases, different forms of autism. These children are born with that good luck or bad luck, depending on how we look at. But the real unknown is to what degree ambition is learned or genetic. Evidence suggests that genetic and biological factors contribute, but ambition is most strongly influenced by social, cultural, and demographic factors.

Behavioral genetics studies, which quantify the degree of genetic versus nongenetic causes of observable traits and behaviors, indicate that ambition is around 44 percent heritable. This obviously seems like a big number and one that is plausible to me. But when you compare ambition to other heritable traits like weight (which is 80 percent heritable) and height (over 90 percent), it may not seem as important. Like many positive traits, it's possible to learn and cultivate ambition.

The Visible Evidence of Ambition

There is one surefire way to improve ambition, and that is to have goals—as I talked about previously, not just goals, but *written* goals. According to a study conducted by researchers led by Dr. Naveen Puri, our ambition peaks around the age of thirty-three. Puri believed that restoring diminishing ambition could be accomplished by creating a series of mini aspirations. Some researchers believe ambition is not something that can be taught, but rather, it is something that must be nurtured and discovered from within.

Ambition is easy to spot. If I asked you to write down the name of three ambitious people, you could probably do so. And people who know them would probably agree. Ambition is out there for the world to see. Some people are quietly ambitious and some people, not. Some of the "not" people can also fall into the category of braggarts.

I believe that I had a certain amount of ambition from a very early age. I told you the story about my tooth being pulled and then going out and buying my paper route. That was the day I remember saying to myself, "I'm going to be self-reliant." However, up to that point, I had already been very industrious. In the second grade, I bought an *Archie Comics* book. On the back of it was an opportunity to sell Christmas cards from the Cheerful Card Company located in White Plains, New York. I sent off to be a representative, and I received a huge catalog with sample cards.

I went all over Lexington selling these Christmas cards. My grandmother, who worked as a secretary for the U.S. Agriculture Department, sold a bunch at work. Finally, when I had run out of prospects, I put on my Easter outfit from the year before and got on a bus and went downtown. Back in those days, a seven-year-old could get a bus and go right downtown Lexington. Times have changed. If my children left the street, we'd have called the FBI.

Once I got downtown, I went from office to office and store to store selling Christmas cards. I'm happy to report I sold a lot and made a considerable amount of money for a seven-year-old. I was hooked.

I also had a lawnmower and a snow shovel, and I spent many hours shoveling snow, mowing grass, and raking leaves. Raking leaves may be the worst job ever. The point is, all of this started when I was seven years old and way before I bought my paper route. Simply put, I was a hustler. I don't think that hustle has ever left my body.

When I think about the paperboys I knew, they were hustlers too. We were all kindred spirits because we knew we were doing something that nobody else was doing, and it was no picnic. It was a job and real work, and we had to show up every single day in the rain, sleet, and snow.

The Ambition Trajectory

It does not surprise me that the peak age for ambition is thirty-three. I have long told my children and their friends that I believe between the ages of twenty-five and thirty-two, your trajectory starts to take shape. Some people are going sideways, some people are going straight up, and others are going straight down. How far, how high, or how deep your rocket ship takes you depends mostly on your ambition and drive. I further believe that by the time a person is thirty-five years old, they are essentially formed.

People usually don't turn things around after thirty-five. Lots of parents, especially helicopter parents, hold out hope. But in my lifetime, it has been my observation that once a person reaches thirty-five, their trajectory in life has been set. The only thing left to determine is how successful or unsuccessful they will be. But thirty-five years old is the witching hour. If you're still in junior college or living at home, you might not be as successful as mom and dad once hoped.

I've told many of the people who work for me and with me that once you are forty years old, you are no longer eligible to be in the category of Golden Boy or Golden Girl. At forty years old, the joke is over. You're a grown adult, and you better have made it by this time, or you're not going to make it all. John F. Kennedy was president at forty-three. Ambitious children known as go-getters, in many cases, grow up to be adult go-getters. Now there are, of course, lazy ambitious people who are willing to take shortcuts, cut corners, take outsized risk, and prioritize short-term gains over long-term success. The lazy ambitious people are looking for easy ways to achieve their goals rather than putting in the hard work necessary to build a strong foundation.

In the great story "The Three Little Pigs," we learned that building a house out of straw or sticks was done so at their own peril. The third pig, Practical Pig, built his house out of bricks, and thank goodness he did. If he hadn't, his brothers Fiddler and Fifer (the first two pigs) would have been eaten by the wolf when he blew their houses down. They escaped to Practical Pig's brick fortress. He was an ambitious pig who had put in the hard work. You will know the lazy ambitious person because they are the person who talks a big talk and wants to live the lifestyle of the rich and famous but is unwilling to do the work to get there. They'll cut people down and do unethical things to achieve their short-term goal. Be on the lookout for these folks. They're not hard to spot.

Three Key Areas of Focus

Now just because your ambition is not extremely high does not mean you won't be successful. And the inverse is also true. Just because your ambition is high doesn't mean you will be successful. Many people have simple goals and achieve them. Many researchers believe that ambition comes down to focusing on three key areas: performance, achievement, and growth. When a leader decides to develop in these areas, they must do so while still respecting the desire of those they lead. In every organization, you will have different levels of ambition and different levels of success.

CHAPTER 11

WALL STREET

It is always interesting while channel surfing to see Jim Cramer, the host of *Mad Money* on CNBC, huffing and puffing and sweating all the while breathlessly doling out stock tips. What to buy. What to sell.

He does it in a very manic way, with his sleeves rolled up, tie loosened, and moving around the TV set in what seems to be pure panic. And these nuggets of wisdom are given out on a nightly basis. The show has run for many years, which means that many people have sat there and listened to his breathless diatribes. Once, I decided to look up his biography to see exactly who he is and where he got his expertise. The Internet tells us that he was a former hedge fund manager. I then decided to do one of my favorite tasks and that was to Google his net worth on *Celebrity Net Worth*.

Now in full disclosure, I understand that these net worths are hard to pin down. How can they know who lost big money and made big money for sure? *Celebrity Net Worth* pegged Cramer's total net worth at $150 million, with the salary of $5 million a year.

Now don't get me wrong, $150 million is rare air. But a net worth of $150 million is chump change for a hedge fund manager. Successful hedge fund managers are some of the wealthiest people in the world. They own gigantic yachts and sports teams. They have homes all over the globe and are buying new homes throughout America at record-breaking prices. If a hedge fund manager like Steve Cohen or Ken Griffin had a net worth of $150 million, they would be devastated.

Instead, Cramer is jumping up and down, holding himself out to be an expert on all things financial, even though he abandoned whatever he was doing in the hedge fund world. I can tell you this: neither Cohen nor Griffin nor Bill Ackman will be closing or resigning from their hedge funds to host CNBC for $5 million a year. In the world of hedge fund managers, it is the equivalent of a batter hitting about .105. The successful hedge fund managers all bat way over .400 and crush home runs on a regular basis.

But millions and millions of people have watched *Mad Money* forever, and some have blindly taken Cramer's advice because he is on TV, bloviating at breakneck speed. Now don't misunderstand me, Cramer is doing nothing wrong. In fact, Cramer is just like the sports experts who come on TV on Saturdays and Sundays to tell us who is going to win the ball games that weekend. Cramer is nothing more than a financial "Jimmy the Greek."

People are so desperate for an edge and inside information that they will listen to anyone who seems authoritative. My first question is, "If he's so smart, why is his net worth so low for a hedge fund manager?"

Hedge Funds

Now before we continue, just a word about hedge funds. These hedge fund managers make so much money because their fees are so high. A typical fee is 2 percent management fee of the money and 20 percent of the profits gained. Even when they lose, they win.

More importantly, the tax laws in America have basically been written by hedge fund managers through their puppets in Washington, D.C., and many of these billionaires pay little or no taxes because of the tax code. The intricacies and the carried-forward interest provisions give them this protection. If making this much money weren't enough, they are also not going to be made to pay taxes on it either. The folks in Washington are not owned by the hedge fund managers; they are simply rented temporarily. There are always ambitious politicians waiting to take the money and to pass on the favors.

I know one thing. Warren Buffett recommends never investing in hedge funds. That is enough for me. There are people who do invest in hedge funds, and some do very well. Universities, pension funds, and the very wealthy have no problem paying these fees as long as they're getting results. I have long held an opinion as to why people invest in these hedge funds in the first place. The fees are shockingly high, but it doesn't matter if the net return is beating the market.

The reason I believe that people invest in hedge funds is because they think, and hope, that the hedge fund is receiving inside information that will benefit them. Now, of course, most people would deny this. Insider trading is illegal—Martha Stewart went to prison for it. We know of so many incidents where insider trading has been busted by the Feds, so we know it takes place. I have friends who were in the hedge fund industry, and when the Feds started sniffing around, they simply closed and never returned. The prospect of jail will do that.

My hunch is that these investors turn a blind eye to what may be going on and, of course, have plausible deniability. If you've ever watched the show *Billions*, it is a fascinating (and somewhat accurate) look inside the world of a hedge fund. I'm sure Hollywood has made it more glamorous than it is, but you get the drift. The best and the brightest are hired to research and find advantages in the stock market. They can do it with analysis, research, and due diligence—and also with inside information. And no institution, pension fund, or individual can ever be found guilty of insider trading because of their plausible deniability. All they did was invest in a reputable hedge fund along with other reputable people.

If It's Too Good to Be True, It's Too Good to Be True

If you don't think it's true, remember this name: Bernie Madoff. Year after year, Bernie Madoff made spectacular returns—10 percent, 12 percent, 15 percent. It was shocking and unbelievable—until the fund fell apart in 2008 and employees (who were also Madoff family members) admitted to the FBI that it was a giant Ponzi scheme.

I had a friend who had sold his ambulance company and made about $10 million. This friend told me that he was investing, through his aunt, with a fund out of New York. He explained to me how well it had done for so many consecutive years.

So you must be wondering how this story ended. Years later, I received a text from my smug friend and the text was simple: *S.O.S. Call me. It's an emergency.* I immediately called him, thinking it could be an injury or a death. When he answered the phone, his voice shook, and I, at first, could not understand what he was saying.

Finally, I did. "I lost everything. All my money is gone." I asked him how that was possible, and he then asked me if I had been watching the news. He reminded me that the fund he had been investing in was Madoff's. It immediately registered with me, and I then had to listen to a grown man, well into his life, try to figure out what to do next.

As the days and months went by, we all watched the slow-motion train wreck concerning all of Madoff's actions. It was hard to watch. Some of the people had very little money, were unsophisticated, and even family members of Madoff. The monster had no conscience. Here is my takeaway concerning the Madoff debacle: I am certain there were many investors and money managers who knew full well that if it's too good to be true, it's too good to be true. For years, many of these investors had received outlandish returns, and many of them could not be hurt, unless there was a clawback, because their gains had outpaced even their investments. In other words, they had already won, and it was just gravy. These people simply turned a blind eye.

Once the search for the money was on, many of the players in the scandal were discovered. Some committed suicide because the investigation was getting too close to them. Some had some of their money clawed back, but not all. The small investors, as usual, just got wiped out.

Madoff reminds me of hedge funds. Hedge fund investors know it seems fishy, but they put on blinders, take the money, and run. They don't want to know because they are making so much money. I believe that people and institutions invest in hedge funds for the same reason they invested in Madoff. Greed and money. And, of course, plausible deniability. That's a big one.

Greed Is the Primary Cause of Bad Luck

If you want a surefire way of enhancing and improving your luck, never forget that advice. Greed is the primary cause of bad luck. Greed blinds our senses and our morality.

Wall Street is a gigantic casino where much of the game is rigged and favors the house, just like in Las Vegas. But the excitement of winning and losing is exhilarating, and the ups and downs are addictive, like cocaine. By the way, I don't know what cocaine does to you. I hear it is a euphoric high.

The endgame for most of these companies is for a very few select people, who control the inner workings, to one day have one gigantic event and then get the hell out of Dodge. Most of these masters of the universe make decent money, but the big money comes during the exit, or the IPO. So they manipulate earnings and sales and they cook the books. There used to be what was called the "Big Eight" accounting firms. I'm not sure there are four now, and certainly not the eight that existed before. Why? Many of these accounting firms turned a blind eye, or a helping hand, in the fraud of these companies. The country is littered with these cautionary tales. Enron. WorldCom. I could go on and on. What basically happens is the same thing that happens in musical chairs in kindergarten. You keep walking and walking around, and when the music stops, you need to find a chair. For some, there is no chair and they're out of the game. That's how I view the world of public companies.

Years go by as they circle the chairs and the music stops, and people keep getting eliminated. But the leaders of these companies have a fix. They actually carry a chair with them so when the music stops, they, and only they, will have a chair. And it's not just a chair, it's a throne. And it's not just a throne, it's a big throne. If you don't believe me, look at the company Countrywide Financial and its former CEO, Angelo Mozilo. When you read that story, you will understand my story.

The Few Ways to Make Money

There are really only a few ways to make money. You can work for someone and make a salary. You can start your own business and invest in yourself. You can take the money from your salary, or from your business, and invest in equities, bonds, real estate, or private equity. I'm sure there are some more sophisticated ways, but that's basically it. The problem with investing in companies is, how do you know who is a crook and who is honest? The short answer is, you don't. The main thing to remember throughout your money journey is that the game can be fixed, is sometimes rigged, and you will never know until it's too late if you've made the wrong choice. You will only know when the music stops and you don't have a chair.

Now there are ways to get luckier. Wall Street is like Las Vegas. There is high energy, lots of thrills, lots of booze, and lots of girls. It's just a different casino located in New York City. And as there are degenerative gamblers throughout Las Vegas, there are degenerative gamblers throughout the stock-market industry. I am always amused when I hear that a person's job is day trading. He wakes up at his house, showers, shaves (presumably), then goes to his monitors where he begins his day's "work." My belief is day traders don't really want to work, they want to gamble. What they should do is just go over to Atlantic City, play craps, and call it work. As we will discuss later, nobody wants to be accused of not working.

Crypto Kings and Day Traders

There are day traders throughout America, losing hundreds and hundreds of millions of dollars on a regular basis.

Many of the day-trader types are now transformed into crypto kings. They promise us riches with Bitcoin and other crypto coins. I have tried to understand what Bitcoin is and how Bitcoin works, but my simple mind just can't understand. I don't feel bad, because some really smart people don't understand it either. Yet it is all the rage as I write this book. Crypto traders and day traders to me are no different than the gamblers in Las Vegas and Atlantic City. They are just hoping for luck, not planning for luck. Planning for luck can be done and should be done. We can improve our chances of winning. In the casino, there are certain rules for the games. And each of these games has certain plays you should make each time a situation arises. Each game has different best practices for that particular game. Dealers and game operators all know what plays should be made according to the book. The book is the Bible in Vegas. Put simply, it's the play you should make to give you the best chance of winning. Remember, though, that in gambling, the house ultimately always wins. The game is set up for the customer to lose over the long haul. But it's very important for there to be winners, because that excitement and buzz is what draws the flies to the sugar. If you've ever been in a Las Vegas casino late at night and liquored up, and see the drunk big winner at a craps table, it is more entertaining than Mardi Gras in New Orleans. The place is electric. You must have winners to ultimately get more losers.

Now, the secret for those uninitiated: I do not consider myself a proficient gambler. I don't like to play games where I know I'm going to lose my money. Even though I know about the book and many of the plays I should make, I don't know them all. So if I don't know what to do, I simply ask the dealer. Why? Because the dealer knows every rule and play in the book, and the dealer is more than happy to tell you. They do so freely and they don't lie. Casino management is okay with this. When you think the dealer is on your side, you are going to sit there for a long time. The house knows that even if you know every play to make, the odds are still against you. Furthermore, the dealer also knows that when you win, especially while drunk, you are going to tip the hell out of them. So one way to improve your luck in the casino is to ask the dealer questions, even if you think they are stupid questions. People don't like to ask stupid questions, because people don't like to seem stupid, naïve, or new. What I hate more than seeming stupid is losing my money. So if you are unsure, ask the dealer the stupid question and improve your luck.

The Investing "Book"

Just as there is a "book" for gambling games, there is also a book for investing.

Over the years, I have learned the hard way about investing in the stock market and the bond market. There are simple rules and methods that, if followed, will give you the best chance of success. But like in Vegas, exuberance and greed sometimes gets the best of us and we quit making bets based on best practices and instead make bets based on our irrational exuberance or intoxication.

Have you ever been at a table in Vegas and watched some poor sap make the most incredibly stupid bet you have ever seen? Often when it occurs, the dealer will look at you with knowing eyes. Her eyes say to you, "This stupid bastard is blowing their money. You know it and I know it, so let's watch the show." Sometimes you actually want to say something to these strangers, because it is so hard to watch them playing the game and not knowing the rules or even the game itself.

The exact same thing happens in brokerage houses and wealth-management firms every single day. People make incredibly stupid and avoidable mistakes, just because Cramer said to buy this or that stock.

Later, I will talk about individual stocks and my thoughts on all that. My thoughts have been developed by consensus, error, and reading about the greats. Two books that were incredibly important in my journey are *A Random Walk Down Wall Street* by Burton Malkiel, and *The Black Swan* by Nassim Nicholas Taleb. I highly recommend these books to help you learn and better understand the pitfalls and the math going forward.

It's also important to understand that I am not and have never been good at math. I struggled mightily. When I would look at algebra, I was looking at hieroglyphics. I am a trial lawyer, real estate developer, and serial entrepreneur. I am the opposite of genius and rely heavily on others and on books. However, as bad as I was at math, once I started putting dollar signs next to the numbers, I became an idiot savant. Numbers meant nothing to me in math class. Numbers with dollar signs next to them were like waking from a coma and having extraordinary gifts. If you ever saw the movie *Rain Man*, I became him once I put dollar signs next to numbers. It really got my attention.

In the next chapter, I'll share with you my "book" for investing in stocks and bonds, and I want to explain how I came up with my advice. I think you will find the information I'm going to share with you compelling, and I hope it helps you improve your luck in investing going forward.

A Cautionary Tale

Let me share a story about my friend's investments in Madoff's fund. He had made some money during the Madoff years that he invested in property and houses, so that was safe. My friend received some money back in the clawback, but he had to basically start all over financially later in life. His endeavors have not been successful, even though he's been able to draw a decent salary for himself from the money his own investors put into his startup company. He is a smart guy. He thinks he is a *very* smart guy. But he never understood "If it's too good to be true, it's too good to be true." He had to have had an inkling that something was rotten in Denmark. But profit and his own greed never let him question that fact. Once I fully discovered his character, I made a very decisive move to disassociate myself from him in life and in business. I don't wish him ill, but I just decided I didn't like the stench around him.

Crime and Punishment

Later in life, I had the idea to build an attraction dedicated to crime and punishment. My thought was that America is fascinated with crime and punishment. All you have to do is look at TV shows, movies, and books to understand America's attraction to crime. I built a crime museum that I named Alcatraz East, located in Pigeon Forge, Tennessee, in the foothills of the Smoky Mountains. In this museum, I have artifacts and museum pieces that are fantastic. I have Ted Bundy's VW, John Dillinger's sedan, the death car from the movie *Bonnie and Clyde*, and the pièce de resistance, O.J.'s Bronco. If you ever find yourself in Pigeon Forge or in Gatlinburg, make sure you check it out. The reason I mention this is because I also obtained letters from the Madoff sons to their father and some artifacts. Madoff's sons were unaware. These sons, who had been paraded behind their father their whole life, proud as punch, were now humiliated and financially ruined. My heart bled for them. Think of the betrayal of a father to a set of sons that has that type of magnitude. The boys' letters and correspondence in the museum say it all. Unfortunately, one of the Madoff sons took his own life and another died of cancer. Their mother was swept into exile, while Madoff went to prison and was a manipulator even then. One of the fascinating things about Madoff to me was the night before he was going to turn himself in to the FBI, he had a party for his firm at MR. CHOW. Wielding a microphone, he praised the employees, passed out bonuses, and had a Christmas party as if nothing was going on. I have thought about that a thousand times. A look inside the mind of a psychopathic criminal. It is just fascinating.

LIFE IS LUCK

More fascinating is the fact that so many people follow these crooks when, in the back of their mind, they know better. You can tell when something is amiss. But greed and money are a powerful aphrodisiac.

CHAPTER 12

THE WOLVES OF WALL STREET

One of the really great movies of all time, starring Leonardo DiCaprio, is *The Wolf of Wall Street*. The main character is an unscrupulous addict who only cares about money, even at others' expense. If you've never seen it, it's certainly worthwhile.

A Word About Penny Stocks

The firm DiCaprio's character leads is what is commonly known as a *penny stock* firm, which operates boiler rooms. Boiler rooms—offices jam-packed with cold-calling salespeople—are a beehive of high-pressured sales. The stocks they are selling are called penny stocks, because you can buy them for pennies. They do not trade on big stock exchanges anywhere and are a highly risky investment. These stocks have much less regulation and transparency. The high-pressure salespeople have a list of names, and they dial for dollars all day long. Once they get someone on the line, the pitch begins. Each stock has a different story, and each story is being told by a penny stock salesperson. There are certainly some companies that came up this way and did well.

Penny stocks get a bad name in large part because of those operating the penny stock boiler rooms and the highly speculative nature of the companies. However, the story they tell (which is a true one), is that some legitimate companies started as penny stocks and erupted into gigantic colossuses.

Some penny stocks that blew up:

- GameStop
- Ford Motor Company
- Monster Beverage Corporation
- Micron Technologies
- Qualcomm
- Amazon
- Tesla
- Advanced Micro Devices
- Apple

So it is not as if these stocks don't have potential. As a matter fact, the success of some penny stocks is the reason wolves on Wall Street have so many takers who buy without even knowing the person on the other end of the phone.

There is nothing inherently wrong with low-priced stocks. They are considered speculative, very high-risk investments because they experience higher volatility and they're harder to sell once you buy them. Few full-service brokerages even offer penny stocks to their clients. That should tell you something.

Obviously, these speculative stocks are not for the faint of heart. If you are able to get past the limited disclosures, warnings, and liquidity issues, real money can be made by investing in these stocks.

The reason I have always avoided penny stocks, even with stories like Tesla and Amazon, is that according to a study by the SEC, only about 10 percent of penny stocks succeed in the long-term. This means 90 percent fail, resulting in significant losses for the investors. Penny stocks are a vehicle many con artists use to take advantage of unsuspecting investors.

The most common reason people buy these stocks is simple: greed. Greed anywhere is a surefire way to NOT improve your luck. Since 90 percent of all penny stocks fail, and it's impossible to know which one will be the next Apple and which one will be the next rotten apple, it seems to me that the best way to improve your luck is not to play the game at all. So my advice for enhancing luck on Wall Street is to stay away from penny stocks.

Individual Stocks

The first real decision is what form the investment will be, whether it is individual stocks, mutual funds, or index funds. There are pros and cons to all options.

Individual stocks come with risk and reward. How one knows which stock to buy and which stock not to buy is a matter for debate. I can't tell you how many individual stocks I bought in my early years just based on tips from friends and brokers. I was walking around with a wad of money looking for slot machines. In retrospect, I had no clue. More importantly, the people who were giving me my tips probably didn't either.

Sometimes someone just sees the future. For instance, my daughter was in college when Kindle and e-books were beginning to be used in classrooms. She and her brothers received some monies from another investment. She insisted on putting it in Amazon (the others banked it) and she has tripled her money.

Mutual Funds

Mutual funds let you pool your money with other investors to "mutually" buy stocks, bonds, and other investments. They're run by professional money managers who decide which securities to buy and when to sell them. Many investors buy mutual funds because they offer built-in diversification, and diversification helps mitigate the risk and volatility in their portfolios. It is a luck enhancer when compared to individual stocks.

You can withdraw your money from most mutual funds any time, unless they have a lock-in period. Relatively speaking, mutual funds are a good way to invest, but there is always a hidden caveat—that is, fees.

It is very important to know what the hidden charges are in mutual funds. Some of those costs include sales and marketing expenses, administration fees, distribution fees, fund manager fees, and so on. Usually, the more money you have with a fund manager, the lower your fee should be. Once again, to the inexperienced, these fees can get blurry, and often newer investors do not know enough to ask.

Index Funds

An alternative to mutual funds are index funds. After many years of trial and error, this is where I decided to place my money.

As mentioned earlier, a life-changing book for me was *A Random Walk Down Wall Street* by Burton Malkiel. Once, as a gift, someone gave me an autographed copy, which I keep proudly in my library at home in Florida.

The book's central theme is the "random walk" theory—a belief that stock prices follow a random pattern and are not predictable in the short term. Malkiel's argument is against the notion of market timing and stock picking, and states that it is nearly impossible to consistently outperform the market over time. Even with mutual funds and single stocks.

What has been proven over time is that by embracing the random walk theory and the principles of efficient markets, investors can reduce risk and increase their probability of achieving long-term financial success. However, the central most important part of index funds is that they charge a very low percentage for managing your money. And they should. They are not picking individual stocks. They are simply buying the entire market. Which markets you decide to buy can vary. There are index funds for almost everything. Large cap. Small cap. Asian-Pacific. You name it, there's an index fund for you. Index funds come in all shapes and sizes to give investors diversity.

Dollar-Cost Averaging

One of the safest rules, which is actually part of my own Wall Street "book," is the idea of *dollar-cost averaging*.

With dollar-cost averaging, every month, or week, whatever time you determine, you send a fixed amount of money to the fund of your choice. John Bogle pioneered all of this with the Vanguard Index. To this day, the Vanguard Index is the gold standard for index funds.

Once a month I send a fixed amount to an index fund known as DFA, and I am then locked and loaded. I don't think another thing about what has happened, and I rarely check the stock market. I don't have to. Because I'm averaging over time and not trying to time the market, it all evens out over the long haul. Much like the games in Vegas, to continue dollar-cost averaging as the market is crashing takes nerves; sometimes nerves of steel. In my investing life, I've been very disciplined, and during the worst times, I have increased the amount I send monthly, hoping to have a better return when the market returns.

In 2008, the economy tanked, and everybody was wondering what would happen next. I want to tell you the story of two men. They had started a home-building company and sold for a big profit. Both of these men were investors with AllianceBernstein and had all of their money there. Both stocks and bonds. When the market crashed, both men took very different paths. One of the men finally had enough of the volatility, and by the time his portfolio of equities had been slashed in half, he pulled the rip cord and jumped. This is what the majority of people do when the going gets rough — they bail.

The other partner had the exact same conversation with the broker, and decided to sell nothing and continue to dollar-cost average — buy a set amount every month and ignore it. He never blinked. The book said to hit, and he hit. The story ends with the market recovering and the one partner gaining not only all of his money back but also having tremendous gains from buying when the market was at a record low. His partner, on the other hand, sat on the sidelines for many years and started to get back in the market once it had fully corrected and had actually surpassed the prices when he sold.

The Millionaire Next Door

Once, I read another great book called *The Millionaire Next Door* by Thomas J. Stanley. The book basically watched two doctors who made the exact amount of money but ended with two vastly different amounts in their savings account. Even though it's old, it's a worthwhile read. The proverbial millionaire next door is very disciplined and has a lot of great habits.

As we discussed briefly in chapter 5, "Marriage," the number-one trait for the millionaire next door, who kept most of his money, was that he was never divorced. Choose wisely in marriage. Divorce usually means sharing half your net worth. Unless you have a prenup. Another hedge for luck is a prenup. All of my children have one. In fact, if they don't have one, they don't receive under the will like the other children; they only receive a certain amount of money each year. Make yourself the bad guy and let your child tell their future spouse it's out of their control.

The Psychology of Money

One of the most successful mutual funds of all time was Peter Lynch's Magellan Fund. Between 1977 and 1990, the fund averaged a 29.2 percent annual return, making Magellan the best-performing mutual fund in the world. Now for the punch line and a bit of psychology. Shockingly, the average investor lost money in the Fidelity Magellan Fund under Lynch's tenure during a period of time when the fund returned around 29 percent annually. And now you must ask yourself the question, why? Before you go to the next paragraph, maybe you want to answer it yourself to see if you are correct.

What happened during those years is a lesson in the psychology of money. When the market crashed, people sold. When the market was at an extraordinary high, people bought. The net result is that only 31 percent of all the investors ever made money in the Magellan Fund—the ones who stayed in for the long haul and didn't react to daily market conditions. The investors who didn't make money failed to read the great Warren Buffett's warning: Be greedy when people are fearful and be fearful when people are greedy. My book for equities is very simple. Stay with dollar-cost averaging, even as the market is going all the way to zero. (By the way, if it ever hits zero, we are living in *Mad Max* days anyway. At that point in time, it's a free-for-all.)

Putting It All Together

So now that you have the warning about penny stocks and the lessons on dollar-cost averaging, let me give you the final big takeaway for index funds over mutual funds. As we discussed earlier, index funds typically have lower costs and fees compared to actively managed mutual funds. This stems from their passive management style involving less frequent trading and lower administrative expenses. The average expense ratio for actively managed mutual funds is between 0.5 percent and 1 percent. They rarely exceed 2.5 percent. The Vanguard fee is currently 0.17 percent. When you look at 0.17 percent next to 1 percent an unsuspecting, unsophisticated investor might not see much difference. But there is a gigantic difference. Do the math. The fee is almost five times more. And some mutual funds charge up to 2.6 percent, making the difference in price astronomical. Over the life of a person's savings, those costs can really add up and have a huge difference in your ultimate retirement goal. But now for the really important news.

The way mutual funds are sold to us is that because they have active professional managers trading every day and living and breathing the market, then you, the investor, will have a better return with active management rather than passive management. Now let's look under that hood.

Generally, when you look at mutual fund performance over the long run, you can see a trend that actively managed funds underperform the

S&P 500 index. A common statistic is that the S&P 500 outperforms 80 percent of the mutual funds every year.

Malkiel gave an example by comparing a $10,000 investment in the S&P 500 index fund to the same amount in the average actively managed fund. From the start of 1969 through June 30, 1998, the index investor was ahead by almost $140,000; the original $10,000 increased thirty-one times to $311,000 while the active fund investor ended up with only $171,000. The bottom line is this: Over the short term, some mutual funds will outperform the market by significant margins, but over the long term, active investment funds tend to underperform passive indexing, especially after taking account of fees and taxes. If you go out ten years, it is almost impossible to find a mutual fund that has outperformed the index fund during that time. When you look over thirty years, it's a no-brainer. The person who is dollar-cost averaging in index funds, with low fees and expenses, will do markedly better than the person with the actively managed mutual fund at higher expenses and costs.

This is possible for the same reason that the person who hits 16 in Vegas will lose more often than they win. It is possible because the person who is buying penny stocks, while still knowing there is a 90 percent chance of losing all of their money, buys them anyway. The reason is good salespeople and greed.

The Wall Street book for me reads like this:

- Dollar-cost average.
- Only use index funds for stocks.
- Don't panic and run. Keep investing.
- Pay attention to the fees associated with your account.
- Sit back and let the market take care of itself.

You will likely need to have a yearly session with your tax preparer to make sure everything is taken care of for taxes.

I have decided against hedge funds. Warren Buffett says no, so I say no. I say no to mutual funds and penny stocks. In the next chapter, I will give you one more piece of investing advice that I use for my retirement.

When it's all said and done, the same rule to improve your luck is the same one we have seen before. If it's too good to be true, it's too good to be true.

CHAPTER 13

ITS HARD TO MAKE MONEY (AND EVEN HARDER TO KEEP IT)

As hard as it is to make money, in many cases it's even harder to keep money. There are many reasons for this. Many people are simply not prepared to start investing, and it takes years and sometimes decades to finally figure it out. It's amazing to read about all the sports stars who had staggering sums of money paid in salaries and are now broke. It doesn't just end with professional athletes. It happens everywhere. The most frustrating part of it all is that most of the fate these folks had was totally avoidable. I can't imagine how many times they must look in the past and think, "What if?"

Like in gambling and the "book" in casinos, the book exists in investing too. However, just as enthusiasm and recklessness causes people to make dumb bets, we make the same dumb bets for the same dumb reasons when we invest.

How we make these mistakes can vary. Unscrupulous financial advisors. People doing their own research and following Jim Cramer off a cliff. Making bad investment choices, not based on research, but caught up in the moment. There are so many reasons and so many different ways to lose money that it is staggering.

One of the most common mistakes people make is they think their ability to make money will never end—that they will be making this money, or more, for the rest of their lives. That is a fatal mistake, because we have no idea what the future holds.

Youth can be a tremendous asset for work. Energy and drive are at all-time highs. But the young do not believe in mortality. A person at thirty cannot even imagine being seventy-five. I'm here to tell you it happens in the blink of an eye. When I look back now at all I didn't do, it makes me sick to my stomach. I am, however, proud of some of the things I did do, because I have been extremely cautious. A childhood like mine can have that effect.

The Great Depression

Many people who lived during the Great Depression were scarred for the rest of their lives. People who lived through it were comfortable but never saw it coming. It is hard to fathom what the Great Depression must have been like. But the people who were impacted in those days had an experience most never forgot and that many used for the rest of their lives. They lived to save. They were not reckless with their investments. The people who suffered during the Great Depression knew firsthand how bad it could all end in one fell swoop and their investing and savings were changed forever. The bad luck of the Great Depression turned out to be good luck for their futures and great luck for their children's futures, who had watched their families collapse firsthand.

While my family never had the degree of suffering that some people had in the Great Depression, we still had some very rough patches. Due to both of my parents' alcoholism, financial security was not something we grew up with. We lost homes and, on many occasions, had the power, phone, and other essentials disconnected. It became a way of life. I would pick up the phone and there would be no dial tone. I would not wonder if the phone company had an outage. I knew that my parents hadn't paid the bill.

Consequently, home ownership and mortgages have been a very focused part of my investment life. Losing our home meant losing our dignity. If you lose your dignity, it can be as scarring as it was for all those people in the Great Depression.

Extinguishing Consumer Debt

The number-one expense in American households is the mortgage. The second expense is the car payment. Once you get rid of a car payment and your mortgage, that is the moment you start saving like crazy. And the sooner you start, the more likely you are to have a happy ending.

You will have to be careful though, because there are many snake-oil salesmen out there hoping to get into your pocket. In doing so, they will sell you lots of promises and projections that look good on paper, but simply are pure speculation and numbers pulled out of the air.

My belief is that the sooner you extinguish consumer debt, car payments, and mortgages, the sooner you start to build your ultimate safety net. Now the advice I'm about to give you runs contrary to some of the smart people's advice.

Leading up to the financial collapse in 2008, there were many people responsible for setting so many other people up for this great fall. It worked like this. A stockbroker and a mortgage broker would take a person to lunch. Over lunch, which may have included cocktails, the pitch went like this: You borrow money on your home and take the interest tax deductions for the mortgage and invest the principal in the stock market. Over time, your house increases in value. At the same time, your stock value increases. All of these assumptions were made based on the past—the past ten years, the past fifteen years, but the past. And all that is fine and good, until it isn't. Until the stock market crashes and home prices fall.

In those days, I had neighbors who were actually borrowing money on their homes to buy speculative condominiums being built. Remember those days of flipping contracts and making easy money? A very respected radiologist in my neighborhood borrowed money to put in the stock market and buy two spec condominiums in Daytona Beach. Almost twenty years later, he is still digging out from that debacle.

The stockbroker and the mortgage broker will not be there to bail you out when everything goes to hell in a hand basket. They will have made their commissions, and you will no longer be invited to lunch because you are broke.

So the conventional methods of keeping a mortgage and investing in stocks dissipated for a while, but people have short memories, and they forget the pain of all they experienced.

Because of my experience growing up, I have the same fears some of those folks had exiting the Great Depression. In 1988, I bought a big house. I bought it after a really great liquidity event happened for us. I paid cash for my home. The house cost $480,000—a staggering sum to me at the time. I could not believe I was living in such a house, and I really couldn't believe that it was paid for. I have never had a mortgage on any of my homes since. The fear of losing my home traveled with me from childhood. The bad luck I experienced as a kid turned out to be good luck for me in my future.

In my past, I had also seen my father have his car repossessed. This was another humiliating moment and more bad luck for the family. Again, that bad luck turned into my good luck, because my further advice in enhancing your luck going forward is to pay off your cars and your consumer debt before you pay off anything. And why? It's really very simple. The interest rates you pay for cars and credit cards are so ridiculously high that there is no way you will make that type of return routinely with your investments. These credit cards are 18 percent and higher. So my advice goes like this. Pay off consumer debt first. Pay off cars next. Once those are taken care of, then—and only then—start whacking down the mortgage.

Life Insurance

I'm here to tell you that this will prove to be one of your best luck enhancers going forward. I might also add at this time that the younger you are when you start buying life insurance, the better off you will be. Young people don't think they're ever going to die. I'm here to tell you that is wrong.

One way to protect your family and increase your family's chances of financial security in the event of your unexpected death is to buy lots of life insurance at a very early age. First of all, when you are young, the insurance is very cheap. Next, assuming you are in good health, the insurance will be much cheaper. Time gives you the opportunity to develop a medical condition that will make insurance prohibitive or impossible, and age only adds to the cost of insurance. Many people, as they get close to the end, buy life insurance as their investment strategy for retirement. And isn't that sad? Older people throwing a Hail Mary pass at the end so that one of them will have enough money to live and not be homeless. I know it seems hard to talk about, but life insurance has to be part of your financial planning. I used to tell people that you knew someone really loved their spouse and children when they had lots of life insurance. They weren't going to be there to enjoy it, but they loved their family enough to sacrifice now for them later.

When I bought that house for cash in 1988, I had another bit of good luck come along with the deal. My neighbor, Mike Furstman, was a retiree from Ohio. He loved to talk, and his conversations turned out to be some of my greatest luck. By the way, the neighbors you have can be great luck or horrible luck.

Tax-Free Bonds and Treasury Bills

What Furstman taught me back in those days was invaluable. The lessons are still with me. Furstman explained tax-free bonds. Tax-free bonds are bonds that are issued to pay for infrastructure and a variety of public essentials. Water. Electricity. The bonds are tax-free because the law is such that we need the investments to build these essential services.

When I started buying tax-free bonds back in 1988, the rates were crazy. When you historically look back at the rates of tax-free bonds, there are periods of low yields and periods of staggeringly high yields. When I started buying, my yields were very, very high. I decided then and there that tax-free bonds were going to be a very safe investment for me and a way to keep my hard-earned money. Depending on the quality of the bond and the municipality, or government that is guaranteeing it, will determine your rates. There are some very good bond managers and bond funds in America. Because I was scarred from my childhood, making money and then keeping that money was paramount. Over the years, I have built a bond portfolio that pays me money every single year. As I write this book, my tax-free bonds are yielding anywhere between 4 and 5 percent. Back in the day, I used to set goals for myself. At first, I wanted $10 million in tax-free bonds. I figured if I had that, I could receive $400,000 to $500,000 a year. As time went on, I kept moving the goalposts. I made a decision to forgo risk and potentially better returns for less risk and security.

Once your home, credit cards, student loans, and cars are paid off, your bills shrink to almost nothing. Now for the good news, which made this a luck enhancer for me when it came to keeping my money. Because I'm always worried about losing my investments, I research things like tax-free bonds and treasury bills. My research showed me that even in the Great Depression, fewer than 1 percent of municipal tax-free bonds defaulted. That fact really stuck with me. The world was on fire, the economy was tanking, but these tax-free bonds kept paying. Now I am still never totally at peace financially. Just because it's never happened doesn't mean it won't happen. Consequently, I have divided my investments into different buckets. The one thing I know from the past is that anything can happen. In my lifetime, there have been events that shook the world and the economy.

- The Korean War
- The Vietnam War
- The recession in the early 1970s
- 9/11
- The Great Recession of 2008
- The coronavirus pandemic, which closed the world

You never know. Throughout all those different crises and world events, tax-free bonds have stood the test of time. My investments in higher-risk equities like stocks have decreased and investments in safer instruments such as tax-free bonds have increased. I consider that a luck enhancer.

In addition to tax-free bonds, I buy lots of treasury bills. Am I nervous about them? Hell yes! I am nervous about everything. I worry about the full faith and credit of the U.S. currency. Especially when you look at these numb-nuts who are in Congress. I would say that I wouldn't hire 95 percent of them to work in any of my businesses. That is frightening. On the other hand, we have to put our money somewhere. Equities. Bonds. Private equity. Real estate. Cash.

All of these vehicles I use. And I use many different brokers and brokerage houses. Bernie Madoff has scarred me forever. If treasury bills are finally worth nothing, then there are many other huge problems that may be the least of my worries. Again, I would be living in a Chernobyl-type world if that ever happens.

I've stayed away from metals, commodities, and Bitcoin, because I just don't understand it; and to me, it's another form of gambling because of my lack of knowledge. If you don't understand something, you are asking for bad luck, and the major thing that is driving you is greed.

The Best Way to Keep Money Is to Not Spend It

Now, I know that much of this advice will be ignored. It always is. People will go with hunches, tips, and just their gut. So many people are trying to get rich quick that they end up getting broke fast.

Making money is hard. Keeping money is harder. And one way to keep money is to not spend money. Credit cards and revolving debt are poison. The interest rates are mafioso-type and sometimes impossible to extinguish. I'm lucky that I'm married to a woman with inexpensive tastes. Ultima shops at Ross Dress for Less and T.J. Maxx. In life, it is very helpful to have one spouse that plays good offense and the other that plays good defense. Which is why one of the best ways to keep money is to not spend it in the first place.

CHAPTER 14

WARREN BUFFETT

Patience Is a Virtue

It's impossible to talk about money and luck without talking about one of the greatest investors ever: Warren Buffett, the Oracle of Omaha. I don't think there is one investor in America that any of us reference as the GOAT other than Buffett.

Buffett was a paperboy in Omaha, Nebraska. He didn't have to be a paperboy; he chose to be a paperboy. His father was successful and was actually a U.S. congressman. Buffett, at an early age, had his entrepreneurial genes working full force.

Today, as I write this chapter, Buffett's net worth is somewhere around $140 billion. Some billionaires are born into immense wealth, while others hustle their way to the top with drive, ambition, and grit. Buffett is the poster child for the hustlers.

At just six years old, Buffett earned his first few cents selling sticks of gum in the neighborhood. He sold Juicy Fruit, Spearmint, and Doublemint. He carried the sticks around on a tray and sold them in packs of five for a nickel. Once, a woman asked for one stick, and little Buffett refused. He told the woman, "We don't break up packs of gum—I mean, I've got my principles. I still, to this day, remember Mrs. Macoubrie saying she wanted one stick. They were a nickel, and she wanted to spend a penny with me."

Later, he found the margins to be better while selling Coca-Cola door-to-door in the summer, even at the lake when his family vacationed in Iowa. Interestingly enough, Coca-Cola would one day become one of Buffett's greatest investments.

Buffett became a paperboy at thirteen years old and made it a competition with himself. Since his father represented a Nebraska district in Congress, Buffett woke up at 4:30 a.m. to deliver copies of *The Washington Post*, and he challenged himself to find ways to serve each of his five buildings faster. Later, he found ways to track when the houses along his route had magazine subscriptions expiring, and he sold new subscriptions on the side, along with calendars. Young Warren was dealing in vertical integration before the term had been popularized.

By the time he was fifteen, Buffett had made $2,000 delivering papers. He invested $1,200 of that in a forty-acre farm where he had a profit-sharing agreement with a Nebraska farmer.

After earning enough money working for other people, Buffett began a company of his own. His first company was Buffett's Used Golf Balls. He bought refurbished balls from a man in Chicago at $3.50 a dozen and turned them around for $6.00.

Later, while Buffett was still a kid in Omaha, his friend's mother introduced him to betting at Ak-Sar-Ben, a local horse track. While he was too young to gamble, he wasn't too young to make money on what other people carelessly threw away. Buffett explained, "They call that stooping." He had noticed that novices were placing bets at the beginning of the racing season. "And they think that if your horse came in second or third, you didn't get paid, because all the emphasis was on the winner, so they'd throw away place and show tickets."

After the races, he searched the stands for discarded tickets mingled in with cigarette butts, beer, and old food. He remarked, "It was awful; people would spit on the floor. But we had great fun. If I found any winning tickets, my Aunt Alice would cash them in for us, because they wouldn't cash them for kids." Later, he had his high school golf coach drive him to some of the races where he would make bets after studying race statistics. Once, he went alone, bet on every race, and lost all of them, as he let his emotions get the best of him.

"I'd committed the worst sin, which is that you get behind and think you've got to break even that day." He went on to conclude, "It was the last time I ever did anything like that." Buffett did not like the odds in gambling and he moved on quickly.

His next venture was titled Buffett's Approval Service, which sold sets of collectible stamps to collectors who lived out of state. He abandoned that business "because it involved manual labor and turned out to be too damn much work."

Later still, he had a new idea that he thought had massive potential. "I bought this old pinball machine for $25." His idea was to put the pinball machine in barbershops. He claimed to be a representative of the nonexistent "Mr. Wilson's Coin-Operated Machine Company."

This venture was a huge success, bringing in $4 in its first night and thrilling the barber, who had allowed him to put the machine in his store. After a week, Buffett walked away with $25 and reinvested in another machine. He continued until he had seven or eight machines. "Mr. Wilson's Machines" were making him money even as he slept.

This young entrepreneur and paperboy began his life hustling and, as I write this today, he is still hustling into his ninth decade on Earth. Clearly, lots of luck went into the genetic makeup of Buffett. The drive of the paperboy is the same drive that has fueled so many men and women later in their lives.

Like hedge funds later, Buffett decided against gambling and focused on picking undervalued stocks and waiting for them to take off and explode. Statistically, Buffett is probably not the most successful investor in history. Others have found quicker and more success in shorter periods of time. Even as you read that, you're probably thinking, "Who are they?"

Buffett's Role Model

Buffett learned at an early age that risks, like gambling, were a likely way to lose his money. Losing money is not part of Buffett's calculus. What made him the most famous investor in the history of America was his patience and diligence. Early on, Buffett saw patience and value as a key to his future. The famous value investor, Benjamin Graham, was Buffett's role model and mentor.

Graham was a British-born American financial analyst, investor, and professor. He is known as the "father of value investing" and wrote two important books: *Security Analysis* and *The Intelligent Investor*. One of Buffett's luckiest breaks was being a student of Graham at Columbia University. It was there that he was introduced to value investing, and that lucky break proved a catalyst for the future. Buffett later worked for Graham's company, Graham-Newman Corporation, until Graham retired.

Graham had rules in investing:

1. Always invest with a margin of safety.

2. Expect volatility and profit from it.

3. Know what kind of investor you are.

Those lessons proved extremely valuable.

Later in life, Buffett had his own five basic rules of investing:

1. Never lose money.

2. Never invest in the business you cannot understand.

3. The favorite holding period is forever.

4. Never invest with borrowed money.

5. Be fearful when others are greedy and be greedy when others are fearful.

To this day, Buffett spends 80 percent of his working day reading and thinking. He spends five to six hours a day reading five different newspapers and combs through five hundred pages of financial documents, and he recommends prospective investors do the same.

Bad Luck That Turned Good

By the way, Buffett was first rejected by Harvard and later enrolled in an undergraduate degree at Columbia Business School. The bad luck of being rejected at Harvard turned into great luck by going to Columbia and meeting Graham. Had he been selected by Harvard, he most likely would never have met Graham, and who knows what history would be. That rejection turned out to be some of his best luck ever.

One of the great books on Buffett is called *The Snowball*, and it is terrific. I highly recommend it. It lays out in detail Buffett's early years, all the way to the present. In that book and in further studies of Buffett, we begin to see what his true strength was.

He invested in companies with potential, but a low value at the moment and with great management. Buffett rarely changed management but instead infused direction and capital. Then he sat back and let the company grow, patiently. Relying on the power of compounding interest, he became the greatest investor in America.

When you do a deep dive on Buffett's investments, you will learn that much of what occurred is also known as luck. What Buffett was especially great at was avoiding situations that were too risky, and also relied on time to heal some of those missteps. Buffett has picked quite a few losers, even though he is known as our greatest investor. What becomes apparent is that a few big investments, held for a long period of time while growing with compounded interest, was the secret to his success.

The Power of Patience

Let me give you a fact that was mind-numbing for me but really makes the case for patience: $81.5 billion of Buffett's $84.5 billion net worth came after his sixty-fifth birthday. You almost have to read it again to really appreciate that fact. At an age when most people retire, that was the age when he really put the pedal to the metal and a lifetime of investments began to pay off. Obviously, now in his nineties, his net worth has ballooned even further. That is the power of patience and compounding interest. It is a vital lesson to us all for enhancing luck. If Buffett had retired in his sixties, I doubt we would be talking about him now. He had a net worth of $1 million or $9.3 million adjusted for inflation at the age of thirty. If he was not as driven and had spent his early life doing what normal kids do and finding his way, it would be a much different story.

If his net worth was only $25,000 at the age of thirty, we would be talking about a totally different animal. That million dollars in net worth at that early age gave him a great chance for great luck. When we look at all of Buffett's financial success, most of it can be tied to his early years as a paperboy and an entrepreneur, as well as the longevity he has maintained as he's gotten older.

His great skill was investing. But his secret sauce was time. That's the power of compounding interest.

Another book I highly recommend and that I was spellbound by is *The Psychology of Money* by Morgan Housel. It points out that Buffett is the richest investor of all time but not actually the greatest when measured by average annual returns. Jim Simons, head of the hedge fund Renaissance Technologies, has compounded money at 66 percent annually since 1988. There is no investor that comes close to this record. Buffett on the other hand has made 22 percent annually, or a third as much. The author of *The Psychology of Money* points out that "Simons' net worth, as I write, is $21 billion. He is—and I know how ridiculous this sounds given the numbers we're dealing with—75 percent less rich than Buffett."

If you're wondering why, it is because Simons did not start really doing well with his investments until he was fifty years old. So he's had less than half as many years to compound as Buffett. The author points out that,

> "Had Simons earned his 66 percent annual return for the seventy-year span Buffett has built his wealth, he would be worth—please hold your breath—sixty-three quintillion nine hundred quadrillion seven hundred eighty-one trillion seven hundred eighty billion seven hundred forty-eight million one hundred sixty thousand dollars."

Now, of course, his luck was bound to run out during that time but, more importantly, it shows the power of compounding interest and the power of time.

What is most often lost with investors is the takeaway that "the counter-intuitiveness of compounding may be responsible for the majority of disappointing trades, bad strategies, and successful investing attempts."

Most of us like the idea of getting rich quick. All you have to do is look at the people who play the lottery each week. More about that later.

What happens, especially as you start running out of time, is that you start making investments trying to earn the highest returns possible. You stop chasing gold and begin chasing fool's gold. Greed and not investing early are two ways to squander your luck.

Earn Good Returns You Can Ride for a Long Time

But it is important to note that, like many penny stocks, 90 percent of them turn to dust. The best strategy for investment luck is earning good returns that you can ride for a long period of time. And when you ride that bull for a long time, that's when compounding runs wild.

If the top twelve stocks Buffett ever bought were eliminated, his success would most likely not be near what it is today. That is not to say that he might not have picked twelve other stocks that would have exceeded his top twelve. Possible, but not necessarily likely. Those top twelve stocks have proven to be very lucky in the overall scheme of things.

We know that Buffett does not always pick winners, because he is very upfront about his wins and losses. His annual letter to investors is must-read advice. His candor and honesty are incredible. He really doesn't take that much credit for being a great investor, but he does take lots of credit for being patient, focused on time and compounding interest, and staying away from gimmicks. Buffett believes in index funds. Buffett does not believe in hedge funds. Buffett believes in sitting on cash; to be ready to pounce when the world is shaken upside down. Buffett's story and life is a roadmap for enhancing luck with your investments. The beautiful part about it all is that it is so simple.

CHAPTER 15

THE PSYCHOLOGY OF MONEY

One of the greatest gifts someone can ever give me is to recommend a book that turns out to be one I simply can't put down. It is the greatest feeling in the world. I'm delighted to read as much as possible every single day and dejected when the book finally ends.

In my opinion, there are very few great books circulating out there, even though so many have been written. I would like to recommend a great book that dovetails into everything I'm talking about. *The Psychology of Money* was written by Morgan Housel. I had never heard of him before I read his book, but boy is he smart. For me, he's up there with Adam Grant and Malcolm Gladwell as thinkers I respect. Much of what all three address is human psychology. Housel has distilled it down in *The Psychology of Money*.

As I read the book, it appeared that it had been written just for me and for the book I was thinking of writing. Luck and risk are weaved throughout his entire book.

Morgan points out that the reason we don't always do what we're supposed to do with our money is for the two following reasons:

1. **WE ARE ALL NEW TO THE GAME.** Most financial tools are very new. 401(k)s were not introduced until 1978, and the Roth IRA was added in 1998. We've only had about fifty years of investing with these vehicles.

2. **WE ALL THINK ABOUT MONEY DIFFERENTLY.** People who grew up in the Great Depression think differently about money than the person who has never had a financial blip. Life experiences play a huge role in how we invest our money.

Luck Matters More Than Skill

A key takeaway is that luck and risk have a bigger impact than financial skills. Nothing is as good, or as bad, as it seems. All success is not due to hard work, and all poverty is not due to laziness. No financial outcome, either success or failure, is purely due to hard work and sound decisions. The accidental impact of actions outside of our control can be more consequential than the ones we consciously take.

For example, you might not know that Bill Gates and Paul Allen started Microsoft together when they were classmates and fascinated with computers. They also had a close friend, Kent Evans, who was also very skilled with computers and math. Evans was part of this trio, and you may wonder why they left him behind when they formed Microsoft. They didn't. He died in a mountaineering accident before he graduated from high school. The odds of being killed on a mountain in high school are roughly one in one million. Both Gates and Evans were very smart and had a passion for computers, but each of them had two extreme ends of luck. One was bad luck, death. One was phenomenal luck, Microsoft. From time to time, Gates has been known as the richest man in the world, and probably most of you had never heard of Evans until this book. Luck can be cruel. One thing is certain: there are countless numbers of rich people who have lost everything because they were not satisfied with the immense wealth they had.

Financial Success Is "Survival"

Bernie Madoff was a success. He was very respected, and yet that wasn't enough for him. He wanted more and more. The only way to get the admiration and success he was looking for was to create a horrible Ponzi scheme. In my life, I have always kept my money separated. I have what I call the A side—that is, money I use to invest—and my B side—which is money I will never touch for the rest of my life. In *The Psychology of Money*, Housel points out, "There is no reason to risk what you have and need for what you don't have and don't need." Housel, like Buffet, is also a big proponent of time, patience, and the power of compounding interest. According to Housel, financial success can be summarized by one word: survival.

1. FOCUS ON BEING FINANCIALLY UNBREAKABLE. If you're unbreakable, you will get the biggest returns because you'll be able to hang around long enough for compounding and time to kick into high gear.

2. WHILE PLANNING IS IMPORTANT, EVERY PLAN IS NOT GOING TO GO ACCORDING TO PLAN. The more you need specific elements of a plan to be true, the more delicate your financial life becomes. If you have enough room to say, "Making 8 percent a year over the next thirty years is great, but if it only does 4 percent a year, I'll still be okay," your plan is a good one.

3. ALWAYS BE OPTIMISTIC ABOUT THE FUTURE BUT PARANOID ABOUT THE OBSTACLES TO YOUR SUCCESS. Andy Grove, the great CEO of Intel, famously said, "Only the paranoid survive."

Buffett is the greatest investor of our lifetime. He teaches us that you can be wrong half the time and still make a fortune. As I pointed out in the last chapter, Buffett made the majority of his money on ten to twelve stocks but owned four hundred to five hundred stocks in his lifetime, and many of those were big busts. The investment decisions you make on 99 percent of days don't matter. What does matter are the decisions you make on a small number of days when something big is happening—the stock market is crashing, or the stock market is frothy, or the stock market is a speculative bubble, and so on. Housel describes the investing genius as an individual who can do the average thing when all those around him are going crazy. If we look at Buffett's wins and losses, we will see more losses than wins. But when he won, he won big, and held on forever with a compounding interest at his back.

Comparison Is the Thief of Joy

Your greatest freedom comes when you have total control of your time. The highest form of wealth is the ability to wake up every morning and say, "I can do whatever I want, when I want, with whom I want, for as long as I want." Once you get control of all of your time, you have won this game.

Some of the things that I believe drives so many of us to make terrible decisions is because of greed and envy. There is a saying: "keeping up with the Joneses." The Joneses' success and your envy of their success can be the beginning of your financial downfall.

"Comparison is the thief of joy." The first time I heard that quote, I really had to sit back and digest it fully. It really hit hard, because if I were honest with myself, I would have had to confess that others' wealth and success had been something in the past that caused me lots of consternation. The question I would ask myself is, "Why them and not me?"

The comparisons we make between ourselves and others are fraught with danger and pitfalls. We see a competitor working out of a beautiful office, dating a stunning person, and driving a Ferrari. That comparison can drive a lot of joy out of our system.

The truth is, we have no idea if it is real or fake. Remember, all that glitters is not gold, and no one is as impressed with your possessions as much as you are. It's called the "man in the car paradox." People don't think someone is cool if they see them driving a nice car. Instead, people imagine how cool other people would think they were if they had that car. People who compare themselves to others believe that if they have this success and wealth, they will be liked and admired. If respect and admiration are your goals, be careful how you seek them. Humility, kindness, and empathy will bring you more respect than a Lamborghini ever will.

Finally, there is often a sad ending to that person you have been admiring and coveting their wealth for so long. In some cases, it turns out that it was all a mirage. The office was rented month to month. The Lamborghini was a lease. And the attractive passenger in the Lamborghini was rented as well.

It turns out that, for some of us, comparison, which stole our joy for so long, was not based on reality. We wasted our time trying to keep up with a crook, a fraudster, or a poser, and in doing so, wasted valuable time making real money and real success. In my own town, I have seen people who I thought had a Midas touch go to prison. Everything they were doing was fraudulent.

In Orlando, there was a fellow who was always driving fast cars and even had bodyguards follow him into restaurants and bars. When he would land in other cities, he would hire police escorts to take him to the hotel. He was flocked by beautiful women. It turns out he had stolen millions and millions from unsuspecting investors and is now serving time in prison.

The truth is, wealth is what you don't see. Rich is current income. Cars. Jewelry. Vacation homes. But wealth is hidden.

Living in Richistan

Another great book I would like to recommend is called *Richistan* by Robert Frank. Richistan stands for the idea that in neighborhoods throughout America, there are three sets of residents: Upper Richistan, Middle Richistan, and Lower Richistan. All these people live in the same ZIP Code and socialize with each other. They're in the same country clubs and the same schools. All together in this world.

The problem is, each set of individuals—upper, middle, and lower—has a much different net worth, yet they are all shopping at the same stores. When one of the neighbors sees another coming back from Neiman Marcus with bags and bags of goodies, comparison becomes the thief of joy, and they want those items. Luckily for them, they have credit cards. And they use those credit cards voraciously to keep up with the Joneses.

At the end of the month, one of the individuals simply pays off the credit card charged that month, and another person makes a minimum payment on a credit card that is charging incredible interest rates. They both bought the same items, but one could afford them and the other should have put them on layaway. Remember layaway?

This phenomenon plays out all across America every day. People joining country clubs when they can't really afford it. People taking vacations when they have no money in the bank.

I remember years ago going to the Super Bowl in Jacksonville. Paul McCartney played at halftime. I remember later reading about the fans from Philadelphia. It was reported that the largest number of third mortgages that had ever been issued in a certain period of time set a record in Philadelphia. What was going on? These Philadelphia Eagles fans were taking out third mortgages on their homes to see the Eagles play in the Super Bowl. When I read it, I wanted to throw up. As a side note, McCartney was fantastic. To add insult to injury, the Eagles lost. Those fans had that one weekend they desired, and probably for the rest of their lives, they will be paying off three mortgages back in Philly.

It's also important to understand that long-term planning is harder than it seems because goals and desires change over time. The truth is, we don't know what the future holds.

Life's Surprises

When I got married, my wife was practicing in Orlando with a good job. I had almost no money, and she had to give me her Mobil gas card to get home for the wedding after I graduated from law school at the University of Florida. I was as broke as broke can be. It reminded me of something a fellow from Alabama told me once about his financial situation at one point in time. He said, "Sweetheart, I was so broke, I needed a cosigner to pay cash." Luckily for me, I didn't need a cosigner because I had my wife, but I was broke.

We went on our honeymoon to The Bahamas. I had a friend who owned a Holiday Inn in Nassau, and we went there for free. Now here comes the interesting part. When we returned from our honeymoon, I had to start studying for the bar exam. Twenty-five percent of the applicants usually fail that exam, so it's a pressure cooker.

Before I took the exam, we discovered that my wife, Ultima, was pregnant. It was a stunning moment, and we lay there in our rented bed, in our rented condominium, watching a broken paddle fan whirl at a very slow speed. It was one of the most helpless feelings I have ever felt. It was game on, and although I had a job lined up, I still had to pass the bar exam. Pressure does not begin to describe what I was feeling. Mike Tyson says, "Everyone has a plan until they get punched in the face." Well, that morning, I was punched in the face.

My wife is a very devout Catholic and does not believe in artificial birth control. She follows the rhythm method. Well, I am here to tell you that the rhythm method does not work on your honeymoon when you've been drinking. We had all four of our children in rapid succession until I took matters in my own hands and visited my doctor. I learned during those years that the rhythm method is no match for Maker's Mark on a Friday or Saturday night. It simply does not work.

The good news is, our four children have given us more joy and pleasure than any money ever could. Our three sons practice in our law firm, and our daughter has a structured settlement business, Monarch Funding. Plans are fine until they're not, and then we improvised and made new plans. That is what life is all about. New wrinkles, twists, and turns will come at you in every stage of your life. You have to adapt, change, and pivot. Sometimes you're right. Sometimes you're wrong. I believe that pure luck has the most to do with everything we do. If someone had told me that getting pregnant on our honeymoon was a good thing, I would have told them they're nuts. Today I'm here to tell you that getting pregnant on our honeymoon was the greatest thing that ever happened to us. We liked our first child so much that we had three more. Money can never buy that kind of happiness and joy.

One thing Housel wants us to remember is that the more we want something to be true, the more likely we're going to believe the story that overestimates the odds of it being true. Cable news has taught us that. People watch Fox or MS NOW because they want to hear what is being said. Not because it is necessarily true, but because that's what they want to hear.

After World War I, most people thought there would never be another world war again. World War II began twenty-one years later, killing 75 million people. Housel tells us that there are many things in life that we think are true because we desperately want them to be true. He calls them "appealing fiction," and they have a big impact on how we think about money, investments, and our future. One interesting fact in the book is that half of all U.S. mutual fund portfolio managers do not invest a cent of their own money in their funds, according to Morningstar. Think about that. Those fund managers are saying, "Do as I say, not as I do." The main thing we need to do is figure out what works best for us and what is the safest path to financial salvation.

Like the casino, there is a book that tells us what our best route and options are. But greed, envy, and impatience get in the way; and every day, people are making terrible financial decisions based on those emotions that lead to financial ruin. Certainly, there are stories where a person has made a wild bet and won big. And we hear about it, and we want to be that person.

Those people were lucky. However, far more were unlucky in making the exact same bets, just on different days. There is a safe path for a safe future. Save. Invest early. Dollar-cost average. Use index funds. Don't invest in hedge funds. Rely on U.S. treasuries and tax-free bonds. But most importantly, invest in yourself.

Invest in Yourself

One of the things I suggest is to get a piece of graph paper, or use the computer, and plot your income for the last ten, fifteen, and twenty years. Then connect the dots on the graph paper to show what that income looks like. Then do the same thing with your savings and net worth over the same period of time. When you look at these two pieces of paper, you're going to be looking at your own personal stock market. I call it "the investment in ME." When you look at that chart, you will see how you are doing in life financially, and also have the opportunity to make changes.

I believe strongly in investing in ourselves. I have made more money investing in me than in anything I have ever done. My other investments are a hedge for the future to give me enough money and safety to make it until the end. Throughout my investment life, I have a number that it takes me to live on, and what I have attempted to do is to have enough investments that produce enough money that I can lead my exact same life as I'm leading now with the interest and never touch the corpus. That was my goal a long time ago and, luckily for me, it happened.

But it didn't happen overnight; it took a lot of blood, sweat, and tears. It's a long climb, but when you get to the top of your mountain, it's a fantastic feeling.

At the end of the day, your financial future rests with you and your decisions. Those decisions will be the time you start investing and what you start investing in. If you play the long game, you will win, more often than not.

CHAPTER 16

THE LOTTERY

The Desire to Be Rich

If you want to understand how desperate people are to be rich, look no further than to all the forms of gambling. If you want to enhance your luck and save your money, you will never gamble again. Gambling is one of the surest ways to lose all of your money in the long run. The fascinating thing about gambling is that the odds are so stacked against you, it's hard to believe you are even participating.

Different forms of gambling give you a better chance of winning. Certain forms of gambling give you almost no chance of winning, yet people spend billions and billions of dollars annually in the pursuit of riches.

The psychology of gamblers is fascinating. We have all heard about the degenerate gambler—the person who is as addicted to gambling as other junkies are to crack cocaine. It is so prevalent that Alcoholics Anonymous actually spawned Gamblers Anonymous. It is a tremendous problem in America and the rest of the world.

What makes gamblers dangerous, especially the degenerate gambler, is that they believe they have figured out a system to win. I have been to horse races with gamblers who come with the preparation of a space launch. They have facts and figures and the racing form, and they are as diligent as any person you will ever find. On many of these days, I have seen these people miss on every single race, but they come back the next day with the same mindset and same certainty. Gamblers usually learn nothing from the past.

Gambling With My Paper-Route Money

The first time I came face-to-face with gambling was when I had my paper route in Lexington. On Saturdays, after I had completed my route, I would go with my crew to have breakfast at the Toddle House in an area known as Chevy Chase. I always loved Saturdays because there was no school, I was going to go home and go back to sleep, and I still had the entire weekend.

Directly across the street was a barbershop simply known as Jack's. Jack was a barber and owned the shop. This is where I got my hair cut.

One day while in the barbershop, a few men came in and exchanged money with Jack for some long-looking cards. When the men left the shop, I asked Jack what it was all about. He informed me that the men were playing a gambling game called a teaser.

When I asked what a teaser was, he explained the rules, a complicated set of rules for predicting final scores of college football games.

Once I learned these rules, I felt like I was going to be taking candy from a baby. It just seemed too good to be true. Remember what I said about being too good to be true? I asked Jack if I could buy a card. As it turned out, Jack and the other barber brother were the local bookies in Lexington.

Jack gladly told me I could have a card and that the price was $1 for three games, and I could win $5. If I picked four games, I could win $10. The amount I could win increased by the number of games I picked. Again, I thought this would be easy. However, I decided to start out slow. I was only going to bet three games, because I wanted to win and get my sea legs for this new form of moneymaking.

I took my teaser card and went across the street to the Toddle House. Every Saturday, I played the same songs over and over again.

"Mrs. Robinson" by Simon & Garfunkel. "Honky Tonk Women" by the Rolling Stones. "Muddy Mississippi Line" by Bobby Goldsboro. Once I got the jukebox cranking and my order made, I sat down to get to the business of making easy money. When I scanned the list, it was every college football game in America, it seemed. Each team was either favored by a certain number of points or not favored. All I had to do was add ten points to three games and I would win.

It seemed so simple. But that entire football season, I only won one weekend. I never bet four games because I was losing just doing three games. What seemed to me to be a slam dunk turned out to be darned near impossible. Those days were a great lesson to me because I learned early that gambling was mainly for fools and desperate people. But boy, was it fun. I've never paid such close attention to college football games as I did that fall season. I lived and breathed them. Back in those days, it was hard to get scores, so sometimes I had to wait for the Sunday paper to scour results from out west the night before.

I saw firsthand, at an early age, how intoxicating gambling could be and how dangerous it was as well. It was so much fun, and it made watching games so much more fun and exciting. What wasn't fun by the end of the football season was the fact that I had lost every single teaser I played except for one. I learned fast why they called it a *teaser*. They teased us into thinking we couldn't possibly lose. What could be easier?

So my paper route introduced me to bookies, gambling, and life lessons that would stay with me forever. One valuable life lesson was the responsibility of running my own business — the paper route. The other life lesson was to stay away from gambling unless I expected to lose the money. Gambling was for entertainment only.

The Allure of Free Money

In my businesses, I have often told people that the best word in America is the word *free*. The second-best word in America is *money*. The two best words together are *free money*. Gambling, in all forms, gives lots of people a perceived pathway to free money.

Gambling is really a chase for free money. Gamblers don't have to work. They can drink alcohol and smoke while they play. They don't punch a clock or go to an office. Many people like the idea of free money with little work. But in the end, they come away with much less, losing money they could ill afford to lose, and in some cases losing everything—including their homes.

Now the one thing operators of gambling businesses understand is that it is essential for there to be many winners. If there are not many winners, there will not be many players. But when you read that a woman in Pennsylvania has won $700 million and will be taking a lump sum after taxes, you begin to think it's possible. In casinos, bells go off and people start screaming when they win. That exuberance causes other gamblers to say it's possible. It is the act of winning and seeing others win and win big that causes gamblers to throw caution to the wind and make bets that are highly unlikely to pay off. But if they've gotten themselves into a desperate situation, the desperation to dig out with yet more gambling is overwhelming.

Crank Games

The psychology in all of this is fascinating. I own attractions all over America. In our arcades, we have games known as "crank games." The crank game has a claw that is lowered into the pit, where you attempt to snatch a stuffed animal, then maneuver it up and over and finally out of the machine. When you get this stuffed animal out of the machine, bells go off, the player starts screaming, and people are drawn to the game like moths to a flame.

There is a dirty little secret about crank games. There is no skill involved at all. The machine is simply programmed to win as often as the owner allows. It can be one out of twenty or one out of a hundred. The owner makes a decision of how many wins to give away to keep the moths coming back to the flame. Keep in mind also that these games, where the price of admission can be anywhere from $1 to $5, only gives the participant the chance to win a stuffed animal that cost 50 cents.

If you go to the fair, bowling alleys, family fun centers, and so on, these games are everywhere. People spend $100 to win a 50-cent giant stuffed pink bear. These crank games go on in arcades throughout America and are one of the top-grossing games ever. People want to win, and they want the bells to go off so that their friends, family, and children can see them win. The psychology in all of this is breathtaking.

Lotteries

The lottery, for me, is the most fascinating form of gambling, because it seems the most risky. I'm sure there are other games that may have more risk, but I don't know which ones.

And they are probably the greatest crank games in the world. Some people are going to win, because if the bells don't go off and the confetti doesn't start to fly, others won't play the game. So lotteries have many forms of winning. With Powerball games, weeks and weeks go by, and people pump billions of dollars into the coffers of the government. Finally, maybe weeks later, there is a winner. Other games vary from state to state—like scratch-off games and lotteries where you pick fewer numbers but have a much lower payout. Just like in the old teaser games, the more numbers you pick, the more money you make, but your odds decrease rapidly as the difficulty of winning increases. Now for some sobering facts.

Americans spent $108 billion on lottery tickets in 2022. Importantly, you only have a 1 in 292 million chance of winning one of the largest jackpots. You probably have a better chance of jumping out of an airplane into the ocean and surviving. Spending on lottery tickets is up 20 percent from 2020, and ticket sales have topped $100 billion.

Americans are becoming much more comfortable spending an increasing amount on lottery tickets, perhaps because so many have become desperate and worried. Forty percent of all Americans have less than $400 in the bank, and 60 percent of all Americans live paycheck to paycheck. Ticket sales were just $69 billion in 2012 compared with $108 billion in 2022. That represents a massive 57 percent increase over ten years. What it means to me is that there has been an increase in desperation and a desire to get rich. To put it all in perspective, I remember hearing about a mathematics professor who told the Associated Press that if someone bought a Powerball ticket—a much harder ticket to win—three times a week for eighty years, they would be far more likely to get struck by lightning than to win the large payout. It's important to note that not only are the odds stacked against you, but it's also that when you spend that money on lottery tickets, you're taking away from investment opportunities that have a far better chance of making you money.

For example, if you spent $20 a month on lottery tickets over thirty years, that totals $7,200 out of pocket. But if you opened a brokerage account and put $20 every month toward an index fund that tracks the S&P 500, you might earn a historical average rate of return of 8 percent per year, giving you $27,400 at the end of thirty years. To the habitual lottery player, $27,400 is peanuts compared to the potential of a lottery jackpot, but it is also far more realistic than hitting it big in Lotto.

According to the North American Association of State and Provincial Lotteries, roughly 65 percent of proceeds from lottery ticket sales go to winners. Just like the crank games and casino games, people need to see winners and lots of them, and they need to hear the bells, the screaming, and the celebration.

Fifty percent of Americans buy a lottery ticket once a year. The purchasing of lottery tickets really increases as the pot increases, making the chances of winning much slimmer.

According to LendEDU's analysis of the most recent data, the average American spends $223 per year on the lottery. And that number continues to rise from year to year. Remember that 40 percent of Americans don't have $400 in the bank, but the average American spends more than half of that on lottery tickets.

In 2021, state and local governments in the U.S. collected about $31 billion from lottery games. Non-Hispanic whites and native Americans had the highest proportion of gambling on the lottery (51 percent for each group). Now for some more news. The lowest-income households spend an average of $412 per year on lottery tickets, more than four times what the highest income households spend. This is why it is known as a regressive tax. The people who can least afford to play, play the most. It seems absurd that the lowest-income individuals play the lottery the most, but they are also the most desperate and are willing to blow their safety nets on something with a one-in-a-million chance of hitting it big.

Scratch-off lottery tickets pay back around 50 percent on average. For every $10 a player spends, they will "win" $5. National lotteries like Mega Millions or Powerball have even worse odds. While a player may occasionally luck out and win, the more they play over time, the likelier it is that their monetary losses will reach the intended average set up by the lottery operators. Plain and simple, lottery tickets are a losing proposition.

A Social Equalizer

One may wonder why those living in the most strained circumstances would waste so much money on these games. Many of us might think that the behavior is just plain old ignorant. But many scientific researchers point to other psychological explanations. In one study, researchers highlighted the inequalities present in the U.S., and noted that low-income players may consider lotteries to be a "social equalizer" in which everyone has an equal chance to win in an otherwise rigged system. Many of us, me included at a certain point in my life, really wondered why I had been dealt such a shitty hand. That kind of thinking can make logic go out the window and then we pour good money after bad. A study in Germany found that although the chances of winning are very low, playing the lottery at least creates hope for improvement in life and a higher social status that players cannot achieve in any other way.

The lottery plays a fascinating psychological study into the minds of human beings. Without being too judgmental, it's also important to note that many of these lottery players are just not bright. The average reading age in America is seventh grade. So we have many adults walking around making decisions every day, including playing the lottery, but read at a seventh-grade level. I worry that these folks are blinded by the hope of digging out of poverty with these fools' errands.

Now there is no doubt that people do win, and some people win big. That is the foundation of the psychology of gambling. When we see reports on the national news of the Powerball amounts, it creates a frenzy. Week after week, the national anchors give us a blow-by-blow on the lotteries that might make one of us one of the richest people in the world.

With that frenzy constantly swirling in advertisements and news reporting, there is no wonder that a society mired in debt and desperation would play this game. Because of the types of people who play the lottery, it's not surprising to find out what they do with their money once they get it.

Losing After Winning

According to the National Endowment for Financial Education, 70 percent of large lottery winners go bankrupt within a few years. Obtaining more money often leads to careless spending and the desire to get more money, and the greed can be destructive to the lives of the winners and their families. The most common mistake lottery winners make is overspending. New wealth encourages extravagant purchases without a well-thought-out budget. Without this financial discipline, lottery winners can quickly spend all their winnings. Many of the large lottery winners have the option of taking it in a lump sum or putting it in an annuity that pays them year to year and avoids financial mistakes while keeping the majority of the proceeds safe. Far more people take the lump sum, pay the taxes, and start spending like drunken sailors.

The type of person who would play the lottery game is generally not a responsible investor and, in most cases in America, is no more than a seventh-grade child with tens of millions of dollars at their disposal. We read about professional athletes who had gigantic contracts and great success, only to go broke a few years after playing the game. The same happens to these big lottery winners who lost it all. Dan Field, a therapist specializing in gambling-addiction treatment, says, "The lottery holds such a prominent place in American culture, because it gives people the opportunity to indulge in fantasies about how their lives could change if they win. These fantasies run rampant throughout our country."

Addiction

My father was a guy who lost a lot of jobs because of alcohol. He also was a gambler—horse racing, sports betting, you name it. One of the saddest things he used to do was to call me up randomly at night and the conversation would start like this: "Do you know what I would do if I won the lottery?" When he would call to ask me that question, I always felt terrible because I knew that my father was over at his apartment daydreaming about a life he wished to have but had no chance of ever achieving. I always played along and said, "Tell me."

He would always start by telling me that the first thing he would do was go to Greece on a trip. I don't know why Greece. We are Irish and have no connection to Greece, but that was his fantasy. He would then talk about setting all of us up financially and buying a new home for himself. Sometimes this conversation would go on for quite a while, and it happened all the time. I never cut him off or cut him short. I knew that there was this man I loved over in his small apartment, daydreaming about financial security and excessive riches. He didn't just want *some* money, he wanted *lots* of money. My dad had an addictive personality to begin with. People with an addiction usually have more than one. Lottery tickets are as accessible as cigarettes and alcohol. They are everywhere. It's also true that winning a lottery can release dopamine in your brain that causes euphoria. The power of winning is incredible. The lure of winning big is intoxicating. There are many reasons for lottery addiction. Genetics. Environment. Brain chemistry. Mental health. It goes on and on.

For people who have a serious addiction to gambling, there is Gamblers Anonymous, an international fellowship of people who have a compulsive gambling problem. They meet regularly to share their experiences, strength, and hope so that they can help each other solve the problems of compulsive gambling. Gamblers Anonymous use twenty questions as a guide to determine whether they are compulsive gamblers. This is not a definitive evaluation and only helps get you started.

Good Luck and the Lottery Don't Mix

In the long run, all of us are better never playing the lottery, especially if we can ill afford it. In my business life, I have had the opportunity to invite many people into my deals over the years. Real estate, attractions, hotels, apartments, and other enterprises. At the end of my presentation, I tell every single potential investor, "If you cannot afford to lose all of this investment, don't make it." Many times, people look at me bewildered and ask me if I think we are going to lose. In all of my investments, I am always the largest investor. I tell them I wouldn't be putting my own money in unless I thought I had a winner. But I want these people, who are usually friends or acquaintances, not to exceed the amount of money they can afford to lose. I have always felt an ethical obligation to add this caveat in my presentations. The security documents my investors receive have all of this language in the fine print somewhere deep in the prospectus. But most people don't read the fine print until they decide to sue the promoter.

The lottery is possible due to the universal desire for "easy" riches. While there are certain ways we can enhance luck in our life, one of the ways that we run from luck is to run into trouble in games like the lottery. As we go through life, everyone looks normal walking up and down the street. Inside their minds, many are churning and thinking of ways to escape the life they now lead and enter a life they have only dreamed up. Unbeknownst to most of these people who cannot afford to lose this money, they lose their rational thinking and diminish their luck to play a loser's game.

The government never loses and the poorest and least educated amongst us foot the bill for many of our services and basic needs. The same people who don't have $400 in the bank spend $200-plus per year playing the lottery.

And I'm sure many of these people call their children from time to time and ask, Do you know what I would do if I won the lottery? The first thing I would do is go to Greece."

CHAPTER 17

CASINO ROYALE

While playing the lottery is one form of gambling, casino gambling is a whole other animal. The way I look at them both is that the lottery player is like the alcoholic who drinks alone at home, escaping reality and dreaming impossible thoughts; the casino gambler is like the alcoholic who needs a crowd, like Norm from the TV show *Cheers*. The casino gambler is there for the camaraderie, the action, and all the other vices that are rolled into a casino setting.

The lottery gambler doesn't have to spend big money to win the Powerball. The allure of a gigantic payout with such little investment probably makes the lottery much more appealing, especially to people who desperately want to live out the Johnny Paycheck song "Take This Job and Shove It." The lottery gambler makes their bets in private at a local gas station or convenience store. When I think about it, I rarely hear anyone talking about playing the lottery. I think most lottery players quietly dream of getting out of their rut but don't want to say anything about it, because it shows their level of discontent and unhappiness.

The chances of winning the lottery are much less than winning with most casino games. The chances of winning the big lottery tickets are almost statistically impossible. Not only does the casino give us the chance to win money, but it also gives us a chance to have lots of fun and fellowship.

Currently, there are casinos in forty-four states and on Native American tribal land. Once upon a time, we had to travel to just a few cities to play in a casino. As a result of governments needing money and wishing for people to tax themselves by playing games that cannot be won, casinos have multiplied all over America.

When you walk into a casino for the first time, it's like walking into a gigantic party. Cocktails are everywhere and often free. The ceilings are high and the lighting and music are designed to boost energy. Scantily clad women are bringing drinks and friendly faces. Casinos and the bars in casinos are also usually crawling with prostitutes. You sit down to have a drink, and a woman sits down next to you looking for conversation. This doesn't happen at home.

The Perfect Recipe for Losing Money

All of the excitement mixed with booze is the perfect recipe for losing lots of money. There are casino games that have certain plays that players should make situationally every single time. Unfortunately, many people don't know which plays to make and are too embarrassed or intimidated to ask the dealer. Additionally, when they add lots of liquor, they are now dealing with a whole different person who will make wild and erratic bets.

Also, being around a lot of people makes gamblers more reckless, because they can get caught up in the moment and in the excitement of the cheering from fellow gamblers. Total strangers sit at a table, and all of a sudden have bonded over gambling games. Cheering each other on and giving each other high fives is commonplace in the casino.

The truth is, casino gambling does not seem like gambling; it seems more like entertainment. After all, when you visit these places, there is great food, great shows, great shopping and, yes, gambling. It doesn't feel like a place that a degenerative gambler would go to, but go they do, in droves. Lady Luck is just one of the ladies many people are looking for in the casino setting. For me, I have always been very circumspect about how I gamble in a casino.

I am well aware that the odds are very much against me, especially if I don't ask the dealer for help. I also understand that if I have had too much to drink, I might make bets that I would not make if I were sober. Over the years, I have developed my own strategy for enhancing my luck and good time in casinos.

My Personal Casino Strategy

No matter what, losing money is never fun and can put you in a foul mood. Losing lots of money can put you in an especially foul mood, and that is one of the reasons I have developed my personal strategy. It goes like this.

When I go to a casino, I take $10,000 with me, which is a decent amount of money. If I'm going to be there three nights, I go to the casino floor with $3,333 to bet—I've divided the $10,000 into three nights. What I usually do then is go to a show, then to dinner, and gamble at the end of the night. I go straight to the Blackjack tables, where I know the best plays, am not afraid to ask the dealer for advice, and go to the hundred-dollar minimum table because I want to win or lose fast.

I start with a single hundred-dollar bet and move on from there. I make all the plays that the book calls for. If, by luck, I ever get to $10,000 in winnings, I'm done for the night. I pick up my chips, go to the cage, get my cash, and go to my room.

If I lose all my money, I do not go back up to the room and get more money. The night is done. The one thing I never want is to have a casino host or a line of credit at a casino. Imagine how many people have lost serious money betting while drunk or betting while showing off. It is incalculable. I can tell you firsthand how many times I have seen people go to use their line of credit or go back up to the room to get more money. Good money after bad has never made sense to me.

Whether I win or lose, I repeat the same routine every night. At the end of my three nights in the casino, I have either won three times what I started with, lost what I started with, or am somewhere in between. In any event, I know how much I will lose as a minimum and I know how much I can win as a maximum.

My biggest downside is losing my starting money. Because I am probably only in a casino once a year, I have figured my amount is what I'm willing to lose for the entertainment it brings me. I have to admit, there is nothing as invigorating as being hot in a casino and enjoying all the camaraderie that goes on at the tables. Over time, I have won; my losses are reduced. There is no way for me to know for sure what my all-time winnings or losses are in casinos, but I am fairly sure my losses have far outpaced my winnings.

I will say that I did have one phenomenal evening at a casino in Las Vegas. I was gambling into the wee hours of the morning with a nephew, and we had a very early-morning flight. My wife and my children were asleep upstairs. That night, I was up $40,000 at a Blackjack table, when the casino manager came over to me and told me that I would have to leave. He informed me that they believed I was counting cards and was a ringer. It was one of the proudest days of my life.

Of course, I have no idea how to count cards, and as late as it was, even if I could count cards, I was probably too impaired to do it. The casino boss was extremely nice to me and actually walked me to the cage to get my money and to the elevator to leave the casino. It was such a beautiful moment to be mistaken as one of the pros. I am here to tell all casinos throughout the world, if you see me coming in, I have no clue how to count cards.

Surviving Sin City

There is a reason Las Vegas is called Sin City and the slogan is "What Happens Here, Stays Here." It can almost feel like a dream, whether as one last party before an upcoming wedding or just the chance to live on the edge and feel invisible. For many, Las Vegas has become a modern-day Sodom and Gomorrah. Big mistakes with fellow conventioneers are often made, and drunk talk can end your career. My grandmother used to say, "What people say drunk, they think sober."

It's also possible to go to Las Vegas, have a responsible time, and lose a little money without breaking your marriage vows, losing your home, and feeling like it's the beginning of the end. And for some people, the best way to enhance their good luck is to never go to Las Vegas in the first place. Those people with addictive personalities are prone to have a mishap in Las Vegas. And people who have addictive personalities usually have more than one addiction. Sex. Gambling. Sports betting. It all goes hand in hand. The toll that casinos take on families everywhere is immeasurable. It's not just the bad luck of losing money, it's all the collateral damage that comes with it. Because of a carefully controlled environment, we seemingly never get tired. I've been playing Blackjack at 3 a.m. fully wired. One thing we know in Las Vegas and in casinos throughout the world, they know their customers and they know what their customers want.

The reason Las Vegas is such a convention mecca is that it is the perfect place to network, receive continuing education, and ostensibly learn more about your business while at the same time writing the entire trip off on your taxes. After all, you are there to work! But all that said, I cannot think of a city in the world that has more potential for bad luck.

Of course, I'm not suggesting that everyone avoid Las Vegas. It is one of the most fascinating cities in the world. You just have to understand that there is more vice and opportunity for bad luck on the Las Vegas Strip than in your entire state.

For most of us, gambling is a certain way to lose money and incur bad luck. When you are going to a casino, or going to Las Vegas, you are going for a reason, and you understand the temptations and dangers that await. While there are many great times to be had in Las Vegas with shows, dinners, and the Strip, lurking in the dark corners is potential for dark times ahead. Lady Luck rarely shines on regulars to Las Vegas. There are gamblers that go into the high-roller salons. The gamblers in those salons are from all walks of life. Many in there have "fuck-you money." Michael Jordan has "fuck-you money." He can have almost an unlimited amount of bad luck and he will be fine. (I will tell you if

Michael Jordan loses big, he won't be in a good mood. He does not like to lose at Tiddlywinks.) The high-roller salon is a very dangerous place to be, especially if you don't have "fuck-you money" that you know you can lose comfortably.

A few things before we leave the casino. In every casino, there are games that are more winnable than others; and in all casinos, the chances of winning can be changed by the casino operators. Different rules make for different chances of winning. Some slot machines are loose, and some are not.

Casino Games With the Best Odds

In an effort to enhance your luck, let me now give you the casino games with the best odds.

- BACCARAT: House Edge 1.06–1.24 percent

  Baccarat is a simple game with a very small house edge for the casino, making it one of the best games to play. All you have to do is bet whether the "player" or the "banker" wins the hand, and if you guess right, you will double your initial wager. Avoid betting on the tie, since it has a 14.36 percent house edge, compared to only 1.06 percent when betting on the banker and 1.24 percent when betting on the player.

- BLACKJACK: House Edge 0.5–2 percent

  In Blackjack, it is very important to understand the rules and the basic strategy. Whether you win or not relies on the luck of the cards drawn. However, there are certain plays you should make in every single situation. Some of those plays are hard to make because they seem counterintuitive. You have to make those plays if you're going to have the edge you need.

  Blackjack dealers are more than happy to give you advice. They work for tips, not the casino. For me, Blackjack is the game I enjoy the most.

- VIDEO POKER: House Edge 0.5–5 percent
  Video poker is played on a machine at the casino, against the machine rather than against other players.

- CRAPS: House Edge 0.0–5.56 percent
  In craps, you're betting on the outcome of a roll of two dice by one of your fellow players, the "shooter." The ways to win are slightly more complicated than Blackjack. The house edge varies in craps, depending on the bets placed. Always check an individual casino's odds and payout tables before playing.
  I must confess, I have never really got the hang of craps, but there is no more excitement in a lively casino than the craps table.

- ROULETTE: House Edge 2.7–5.26 percent
  Another simple game of chance with pretty good odds of winning is roulette. The ball rolls, it falls into a numbered slot on a wheel. You pick a number, a group of numbers, or high or low, odd or even, red or black—or you don't. There are multiple roulette variations: European roulette has one zero field on the wheel and features a 2.7 percent house edge, and American roulette has a double zero field on top, which makes the house edge a whopping 5.26 percent. Avoid that one.

The real takeaway from all of this is that different casinos with seemingly the same games have different edges for the house based on different nuances in the games played.

Casino Games With the Worst Odds

- SLOTS: House Edge 2–15 percent
  Slot machines are hugely popular with casino goers because they are easy to play, entertaining, addictive, and if you get lucky, you can win *a lot of money*. There is nothing you can do to improve your win rate though, as they are totally random. So if you want

to gain an edge over the casino, consider playing a game where you can actually use a strategy.

As I walk through casinos, I often see a lot of older people playing slots. Sometimes in wheelchairs. But I believe it is popular because when those bells go off and all hell breaks loose, there isn't a more action-packed spot in a casino that in front of a slot machine.

- WHEEL OF FORTUNE: House Edge 11 percent
  In Wheel of Fortune, you bet on whether the wheel stops on $1, $5, $10, $20, or a Joker. But even if you bet that the wheel will land on a $1 mark—the safest bet—the house edge is still 11 percent. Bet on a Joker, and the house advantage is as high as 24 percent.

- KENO: House Edge 20–40 percent
  In Keno, there are eighty numbers. The house picks twenty and you win according to how many of that twenty you selected. Just don't start looking at the actual mathematical probabilities involved; they will make your eyes spin like a slot machine. This is usually the *worst* game to play at the casino in terms of your odds of winning.

Bottom line to all this: go to Las Vegas to have fun. Maybe you've saved up for your trip. You just need to know that the money in your pocket you've allocated for gambling in advance most likely won't be there when you head to the airport, especially if you've been drinking.

The Pros (and You're Not One of Them)

In all fairness, there are certain professional gamblers who have made a career out of gambling, and they are fun to watch. We see these incredible poker pots now televised, and we watch these games like we watch sports. The players all have distinctive outfits and personalities, and have become celebrities unto themselves. There are so many variations and so many games, you really have to be on top of your game to play poker. Years ago in Maui, my sons and I were invited to Willie Nelson's home to play poker. The great basketball coach, Don Nelson, invited me to go. Until you have played poker with Willie Nelson, you have never played poker. First of all, I have never met a nicer guy. Everyone was required to bring beer and something to eat. We listened to Willie Radio.

These guys were playing so many variations of poker that my head was spinning. I believe Willie has a PhD in poker. And, yes, we were able to enjoy some marijuana, just in vape form. Toward the end of the night, my son, Dan, was down to a hand with just him and Willie. At the end, it appeared Willie had won, but Dan pointed out some cards, and he actually won the hand. Willie was reaching for the chips when Dan pointed out his hand. Willie just smiled and said "cool."

The idea of gambling for a living and becoming very wealthy has great appeal. It doesn't seem like work, but it is work. For the successful gamblers, and there are a few, they also have very bright minds that are able to compute lots of numbers in a rapid-fire succession.

Kerry Packer was one of them. Born on December 17, 1937, in Sydney, Australia, he contracted polio at age eight. Despite these troubles, Packer developed a strong desire to gamble. Packer loved Baccarat and often visited London's MGM Grand, Bellagio, and Crockfords. During one visit to Crockfords, he lost $16.5 million in three days. The Australian tycoon made his mark in the gambling world when he showed off his mastery of Blackjack, reportedly winning around $20–$40 million at the Las Vegas MGM Grand Casino in 1997. He also lost nearly £22 million in 1999 while playing at a London casino, one of the biggest betting losses ever recorded in British gambling history.

Bill Benter gained fame for defying the Blackjack odds in casinos. He pursued a physics education at the University of Pennsylvania to refine his abilities. Although he had no experience in casinos, Benter used Edward Thorp's book *Beat the Dealer* to master how to count cards successfully. He began winning thousands of dollars playing Blackjack in no time. Benter later became friends with another gambler and mathematician, Alan Woods. In 1984, the two would profit from Hong Kong's horse racing betting using their mathematical models.

Thorp is known as "the man who beat the house." He's known for his expertise in card counting. Through his mastery of the various games, Thorp achieved global renown for his victories against casinos, earning himself a place in Blackjack history as part of the esteemed Blackjack Hall of Fame. Stories of these people, many who were independently wealthy, make the rest of us want to explore that path. After three cards, I think my card-counting ability would have ended—processing was never one of my strong suits.

So yes, there are professional gamblers who have become celebrities. But the simple truth in all of this is that over time, with very few exceptions, you will lose.

THE ALLURE OF SPORTS BETTING

In my lifetime, I have had the opportunity to play all sorts of sports. I was never great at anything, but good at everything. Sort of a jack of all trades. I have also had the opportunity to be around a lot of youth sports as a participant and as a father. Watching youth sports as a father was an eye-opening experience.

My children played everything. Baseball. Basketball. Football. Soccer. Lacrosse. I wasn't really much for lacrosse, as it's a game that became more popular after I got older. But I've spent many days watching practices, games, and All-Star games. All of my children are grown now, and their own children are now playing youth sports. One observation I can make after my years as a parent watching those games is that while some youth coaches were great, others were the biggest assholes I have ever met in my life. You would've thought they were coaching the final game of the World Series the way they carried on. On many occasions, coaches were thrown out of the facility because of their outlandish behavior.

Small Businesses and the Desire to Win

The one thing I took away from all those years watching youth sports is that Americans have a tremendous desire to win. I think why this desire is so prevalent among adults who volunteer in youth sports is that most Americans get up every day and never get to compete, win, or lose. They go to a job. They do their job. Receive their paycheck. And at the end of the year, maybe receive a bonus and maybe receive a small raise. That is the extent of their winning and losing.

No matter how many letters the mailman delivers, his salary is all he's getting, with the exception of overtime. Nowhere in their work life do they get to win or lose. The owners of businesses get to win and lose every single day. Unfortunately, many of them lose.

A game I play with myself is, as I'm driving down roads and seeing a new business popping up, I ask myself, "Will that business make it or not make it?" It's a good way to kill time. But the simple truth of the matter is, building and maintaining a successful business is hard, and if you are able to win until you lose that business, then you have lost.

Getting in the Game

The one thing that remains true is that people are competitive by nature and they want to be in a game they control and can win. That is the reason we see so many jerks coaching youth sports. For them, this is the moment where they get to be in charge and successful. Even though they are coaching five-year-olds in T-ball, I'm here to tell you that some of those coaches came out of the dugout like Tommy Lasorda in the World Series—kicking dirt, screaming, and sometimes being ejected from the field.

During my time watching and volunteering with youth sports, it was not uncommon to see the coach's child pitching, starting, or at quarterback. It was funny to watch how often the child of the head coach was the player at the most key position. Most of these parents (most often dads) were living their own childhoods through their children. They really believed that they had the next Peyton Manning or LeBron James. Over time, that expectation wanes as the reality of life and their children's abilities sets in.

When your children are playing T-ball, it's almost impossible to get a seat in the bleachers. By the time your child is thirteen years old, you can lie down on the bleachers, because not many are coming to these games. Reality has set in, and the survival of the fittest has made its way to the thirteen-year-olds team. And that's before we even get to high school. Many more kids will be eliminated by the time they get to high school.

Luckily for me, I was circumspect about my children's chances for Division I sports, much less professional sports. Genetically, I was able to look at my wife and myself and our abilities and realize that we would not be hosting draft parties later in life. I came to that conclusion early. Most don't. Most parents believe they have "the one." I have so many stories from so many games and so many All-Star tournaments. It was on those fields when I first developed my theory that youth sports was the place parents came to get winning and losing out of their system. One day my son's team had a scrimmage against another team. They weren't even in uniform. One of the coaches on the other team asked me if I would mind umpiring and, of course, I said sure. I had umpired a little bit in college and high school, so I believed I was up for umpiring a twelve-year-old's scrimmage.

Because it was a scrimmage, I stood behind the pitcher to call balls and strikes, as well as watch the bases. A kid came up to bat with a very awkward walk. The count got to 2–2. The next pitch was right down the middle, and I called strike three.

No sooner had I called strike three, than the manager from the other team came running straight toward me, and I thought he was actually going to tackle me or hit me. Instead, he turned his ballcap around and started yelling at me nose to nose that I had missed the call. I immediately did what needed to be done.

I told the little boy to go back to the batter's box because I was changing my call. I informed the coach and all the parents watching that I obviously had missed the call because I was standing behind the pitcher's mound with a direct view, but George, the opposing team's coach, must have had a better view from inside the dugout. I then told George, "Go fuck yourself," and I placed the ball-and-strike counter in his top pocket. He started telling me he did not want me to quit and to please stay. I informed George that not only did I not give a rat's ass about this scrimmage game, I didn't even care about the regular season.

George was left to call the game himself from my old perch behind the mound. With the count 3–2, the little boy stepped back up to the plate. The next pitch was a mile over his head, but he took a gigantic cut that looked like a tomahawk chop and struck out. As I settled into my seat, I thought, "There is a God."

The Desire to Lead, Manage, and Win

All of those days watching these men and women coaching youth sports taught me that all of us have a tremendous desire to lead and manage and have the opportunity to win. Most of us want to have our day in the arena but often never get that chance in business. And if we do get the chance, the odds are we're going to fail.

The same holds true for high school, college, and professional sports. Especially college and professional sports. You go to football stadiums in the dead of winter and grown men are shirtless, with their bodies painted in team colors and often wearing masks or funny hats. In Cleveland, they call it the "Dawg Pound," and fans actually wear dog masks and bark in the end zone. These types of fans are in every college and pro town in America.

When their team wins, they win. They feel the euphoria as if it were them. Sometimes fistfights break out between opposing fans, and sometimes people are badly injured and even killed. Soccer games in Europe and South America are notorious for riots after games.

What is amazing to me in all this is how personally people take team sports that they have no influence over or are a part of in any way other than being a fan.

Once again, like the youth sports, these fans really want to win or lose. The Buffalo Bills fans come to mind when I think of fanatical fans. They are in weather that could kill livestock and many times are shirtless after drinking a six-pack in the parking lot and having a few chicken wings. Year in and year out, the Buffalo Bills have gotten close to and even in the Super Bowl. Year in and year out, these Buffalo Bills fans, the Bills Mafia, are undeterred. They are coming back next year with the same hopes they have had since they were children. Fathers and mothers pass this fanaticism down through the generations.

Some parents won't allow their children to go to a rival school because that school had a rivalry with their alma mater. It is all just batshit crazy. But it's instructive. It has shown me empirically the desire to play the game, to win the game, and to always be in the game, even if you're just doing it as a youth coach or as a fan semi-naked in the stands of Buffalo or Cleveland.

Sports Betting

With this as our backdrop, there is no wonder that sports betting is such a big business in America. It's one thing to get a thrill from coaching your kids or watching your team play, but the real thrill is when you have money riding on the game. You get to win and lose for real. It also makes the game more interesting and urgent, because you now have skin in the game, and psychologically, you *are* participating. You will be winning and losing.

For years, professional sports teams and college sports teams tried to pretend like gambling was taboo, but they knew darn well that bookies throughout America were feeding the interest in their games. I had Jack the barber in Lexington as my bookie when I was eleven years old. Bookies are everywhere. I had a bookie in my fraternity at college. He also sold marijuana. I would not be surprised if he had also been a paperboy. Today he is the successful owner of a very large construction company. I believe the statute of limitations has run out on his drug dealing in Gainesville, Florida.

Sports betting allows the bettor to be very involved in the game. Most recently, sports teams everywhere have stopped pretending that gambling is taboo. We now have sports betting all over America. Companies such as DraftKings are now luring bettors in to win or lose on games.

Human beings' desire to participate, compete, and have the chance of winning is powerful. That desire to triumph and celebrate victories is real. Therefore, it is not surprising that sports betting is such a big business and gives Americans another opportunity to lose their money on a regular basis if they elect not to play the lottery or to go to the casino. Sports betting is yet another way for Americans to have bad luck.

The Popularity of Sports Betting

In 2023, Americans wagered a record $120 billion on sports betting.

In 2018, the Supreme Court loosened restrictions on the sports-betting industry. Since that landmark ruling, Americans have lost a shocking $245 billion betting on sports. The NFL is the most popular sport in America, and the one most Americans bet on more than any other. According to data collected by CRG Global for Variety Intelligence Platform back in October 2022, 81 percent of bettors that were eighteen or older placed an NFL wager. Once again, many governments collect revenues just like they do with lotteries.

About 85 percent of U.S. adults have gambled at least once in their lives, with 60 percent having gambled within the past year. Shockingly, one in five American men are or have been in debt from betting on sports. That's 20 percent of our adult male population. If five guys walk into a room, the odds are one of them is in debt, or just out of debt, due to betting on sports. Once again, we see clearly that luck does not favor the bettor, but the game itself is too compelling for them to ignore. By betting, it's almost as good as playing. And then they read stories about people like Jim "Mattress Mack" McIngvale, owner of Gallery Furniture in Houston, who won approximately $75 million off $10 million in bets on the Astros to win the World Series. It is believed to be the largest payout in American sports-betting history, with the bulk of the haul coming from Louisiana sports books. You can read up on this fellow on your own, as he has made other outlandish bets.

Now it is true that there are some people who have made large sums of money gambling and betting on sports. But very few do. A good winning percentage in sports betting is 55 percent or higher. At 55 percent, you're winning just over half your bets, but with the fees charged by the sport's books, 55 percent may still not be enough to overcome the built-in house edge. You need a higher win rate, solid money management, and the discipline to pick the right sport. It is estimated that over time, only 3 percent of sports bettors win. And those 3 percent put in a ton of work studying statistics, matchups, and trends to gain an edge. They usually specialize in certain sports or leagues and become true experts. They also exhibit patience and discipline, never chasing losses or deviating from their system. Everyone has a system.

Sports betting on team sports is one thing, but there is also lots of betting on horse racing and boxing.

Horse Racing

If you want to really lose money, you need to think about horse racing. Horse racing is called the "Sport of Kings" because, in past days, royal families enjoyed the sport. Queen Elizabeth, when she was alive, always went to the Royal Ascot.

What is true in horse racing is that many of the tracks are some of the most beautiful and grand structures in the world. Places such as Del Mar, Saratoga, and Keeneland are sites to behold. As a boy, I grew up in Lexington, and was surrounded by horse farms. Because we were not well-off, I only went to the track once as a child and won $44 betting the daily double.

All the years I lived in Lexington, we never went to a Kentucky Wildcats basketball game or football game. We simply didn't have the money. However, we listened to every Kentucky basketball game on the radio, huddled around the stereo. When the Kentucky football team would rally and the other team would call timeout, my brothers, my father, and I would rush to the front stoop of the house where we could listen to the Kentucky fight song and hear the crowd going nuts. It was almost as good as being there.

I was such a die-hard Kentucky fan that when the Kentucky basketball team was beaten by Texas Western in the NCAA finals in 1966, I didn't read the paper for two weeks. Even though my paper route allowed me to keep and read the paper every day, I avoided the sports page because the pain was too great. I remember crying myself to sleep the night they got beat. The team was nicknamed "Rupp's Runts" and one of the guards, Louie Dampier, actually presented me with a tennis trophy one summer.

Horse racing is a sport for bluebloods. Women wear their best dresses and hats, and men are decked out to the nines. The Kentucky Derby or any other big race is like a fashion show. Wild hats. Flashy suits. Gorgeous people all together at one time.

Like a casino, horse tracks can get gamblers revved up by being with other gamblers. When I think of the degenerative gambler, I most often think of racetracks. These degenerative gamblers seem to know everything, but in reality, they know nothing. Okay, they know a lot more than I do, but it never seems to matter.

Horse racing and betting on the horses is a good place to have bad luck. Staying away from racetracks enhances your good luck. Going to the racetrack enhances your bad luck. Let's start with some reasons why.

Professional gamblers hang around the track talking to jockeys, trainers, and horse people. Perhaps they can glean things that the general public does not, like a small injury or bad training. Needless to say, all of them are looking for an edge to give them a win.

The disarming thing about horse racing is the atmosphere and the beauty of the tracks. It seems like you have gone to a fancy party and everyone is happy. There is a half-hour between each race, and many times that calls for another drink and then another drink. By the time you end the day at the track, it is very likely that you are lit. Drinking and gambling is always a bad idea, whether in a casino, sports book, or racetrack. We do lots of crazy shit drunk.

A day at a racetrack, if the weather cooperates, is one of most beautiful days of your life. It's important that you treat it as a party, unless you are a professional gambler and really dialed in. For most of us mortals, going to the racetrack means losing more than we win, and in a disproportionate way. Horse-racing betting is a sure way to increase your bad luck.

Big Names, Big Numbers, and Big Odds

Our old friend, Jim McIngvale, aka "Mattress Mack," who is known for his gambling of large sums of money, is not a stranger to losing big money. He lost $2.4 million at a Kentucky Derby after he bet it on Essential Quality to win but ended up finishing fourth. Another famous sports bettor placed a $1.5 million bet on the horse Epicenter to win the Kentucky Derby, only to miss out narrowly in the run.

As in all gambling there are some people who make a living at it, and quite a good living. Horse racing is no exception. William Venter is an American professional gambler who focuses on horse racing betting. He earned nearly $1 billion through the development of one of the most successful analysis computer software in the horse racing market and is considered to be the most successful gambler of all time. Venter once served as president of the Hong Kong Rotary Club, founded the Venter Foundation, and occasionally lectures on subjects such as statistics and mathematical probability. He grew up in Pittsburgh, Pennsylvania, and wanted to use his mathematical talents to make money. After finishing a university physics degree in 1997, he headed to Las Vegas and used his mathematical skills to count cards. He found a book known as *Beat the*

Dealer by Edward O. Thorp, which helped him hone his skills. Seven years later, he was banned from all of the Vegas Strip's casinos.

Venter then met a fellow by the name of Alan Woods, who shared his enthusiasm and expertise in horse racing, and both relied on computers. The two became partners, and in 1984, moved to Hong Kong. They started with $150,000, which would be the equivalent of $400,000 today. They then used their mathematical skills to create a system for picking winners. The key to his success was using a statistical model that identified factors that could lead to successful race predictions. He found that some came out as more important than others. In 1988, he won $600,000, and the next year made $3 million. In time, William Venter became a billionaire. Stories like this and other successful gamblers can make one interested in it as a profession.

The idea of being a professional horse racing gambler sure looks fun. It's not like a job, and it seems more like a constant party. Beautiful people. Cocktails. Beautiful settings. Great food. What could go wrong? What could go wrong in horse racing is that only 5 percent of the people ever win. It's very important to keep that in mind if you decide to mortgage your house and head to Saratoga anytime soon.

It should be clear that horse racing is a losing proposition for almost all bettors, and making matters worse, most bettors are amateurs. If you really want to lose money in horse racing, you need to actually buy a horse or a share of a horse. The reason I know this is that I am one of the people who did just that.

When you are in life and trying to optimize luck, which optimizes not only your financial security but in many ways your happiness too, you might find it surprising that I am a horse owner.

Fuck-You Money

Lots of people use fuck-you money to buy boats. I am not a boater, and every time I've been on a yacht, I want off. They say that the two best days of your life are the days you buy a boat and the day you sell a boat. Once I was advised that if it flies, floats, or fucks… rent it. It is a bit crass, but airplanes, boats, and boyfriends or girlfriends can be very expensive. The key is to know when to say no, and when to say, "I can afford to lose it."

My Introduction to Horse Racing

Growing up in Kentucky, horse racing and basketball have a special place in our hearts. It is what gives us great pleasure and great pride (although Kentucky also grows lots of tobacco, which is nothing to be proud of). In my later years, I was introduced to some horse people in Lexington, who own a farm called Ashford Stud. The great Justify and American Pharaoh stud there. Also, Uncle Mo, a tremendous sire, shares a barn with these two Hall of Famers.

To make a long story short, once I expanded my businesses into Kentucky, I started going home more often and met up with a fellow by the name of Charlie O'Connor, who runs Ashford Stud. Ashford Stud is owned by the Magnier Family in Ireland, who also has Coolmore Farms there. Over time, I developed a real trust and friendship with Charlie and trusted the Magniers and all of the people associated with the organization.

Knowing full well that I would most likely lose all of this money, I started buying partial shares in horses years ago. I would buy between 25 and 50 percent of each horse in a syndicate. Coolmore and others usually participate with me in these purchases. I am sorry to report that as of this writing, I have lost much of the money that I invested, but I've had some bright spots. One of our horses, Ultima D, named after my wife, ran in the Breeders' Cup and has had several fillies and a colt with American Pharaoh as the sire. As I write this book, I plan to go see one of their offspring, Ultima Grace, race at Keeneland in the spring.

Genetics is everything in horse racing. The great sires command astronomical prices, as do broodmares who carry the foals. Two Triple Crown winners live and breed at Ashford Stud: American Pharaoh and Justify. Each of these horses breeds three times a day. They are paid

$250,000 for every successful insemination. American Pharaoh has two goes at it, then a massage, then one final romp before bedtime. The same for Justify.

One other stablemate of these two champions is a horse by the name of Uncle Mo, who is one of the great sires in American racing. Uncle Mo was at one time commanding $300,000 per successful insemination. These horses are making their owners almost $1 million a day. The reason for it is the success that great horses have in siring and delivering future champions.

Most people who are heavily involved in owning horses have serious fuck-you money. It is a gigantic game that comes with a gigantic rush. One of my partners, Dick Brody, an industrialist from Detroit, once remarked that with all the success he has had in his business life, nothing compares to the rush of your horse crossing the finish line first and then going to the winner's circle. I've had the opportunity to do this on occasion with Dick. He's right, it is a wonderful feeling, but one that comes with a significant cost.

The Human Psyche and the Desire to Win

All of these forms of gambling (the lottery, casinos, and sports betting) are rampant. Our innate desire to win and compete is baked into the human psyche. These games of chance, especially involving sports, gives many people that ability to be in the arena—to suffer the agony of defeat or the ecstasy of winning. It has gotten so crazy that grown men go off on weekends to have fantasy drafts where they pick players in a mock draft. As the season plays out, their players' results give them the opportunity to win their fantasy league. They have these fantasy leagues for all sorts of sports.

Grown men are huddled in locations all over America, conducting drafts and treating them as if they were real. It is astounding to watch. It has also reinforced something I have known after my days on those youth sports fields when my children were young. People want to win.

People want to be in the game. People want to be the boss and to be in charge. People want to be part of something and win together. Sports gives them that, and sports betting is an accelerant to that fire.

Families and lives have been ripped apart because of gambling. Homes lost. Marriages dissolved. Families in tatters. Gamblers Anonymous is much like Alcoholics Anonymous, as the members are addicts and the addiction is gambling. The underlying addiction is actually the desire to win and the desire to be rich and the desire for a better life that they see no other path for.

My advice is only gamble with the money you can afford to lose. Treat it as entertainment and not an investment vehicle. And get a great dress or a great suit, a great hat, head to the track, and enjoy the races — the sport of kings.

CHAPTER 19

LUCK AND SPORTS

Nowhere is luck more seemingly prevalent than in sports. How many games have you watched that came down to the wire? How many improbable shots have gone in that seemed impossible. The sports bet bookies have trouble picking teams straight up, much less with points added. Sports is a game of inches, and with inches, luck is paramount.

I've seen golf tournaments where the ball is balancing on the edge of the cup and then rolls in. I've also seen Tiger Woods hit the ball way into the woods and I wonder, how did that happen? If Tiger Woods is hitting balls in the water and the woods, it doesn't seem like a game for me.

At the end of every *SportsCenter* program, the top ten plays of the day are shown. These are amazing shots and athletic feats that seem to be more luck than skill. But much of what we see on *SportsCenter* is not necessarily all luck. The great Texas football coach, Darrell Royal, used to say, "The harder we worked, the luckier we got." That seems to make sense, until you see someone heaving a basketball the length of the floor and it miraculously goes in. How do you practice or work hard for that type of luck?

Luck and Basketball

I grew up in basketball country. People in Kentucky live and breathe Kentucky basketball. I sure did. In Kentucky, basketball is a religion, and we take it very personally. I previously referenced the loss Kentucky had to Texas Western in 1966. Lots of people believe that game involved lots of luck. Looking back, I don't think so.

Texas Western was the first all African American basketball team. Kentucky was all White. I don't believe luck played a role that night. What actually happened is that the Texas Western players were not appreciated because they were not known. When I grew up in Lexington, Adolph Rupp finally recruited a center by the name of Tom Payne, who was the first Black player to play for Kentucky. Looking back in retrospect, luck had nothing to do with that night. The best team won.

Later in life, I became good friends and business partners with one of college and pro basketball's greatest players, Grant Hill. We have real estate deals together and started two mezzanine funds. Meeting Grant changed my life in many ways. First, I got to meet his mother, Janet Hill, who became one of the most important and influential people in my life. She might not even know that, but her wisdom, compassion, and kindness were awesome. I also got to meet and know Calvin Hill, the great Cowboys and Redskins running back. One night, the two of us drove for hours and he told me stories that I relish to this day.

The interesting thing about Grant Hill is that he was involved in a play that caused me more consternation than many events ever in college basketball. In the NCAA tournament, Kentucky was playing Duke and had Duke on the ropes.

There were seconds left on the clock, and Hill needed to make a pass to Christian Laettner who was at the top of the free-throw line at the other end of the court. There was no way they were going to make that shot, so I wasn't worried. The game was in the bag.

Hill took the ball and threw it the length of the floor to Laettner, who turned around and fired a shot at the buzzer. The shot went in, and the crowd went wild. It was, to me, the most devastating loss in Kentucky's history. After all, the game was in the bag. How lucky could one get?

One night, Hill and I were traveling home from a business trip, and I asked him about that play. To my surprise, he told me that not only was that play designed, but they practiced it every day. In fact, he said that in a game against Wake Forest, they tried it but failed, as he threw the ball down the side of the court instead of to the free-throw line. It did not work against Wake Forest. So they went back to the drawing board.

They decided that the best way for this play to work was to throw it the length of the floor to Laettner at the top of the key. Just a little wrinkle to give them a better shot at the goal. Hill told the story this way.

As they huddled during a time out, Coach Krzyzewski looked at Hill and said "Grant, can you make the pass?" Hill said, "I can make the pass, Coach." Coach K then looked at Laettner and said, "Christian, can you make the shot?" Laettner looked at Coach K and said, "I can make the shot." Coach K then looked at the team and said, "Okay let's go win this game."

And by God they did. If you ever watch the NCAA tournament known as March Madness, you will see this play over and over again. I believe it is the most iconic single play in all of college basketball. And when you look at it on film, it looks like some schoolyard kids had designed a play that they had never run before and pulled it out of their ass. Nothing, it appears, could be further from the truth.

Preparation Leads to Luck

It was preparation that allowed them to win that game and, yes, to be lucky. If you run that play a hundred times, I don't know how many times Laettner makes that shot. If Kentucky had known about that play, he never makes that shot from the top of the key. They would have been prepared for that.

Hearing that story that night was incredible. All these years, I had believed it was 100 percent luck. In actuality, practice makes perfect.

We, the sports watchers, see incredible plays in many different sports on TV all the time. Many of those plays also seem like pure luck, but they're not. In football, you have an onside kick that gives the kicking team the ball if they recover the ball after touching an opposing player's hands or body. When you talk to football coaches, this is something they practice over and over and over again. When you see it work you exclaim, "Those lucky bastards." And, yes, there is a degree of luck, depending on how the ball bounces on that particular day. But without that practice, luck is not remotely possible. We see football teams down with two minutes left in the game. Those teams then go into their hurry-up offense needing to march the length of the field in less than two minutes to win the game. As you are watching it transpire, many times these teams march straight down the field like a steamroller. It is amazing and seems very lucky. The truth of the matter is that, once again, preparation, and lots of it, has gone into these wins at the last second.

And this train of thought applies to all sports, professional and college. Situations that might arise later in the game have to be prepared for. If Grant Hill had not thrown that same pass multiple times in practice, what are the odds of him being successful that day? The same for two-minute drills and onside kicks.

Many times, in all sports, we see "gadget plays" — trick plays that catch the other team off guard. A fake punt when you don't see it coming and they are deep in their own territory. Baseball players coming home on a suicide bunt and crossing home plate safely.

In sports and in life, we have to be prepared for all situations. I have urged Hill to write a book about preparing for the pass. It's a story that's not just about sports or basketball, it's a story about life. And the story goes like this: for us to enhance our luck, it is imperative that we practice, practice, and practice. Preparation, preparation, preparation. The same strategy for sports is the same strategy in life and in business.

Nobody Plays Boxing

I got to watch preparation in sports years ago. I owned a nightclub in Orlando called Tabu. One night while in my club, I met an amateur boxer by the name of Antonio Tarver. He was personable, from Orlando, and was then the world light heavyweight amateur champion. As we talked, he informed me that his dream was to go to the Olympics, but he needed help and some sponsorships. I told him to come to my office the next day and he did. I decided to help Tarver reach his dream and win an Olympic gold medal. It wasn't a stretch; he was the current world champion. So off we go to the '96 Olympics in Atlanta. The one thing about Tarver is he does not lack self-confidence. We had so many great times together during his career. I have laughed until my belly hurt with that guy. Atlanta turned out to be a tremendous lesson for Tarver and for me.

He was the overwhelming favorite to win the gold medal. I had watched him train, and the training was intense. During the Olympics, I went to the boxing venue one day and he was eating a bag of McDonald's food, a big no-no for an athlete participating in the Olympics. I actually said something to him, but he blew me off in a very friendly way.

In short, he fought a man from Kazakhstan and lost in a split decision. I don't even remember the guy's name and am still so upset about it I have decided not to look him up for my book. And just like that, Tarver was not a gold medalist, but a bronze medalist. Everything changed that night.

Had he won the gold medal, Bob Arum had a deal that would have guaranteed him $1 million. Instead, he started from scratch, and we began anew. His first professional fight was in Philadelphia at the Blue Horizon. Joe Frazier and his daughter sat with me during the fight. The Blue Horizon is something right out of a *Rocky* movie. Tarver won that night and then began his quest to redeem himself. It was a long, hard slog.

Ultimately, he won a lot of fights and got a title fight with Roy Jones Jr. Jones was pound for pound the best boxer in the world at the time, although Floyd Mayweather would have taken exception. Mayweather was on Tarver's Olympic team, and I really enjoyed talking to his uncle and father. They were right out of central casting. And great people.

Jones had to lose weight for this fight but won the fight on a decision that was highly controversial. Everyone thought that Tarver had won. I believe Jones thought Tarver had won. But boxing is boxing. A rematch was made.

We all gathered back in Las Vegas for the rematch. Jones was very upset because Tarver kept taunting him by telling everyone who would listen that he won the first fight. Jones's response was, "I had to lose too much weight, but I'm going to kick your ass this time." At the weigh-in, Jones looked great, but so did Tarver. Jones was ready to take Tarver's head off.

After the weigh-in, we went back to Tarver's hotel room to talk as he rested before the fight. I said, "Tony, Roy Jones is madder than a wet hen. He's going to try to take you out early tonight."

And then Tarver looked at me, the way a man looks when a man knows. He said "John, I hope he do, because if he do, I'm going to knock the bitch out."

I was dumbstruck. I was afraid for Tarver, but Tarver was not afraid for himself. Why? Because he had prepared, and he believed in himself.

I went down to the sportsbook and made a big bet on an early knockout. I bet on Tarver. I had seen him train, I had seen him prepare, and I saw his eyes that afternoon. He was going to win.

I had a seat in the corner right next to Magic Johnson. Johnson had barely sat down to watch the match as it began. Right before the fight, the ring announcer, the guy who says, "Let's get ready to rumble," asked both fighters if they had any last-minute comments. Tarver took the microphone, looked at Jones, and said, "What's your excuse going to be this time, Roy?" The entire arena erupted.

Tarver knocked him out in the third round. If you go to the HBO tape, you will see me in the ring rubbing his shoulders and screaming, "We shocked the world!"

Later that night at the Forum Club, Don King came to our after-party. He opened a briefcase filled with $100,000 and told Tarver that it was a bonus for the knockout. Tarver kept telling me to touch the money, but I informed him I did not need to touch that money because I had already made my own money. I opened my coat filled with hundred-dollar bills totaling $40,000 from my bet on the knockout. I believed in Tarver because Tarver believed in Tarver. I believed in Tarver because I had watched firsthand the preparation that went in to getting there.

The Olympic loss. A broken jaw in an early fight. Sleeping on a futon in Tampa. The sacrifices were immense. Boxing is a different sport. Once Tarver said to me, "People play basketball. People play baseball. People play football. Nobody plays boxing." And I have to tell you, sitting in those corners all those years, nobody plays boxing.

My family would travel the country watching Tarver fight. He was part of our family, and we were part of his. His son, Little Tony, now has a career of his own.

Too many people watching that fight that night may have thought Tarver was lucky. No one believed he could beat Jones. To tell you the truth, I didn't either until that afternoon in his room when he told me that he was going to "knock the bitch out."

I had been in many training sessions with him. I don't know of any sport where the training is more rigorous. I had watched him train, run, and diet. I had watched him spar over and over again. I had watched him prepare for that night.

When we left Las Vegas, Tarver was not necessarily lucky. Tarver was, however, the light heavyweight champion of the world.

Putting Yourself in the Position to Win

The next time you're watching a sporting event, think about all that went in to making that impossible shot or goal or hit or catch or knockout punch in a title fight. Whether in sports or in life, we can put ourselves in a position to win and to be lucky. There are all sorts of flukes and twists and turns in life. I believe that one of the twists and turns Tarver took in his quest to be the best in the world was the loss to the Kazakhstani in Atlanta. Like preparation, failure can also propel you to greater things and put you in a position to be luckier. Not lucky, luckier.

Putting yourself in a position to win does not just happen. Many hours and many disappointments lead up to that moment. We will talk about failure and the value of failure later. But failure, coupled with preparation, coupled with believing in yourself, are powerful components that give us our best chance of winning.

Janet Hill

Before we move on, just a short note about Grant Hill's mother, Janet. Janet was a force of nature. She was a suite mate of Hillary Clinton's at Wellesley. She served on the boards of Carlisle, Duke, Wendy's, and Sprint. To me, she was the wisest woman I ever met, and for some reason, she took a liking to me, and I loved her. One day, I received a phone call letting me know Janet had been diagnosed with glioblastoma and would be receiving treatment at Duke. My legs literally buckled from underneath me.

I knew how serious glioblastoma was because earlier in life, I had been partners with Johnnie Cochran, and he had the same cancer. I knew immediately that it was a death sentence. Johnnie didn't last a year.

When I heard the news, I cried, and I couldn't remember crying for someone other than a family member. That's how I knew what she had meant to me. Charles Barkley once said that Grant's mother gave him the best advice ever and that was, "Don't give your money to friends and family, they'll just use you."

By the way, Grant did not hire a sports agent. Instead, he hired a lawyer by the name of Lon Babby, a tremendous lawyer who did his contract on an hourly basis. The money Grant has today is tremendous. A large part of that fortune is a result of the compounding nature of the money he saved by not paying a sports agent's 3 percent, 4 percent, or 5 percent, or 20 to 30 percent for sponsorships. Grant had two big deals with Sprite and FILA. He paid his lawyer by the hour. Why more sports stars don't do what Grant did is beyond me, because most of these salaries after the draft are slotted anyway. But then again, Janet was not their mother.

The last time I spoke to Janet was on FaceTime and she was in a facility in Virginia and was weak. When the call ended, I knew I would never talk to or see her again, and I cried one more time. We don't know how lucky we are to have people like the Hill family come into our lives. People call it a blessing but I call it luck. Meeting Grant Hill and his family and their friends turned out to be one of the luckiest days of my life.

CHAPTER 20

BASEBALL

While football has clearly taken over as "America's pastime," baseball is still very close behind. As a Floridian, there is nothing more glorious than a spring training game in one of the many ballparks scattered throughout the Sunshine State. The great thing about spring training is you don't really care who wins or who loses, and you get to spend some great time with whomever you have gone to the game with.

In Tampa, they sell out constantly because that's where the Yankees play. If the Dallas Cowboys are America's football team, the New York Yankees carry that moniker in baseball. I used to go to a restaurant in Tampa, Malio's, and that was the hangout for the Yankees, and particularly, George Steinbrenner. The Boss, as he was known, was always very nice to me and my friends. Malio, himself, was a Tampa icon and one of the great restauranteurs of all time. During spring training, Malio's was a mecca for Hall of Fame baseball players.

Later in life, Mr. Steinbrenner's pilot, Dean, came to work for me and manages and operates my jet. The stories he has told me about Steinbrenner are just classic. Once, Dean told me that Steinbrenner had a rule. If you weren't on time, he left without you. I asked Dean once who the most important person Steinbrenner ever left. His response, "His wife!"

If I left my wife behind for being late, I think I would look out the window midflight and she would be flying, like Superwoman, right next to the jet. Steinbrenner is braver than I am. On another occasion, when

I took two of my children, Kate and Mike, to Plains, Georgia, to see Jimmy Carter preach, we stopped and got a bag of Krystal hamburgers for our ride home. Dean told me that reminded him of Steinbrenner. He said Steinbrenner's favorite food was White Castle hamburgers. I must admit it's hard to resist a good slider.

Moneyball

Because baseball is not as strenuous and injury-riddled as football and basketball, the season lasts a lot longer. The Major League Baseball season's schedule consists of 162 games for each of the thirty teams divided between the American League and National League, and it is played over approximately six months for a total of 2,430 games, plus postseason.

The average MLB team is worth $2.36 billion, according to data compiled by Sportico. The New York Yankees rank first at $7.13 billion, while the Miami Marlins rank last at $1.07 billion. The thirty teams are collectively worth more than $70 billion and are generally owned by billionaires.

Most MLB teams make money. Revenue is generated from several sources such as broadcast rights, merchandise sales, ticket sales, and sponsorships. But some years, some teams do lose money. The New York Mets posted the biggest loss in the 2022 season, losing $138 million. Luckily for Mets fans, billionaire and hedge fund guru Steven Cohen bought the franchise in 2020 for $2.475 billion and has the means to handle those losses. Even teams that lose money over the years are usually made whole when they sell the team at a later date. Professional sports teams are like yachts. It is an opportunity for the very wealthy to show just how wealthy they are.

Owners consistently say they are not making money to get concessions from local and state governments. Whether it's building a new stadium, parking garage, or other freebies, poor-mouthing is a tactic used to get free money from taxpayers. And while some teams do make a very handsome profit, the real game is asset appreciation.

Making It to the Majors

Like all sports there is much luck, both "planned luck" and "pure luck," involved in the games. There is also lots of luck involved in any player making it to the major leagues. Every spring, a new group of kids start to play T-ball and their dreams for the major leagues begin. If it doesn't begin with the kids, it certainly begins with their parents. So many parents think they have the next great player. Unfortunately, in most cases, nothing could be further from the truth.

One of the businesses I founded and that I enjoy a great deal is our baseball player management company. Years ago, I co-owned some nightclubs and restaurants in Orlando and had a young man by the name of Tom O'Connell who worked for us. We built a restaurant called 3-D's from Downtown. It was at a time when the Orlando Magic were very popular, and Dennis Scott was awesome when it came to shooting threes. We partnered with Dennis and put his name on the restaurant. Tom, who ran our bars, was in charge of finding memorabilia, and did a stellar job. I don't know how he got all the jerseys from all the different stars, but our restaurant was packed with beautiful jerseys, balls, and sports memorabilia.

I wish I could tell you that 3-D's was a financial success, but I don't think I even got a dollar back from my initial investment. One of the reasons may have been that we allowed the Orlando Magic players to eat for free. Unfortunately, at that time, Shaquille O'Neal was the star center for the Magic. If Shaq ate lunch every day there, we would have gone out of business faster. The guy can eat.

Shaq was a wonderful addition to our city and is a magnificent human being. Shaq and I co-hosted the first fundraiser for a fellow by the name of Jerry Demings, who became Orange County's sheriff. His wife later served as a U.S. congresswoman, and today Jerry is the Orange County mayor. Lots of fond memories with the Demingses, Shaq, and all the Magic players. Scott Skiles also became a really good friend.

Like I said before, 80 percent of all restaurants go out of business within five years. I wish I had written this book before I opened up the restaurants and bars. I didn't make much money and I didn't lose much money, but I did have a really good time. Remember the section on "fuck-you money?" That was some of my fuck-you money, though I did not have it at the time!

I really believed in Tom, and I knew he could be successful at whatever he set out to do. Tom had a strong desire to be a sports agent. So with my backing and Tom's hustle and drive, we founded a baseball management company: Legends Sports. I can tell you that we probably made every mistake known to man, or woman. We hired people we shouldn't have hired and paid bonuses we shouldn't have paid and signed players we shouldn't have signed. We were the blind leading the blind. But once again, we were having a great time, and it was worth it, and I'd do it again.

Ultimately, we got our bearings straight and became a real company. We changed the name from Legends to O'Connell Sports Management, because Tom was the face and the heart of the entire organization; it was only fair. As I write this chapter, we have a very healthy stable of minor league and major league players. Obviously, there is only one Scott Boras, and he is the King Kong of baseball sports management; but we have carved out a very healthy business with some very good players and, most importantly, we have had such fun doing it.

Think about if your job was going to Major League Baseball parks to watch your clients play. You sit there with a beer and a hot dog and some popcorn and you are working!

Before we talk about some of the wild and seemingly impossible finishes in Major League Baseball, it's important to understand how hard and lucky it is to get there in the beginning.

A Look at the Numbers

The world has over eight billion people populating planet Earth. Out of all those people, there were a total of 945 players on opening-day rosters for all of the MLB teams for the 2023 season.

Each MLB team is allowed to have forty players on their roster that are protected—signed to major-league contracts with that team. The forty-man roster contains all twenty-five active major league players, as well as fifteen others that are in various spots in the club's minor league system or on the MLB injured list.

There are only 750 players that are active at any given time in Major League Baseball. Compare that number to the number of people in the world. You almost have a better chance of being born, as risky as that is, as playing in the major leagues.

There are 28.5 percent of the total number of players on opening day that were born internationally; 70 percent were born in the U.S. It just goes to show that statistically, it is extremely unlikely for any of the little leaguers to play in the MLB.

The most represented foreign country in baseball is the Dominican Republic, which today has 171 players that have been called up to the twenty-five-man rosters.

According to a report by the Institute for Diversity and Ethics in Sport at the University of Central Florida during the 2021 season, Major League Baseball was made up of approximately 57.5 percent white players, 31.9 percent Latino players, 7.3 percent black players, 2.7 percent Asian players, and .6 percent other. The Dominican Republic produces more major league players per capita than any other country in the world. It is baseball heaven.

So now we have all those children hoping to one day play on a major league field and, based on reality, that is darn near impossible. Then there is another factor that is also important to note if this is your dream, or your dream for your children. The average career of a Major League Baseball player is 5.6 years. Also, one in five position players will have only a single-year career, and at every point of a player's career, the player's chance of ending his career is at least 11 percent.

If a player can last ten years, that's a very big deal. Any player, coach, manager, or trainer that has worked within the league for at least ten years will receive a pension payout for the rest of his life. Everyone is allowed to start withdrawing $68,000 annually by the age of forty-five.

However, if you wait until you turn sixty-two, the annual payout bumps to $220,000. One of the most important things for us as representatives of these elite athletes is to try to finish the career with ten years in. It makes a huge difference in retirement.

The 2023 minimum salary in the MLB was $720,000. This also means that a minor-league player who was called up to the majors will be paid $780,000 for each season he spends on the major-league roster.

Many of the players make the league minimum and some only come up for a cup of coffee. The average salary for a player in the MLB stood at $4.9 million in 2023. This average is so high because there are a few players who are receiving astronomical salaries that skew the results.

Recently, Shohei Ohtani, who was just picked up in 2024 by the Los Angeles Dodgers, will make $70 million in 2024. Max Scherzer of the Rangers and Justin Verlander with the Astros make $43.3 million, and right fielder Aaron Judge of the Yankees makes $40 million. When you go down the list of the highest players by position, you'll see some astronomical numbers, but not that many players.

The astronomical salaries at the top of Major League Baseball actually skew the perception of reality. The truth is that many players have a very short career, and even with that career, after taxes and expenses, many do not have enough to retire, especially if they have not played in ten years.

Here are some statistics that are sobering. According to the Little League World Series Tournament, there have been just sixty-four players who appeared in the Little League World Series that have made it to the major leagues. That is less than 1 percent. Approximately one in 200, or approximately .5 percent, of high school senior boys playing interscholastic baseball will be eventually drafted by a major league team. And being drafted by a major league team is just the beginning. Then there is the long climb from instructional ball all the way through A, AA, AAA, and then finally the major leagues. Only 5.6 percent of high school players advance on to college to play at some level of college baseball.

And as certain players continue to rise, there is always the unlucky part of the sport, which is injuries. Unfortunately, we've had many players that we believed to be surefire Major League Baseball players who were thriving in the minors, only to have an injury or a Tommy John surgery. Many of these players have had coaches who were more interested in winning than in preserving the health of these young players, and arms are thrown out and careers destroyed. Some good news along the way is that for players who make it all the way to their senior year in the NCAA, 10.5 percent of those players will then get drafted by an MLB team.

There are many more players drafted in baseball than other professional sports because many of these players bloom much later than in baseball and football. The major league draft consists of twenty rounds for all thirty teams. In a sport like basketball, if you're not drafted in the first round, you probably will not be playing in the NBA.

We now know of the almost impossible journey to Major League Baseball. If you want to know why the players are so good, it is because it is so hard. Major League Baseball is an allure for children all over the world. It's a dream for their mothers and their fathers. Especially when you get into countries like Cuba and the Dominican Republic, where it is a path out of poverty. Life is truly luck when it comes to the Major League Baseball player. They were blessed with athletic gifts, great coaches, and parents along the way and, most importantly, good health. One variable can mean the end of that career or that potential. So the next time you go to a Major League Baseball park, be thinking of what it took for that young man to make it that far.

Home-Field Advantage

Home teams have home-field advantage in Major League Baseball. *Real Sports with Bryant Gumbel* on HBO aired a special looking at called strikes and actual strikes. Yale Professor Toby Moskowitz analyzed every pitch — about a million of them — over the last three and a half years for

Major League Baseball before the 2013 airing of this story. Moskowitz found that since 2013, the umpires are only about 88 percent accurate, getting one out of every eight ball/strike calls wrong, which adds up to more than thirty thousand mistakes a year! Moskowitz did this by using video to see if the ball was in the strike zone or not. Purists do not want machines calling balls and strikes, or umpiring the bases. There is a machine that could call, accurately, every ball and every strike. The technology has been available for years. The most frustrating part of all this is when we watch it from home, we know when the umpire has blown a call.

What the HBO special really showed was that most of the missed calls went against the visiting teams. In other words, the umpires missed more calls when it was to the advantage of the home team. And that discrepancy was gigantic. The simple fact is this: humans are not perfect, and they can't see like a computer. Balls and strikes are being missed on a regular basis, and games and championships are being decided. There is a way to fix it and settle it for good, and that is the computer. It seems that Major League Baseball would rather have the excitement and the challenges and the managers storming out of the dugout than accurately calling balls and strikes. It does make for great water-cooler talk the next day at work, but it just goes to show how much luck there is in all sports. Referees and umpires are human. They like to be cheered. They feel cheered when recalling the third strike on the visiting player or calling that same visiting team out at home plate. Some of those umpires feel those cheers are for them. The opposing team feels otherwise.

A Few Memorable Games

There have been so many memorable games in baseball that an entire book would not be sufficient to do it justice. And depending on your team, and the time and the place, we are going to have different favorite MLB moments. When we look back, we see that luck had a lot to do with it. One undisputed important moment in MLB history occurred when Jackie Robinson became the first African American player to enter the league. After that, he paved the way for countless other players of color to join, and broke down barriers that existed far too long.

I will only focus on a few memorable games here, but I bet all of you have your own favorite moment in baseball.

On October 3, 1951, the New York Giants and Brooklyn Dodgers faced off in a deciding game for the National League pennant, and in the ninth inning, the score was tied at 4–4. Giants' outfielder, Bobby Thomson, hit a walk-off home run off Dodgers' pitcher, Ralph Branca, sending the Giants to the World Series. This moment is so memorable because it was the first ever playoff game to be televised and became forever known as the "Shot Heard 'Round the World."

If you're a Pirates fan, you will know Game 7 of the 1960 World Series when the Pirates were playing the New York Yankees. With the score tied 9–9 in the bottom the ninth, Pirates' second baseman, Bill Mazeroski, hit a walk-off home run, making it the only walk-off homer in the World Series Game 7, ever. The Pirates won the game 10–9 and clinched the World Series.

Growing up in Lexington, the Cincinnati Reds were my team. I played on the Perry Lumbar Tigers in little league and once a year, we would all go to Crosley Field to see the Reds play. It was always one of the best days of my year. Standing on the field with people like Vada Pinson, Frank Robinson, Tommy Helms, and Pete Rose; I couldn't believe it was happening! Obviously as a Reds fan, Rose became my hero.

On September 11, 1985, it was a historic day for Reds fans and for Rose, as he broke Ty Cobb's all-time hit record of 4,191 hits. Rose played over twenty-four seasons and hit an incredible 4,256 hits, a record that stands today. Later, he was banned from eligibility for the Hall of Fame because he bet on baseball. With all the dirty antics that have gone on in all professional sports, it's time to let Rose in the Hall of Fame. Most are not choirboys, and Rose certainly isn't; but he is the greatest hitter of all time.

Game 5 of the 1956 World Series is another baseball greatest moments. It was the first time a pitcher, Yankees' pitcher Don Larson, threw a perfect game in the World Series. He threw ninety-seven pitches for the game, striking out seven batters and not allowing a single hit or walk. When you talk about luck, there's a lot of luck that goes on with pitching a perfect game in a World Series. There's a lot of luck that goes along with pitching a no-hitter on any given day.

Perhaps one of the most iconic moments in baseball was in Game 3 of the 1932 World Series when the great Yankees' outfielder, Babe Ruth, famously pointed to the centerfield before hitting a home run in that very spot. Years later, many aficionados debate whether he actually called his shot, but for me I'm believing it.

And for Cubs fans everywhere, they can never forget 2016. The Cubs had not won a World Series since 1908. It seemed they never would. But all that changed as the Cubs faced off against the Cleveland Indians in the World Series. The Cubs found themselves down three games to one but refused to give up. In Game 5, they rallied back to force extra innings and, in Game 7, they fought tooth and nail and won the game. The curse was broken and Theo Epstein, the young brain who transformed previously the Boston Red Sox, had done it again. This time for the Chicago Cubs. If you've never been to Wrigley Field or Fenway Park, I urge all of you to go before they're gone. It is a day you'll never forget. Baseball is a game of inches and a game of skill. Getting to the major leagues is almost impossible, and staying in the major leagues for ten years, very difficult. Games have been won and lost over bad calls, bad pitches, and just blatant errors—errors that are usually not made, but are made in that particular situation.

My Favorite Moment

My favorite moment in baseball was in the 1988 World Series with the Los Angeles Dodgers facing the Oakland Athletics. Kirk Gibson was initially held out of the Dodgers' lineup with injuries to both legs, but after being called upon to pinch-hit in the bottom of the ninth inning with two outs, he hit a two-run, walk-off home run against Oakland Athletics superstar pitcher, Dennis Eckersley. It's worth going to your Google app and watching this homerun. He could barely walk to the plate and had trouble rounding the bases as he pumped his arm. I can watch that moment over and over again and hear famous Dodgers' announcer, Vin Scully, exclaim as Gibson rounded the bases, "In a year that has been so improbable, the impossible has happened." Or was it just luck?

Whatever your favorite baseball moment in MLB or watching your children play the sport, baseball is and will always be a part of America and Americana. Baseball is the fabric of our sports world and where it all really began. If you've ever been lucky enough to go to a Major League Baseball game, consider yourself very, very lucky.

CHAPTER 21

BASKETBALL

It's impossible to talk about major sports in America without taking a dive into basketball. It is my belief that none of the major sports come close to basketball when it comes to pure luck determining the outcome of many games.

All you have to do is watch the highlights on ESPN to know what I'm talking about. Some of these players make outlandish shots that actually bank in off of the backboard. It is clear in watching the shot that they did not mean to use the backboard. It is even clearer when you look at their teammates rolling in laughter after those shots are made.

Many shots are made on the other side of the half-court line. It seems miraculous. Now in all fairness, many of these players routinely make some of these Hail Mary-type shots in practice. They are skilled athletes. If I made one of those shots, that would be one thing; coming from an elite athlete, some skill must be involved.

The Harlem Globetrotters

Once upon a time, I represented the Harlem Globetrotters' players in a case against FUBU. Merchandise was being sold using their likeness and they were not being compensated. The stories the Globetrotters told were amazing. These clown princes of basketball were actually good players in their own right. Wilt Chamberlain and other future NBA stars actually played for the Globetrotters.

The Globetrotters could make outrageous shots from all points and angles. One of Meadowlark Lemon's shots involved drop-kicking the basketball from center court into the basket. He made it enough times to understand that it was not all luck but lots of skill and, more importantly, lots of practice. Practice, of course, is a luck enhancer. And practice moves us from pure luck, to practice luck, to actual skill.

The Role of Genetics

Another interesting factor in basketball and in many other sports as well, is the number of players whose parents were also college or NBA players. Genetics plays a huge role in talent and ability. And if your parents played a sport, then odds are they will have you playing the same sport as a child—so both nature and nurture at work. I'm sure you can think of some great players whose parents were also tremendous athletes. It applies to all sports, but basketball seems to have a lot.

Over 250 father-and-son combinations have made it to the major league-level in baseball. Some famous players include Moisés Alou, Ken Griffey Jr., Barry Bonds, Prince Fielder, Roberto Alomar, Ray Boone, and Buddy Bell. And the list is even longer when you're talking about college players who played Division I baseball just as their father did. Football offers similar advantages to the son of a great athlete.

But basketball takes this trend to a new level. Kevin Love, Steph Curry, Klay Thompson, and Kobe Bryant aren't the only NBA players with a father who played in the league before them. According to a *Wall Street Journal* analysis on biographical data on every NBA player, 48 percent are related to current or former elite athletes—defined as anyone who has played the sport professionally, in the NCAA, or at a national-team level. While other sports feature notable dynasties like the Mannings of the NFL, only about 17.5 percent of NFL players and 14.5 percent of MLB players are related to other elite athletes, based on a similar study.

According to the report, there are a number of possible explanations. Obviously, being tall and having a large wingspan makes it more likely for a player to make it in the big leagues. There are also the environmental factors too, which we can only assume includes the inherent desire to one-up one's sibling at all costs.

Go to Wikipedia to see a list of father-and-son combinations who have played in the National Basketball Association. The list goes on and on, and that doesn't count all of the elite players who have played basketball. One thing is for certain: the day I was born, everyone knew that I would NOT be playing in the NBA, NFL, or even Major League Baseball.

Genetics gives us height, speed, and many other factors that award these people an athletic edge. Shaquille O'Neal is not Shaq unless he is 7'2" and runs like a gazelle. Living in Orlando, I frequently went to the same carwash as Shaq's mother, Lucille. Shaq can thank Lucille for his genetic advantages. This pure genetic luck plays such an outsized role in so many athletes and in so many sports. And that's before we take into consideration other X factors such as drive, ambition, and heart—many traits that aren't learned but are born with us.

So when we talk about sports in general, it is impossible not to give lots of credit to pure luck for these players who were born with these incredible gifts. Their gifts are as striking as Stephen Hawking's and Albert Einstein's mathematical genius. And when you add environment to the mix, it even gets better. These little boys have been tagging along with their fathers to gymnasiums all around the world playing pickup and shooter rounds with the best players on the planet. Before we even get to the first game and the first shot, lots of luck has been involved. Once we get to the games, then luck really becomes important and prevalent.

NCAA Basketball

One of the most exciting times of the year for sports is known as March Madness — the tournament that determines the eventual NCAA winner. Each year, it nets the NCAA almost $1 billion in profit. That's how much we enjoy watching these games.

The thing about March Madness is that it is so unpredictable, and brackets are ruined immediately after one game. Kentucky's loss to Oakland probably upended 98 percent of all brackets in one game. And so it goes from there.

The teams are seeded based on their performance during the year and then the tournament progresses. During these games, the wildest and most improbable plays are made. At the end of the tournament, there is the famous collage with a familiar song that recaps the great moments of March Madness. I would submit to you that many of the plays we watch in that recap can only be described as pure luck. And some as practiced luck. In any event, just the way a ball bounces off that rim is not certain or exact.

In the history of the NCAA, we have had several eventual champions who I don't believe could have ever done it again if they played a hundred games. A few notable ones come to mind.

One great one was the improbable win by North Carolina State coached by Coach Jim Valvano. The 1983 NCAA Division I Men's Basketball Tournament involved fifty-two schools playing in a single-elimination play to determine the national champion. The Houston team was coached by Guy Lewis and was a gigantic favorite. Hakeem Olajuwon of Houston was still named the tournament's most outstanding player, becoming the last player to date to earn this award while playing for a team that failed to win a national title. The team was so dominant that the thought of North Carolina State prevailing seemed impossible.

NC State's victory has often been considered one of the greatest upsets in national college basketball history and it's the fourth biggest point-spread upset ever. The No. 6-seeded Wolfpack won on Lorenzo

Charles's buzzer-beating dunk after a missed desperation shot. This was not planned luck; this was pure luck. If you don't believe me, watch the tape of Valvano wildly running around the court after the game was over. He couldn't believe it had happened. Google the final minute of that game. I believe that Houston would win that game the next ninety-nine times they played. However, on that night, everything went NC State's way, and Valvano and company became basketball immortals.

Similarly, Villanova's historic upset of Georgetown in the 1985 NCAA championship game remains one of college basketball's most memorable and compelling moments. Villanova won the title game by a score of 66–64. The Wildcats had the highest field-goal percentage in Final Four history, winning their first national championship in men's basketball. Some nights everything you shoot goes in. The Wildcats held off star center Patrick Ewing and the defending national-champion Hoyas in the title game as eight-point underdogs. Villanova essentially played a perfect game against Georgetown. That's what I call luck.

Probably the biggest upset in March Madness history was when No. 16 Fairleigh Dickinson beat No. 1 Purdue. It was shocking.

The NBA is not as susceptible to these big upsets because they play the best-of-five or the best-of-seven games. It is very hard for a lucky team to win four out of seven games, as is needed for NBA championship. I highly doubt that Villanova would have beaten Georgetown the best four out of seven or that NC State would have beaten Houston four out of seven. As a matter fact, I think NC State and Villanova would have lost all four games, if I were a betting man.

All of this goes to demonstrate that just like in life, luck in sports plays a huge role. It plays a role in the player ultimately reaching an elite level and a role in some key games at key moments in time.

There are broken hearts scattered throughout the annals of basketball history with lucky shots and lucky plays. And there are also so many great players who were just fortunate to have mothers and fathers who were great athletes. Warren Buffett called this type of luck the "Ovarian Lottery."

The Miracle of Sports

Americans are fascinated and addicted to sports. It is tribal to us. We call them "my team." It is as if we are a part of that team and take the losses and wins just as personally as the actual players. Again, our desire to win and succeed is oftentimes materialized as a spectator for sports. In sports and in life, there is practiced luck and pure luck. Either way, this luck has broken hearts, made careers and, most importantly, left all of us with enduring memories that we take with us to our grave.

Do you believe in miracles? I do!

CHAPTER 22

FRIENDS AND NEIGHBORS

There may not be any luckier moment in your life than when you meet that friend who turns out to be your lifelong friend. We make these friends at every stop in life. It is amazing how many childhood and high school friends stayed with us forever. I know firsthand that some of my college friends remained friends for life and some came to work with me in various endeavors. What I often say to others is, "Our best friends are our first friends. Because they loved us for no reason other than us." As life goes on and people's status in life changes, it is hard to find those kinds of friends. Mark Cuban still has get-togethers with his friends from Indiana University. They are thick as thieves and happy for Mark. Real friends are happy for our success.

While I was at the University of Florida, I was a member of the ATO fraternity, and there I met friends who are still with me fifty years later. We are connected on email chains and funny jokes. I remember the night before I was leaving UF after undergrad and had no clear prospects of what I would be doing next. I wanted to go to law school, but I was graduating early and just needed to make some money.

On that last night, I took a long walk reminiscing about those four great years spent in all parts of the campus. My walk concluded in the ATO parking lot. I remember thinking to myself, "Will I ever in my life have these kinds of friends and these kinds of times?" Fortunately for me I did, and further fortune shined on me as those fraternity brothers I was close to, I'm still close to.

We go through life picking up friends, having acquaintances, and at some points along the way, even discarding some of them. Friends give us that human connection and stop loneliness. Loneliness is one of the greatest causes of mental illness. There are many of us who depend on that human connection to survive. I am one of those people. I am Irish, and people are like gasoline for my vehicle. If I don't have gas, my car won't run.

I will confess, as time has marched on, I have had less and less desire for social interaction. I used to wonder how people like the fitness guru Richard Simmons and the great actor Jack Nicholson could just disappear. I'm not ready to disappear, but sitting on my deck at home and watching my dogs run, today I'm okay alone.

One at a Time

When Bill Clinton ran for president, I was his state finance chair in Florida. I got to watch this guy very closely. During the pandemic, he and I became pen pals and had some great conversations by text and by phone. Clinton needs lots of human interaction to energize him, and he loves every minute of it. Once when we were together, I asked him for his best piece of advice. He told me to treat every single person as if there were an election tomorrow, that I was running, and that person was going to have a vote.

Now I'm not planning on running for office, but I do practice "one at a time." I still have businesses that are heavily dependent on referrals and help from people I know. Not only is "one at a time" good karma, it's also good business.

I've been collecting people and friends my whole life. They are very important to my mental health. If you are someone who doesn't have enough friends, you know firsthand the misery that loneliness can bring.

The Cost of Loneliness

Loneliness is not a mental illness, but it is a significant and growing problem with substantial physical-health and mental-health impacts. Research by the American Psychiatric Association shows that loneliness and social isolation may be as bad for your health as obesity or smoking fifteen cigarettes a day, and loneliness significantly impacts mental health. The restrictions of the pandemic increased the problem and increased public awareness of the issue.

Persistent loneliness is associated with higher rates of heart disease, obesity, depression, anxiety, and dementia. Much of the research tends to focus on older adults, but recent surveys suggest loneliness is especially high among teens and young adults.

For years I have supported the charity Meals on Wheels. While the meals are very important to the shut-in people who receive them, more important is the social interaction they get to have with the volunteer dropping off the meal.

One of the primary reasons children and young people may be feeling lonely is the inability to socialize and mix with friends in and outside of educational settings. Seventy-six percent of young people have said not being able to see friends had a negative impact. More concerning is that many of these young children have no friends at all. When you couple that with watching others on social media having the time of their lives, one can only imagine the pain that causes.

I am convinced that school shootings arise out of loneliness. Many shooters are misfits and somewhat odd. They are outsiders and outcasts, and they go through life watching others seemingly have the time of their lives. And then they snap. I think their thinking goes like this: "If I'm not going to have a good life, neither are you." Even before there were school shooters, we still had kids in our classes who were odd and troubled. I had a boy in my sixth-grade class named "Bruce." I don't want to reveal his real name. He was very strange, and many of us felt that, in science class, he often had his hand down his pants and was masturbating. Bruce was a weird dude.

Even at that early age, I was always looking for someone who could go nuclear. I always sold candy in the schools I went to. It was a way to make between 25 and 50 bucks a week. Whenever I would pass by Bruce's desk, I used to give him a Jolly Rancher candy, for free! My thought was that if Bruce decided to go off, he would shoo me out of the classroom before wreaking havoc. I don't know whatever happened to Bruce, but I do know he was a weird cat.

From 2000 to 2020, more than 800,000 people died by suicide in the U.S., with males representing 78.7 percent of all suicides that happened between those dates. In 2022, a record high of 49,500 people died by suicide, and the suicide rate reached its highest level since 1941 with 14.3 per 100,000 persons. Interestingly enough, Casper, Wyoming is the city with the highest suicide rate in the U.S.

The highest suicide rates among professions are:

1. Medical doctors

2. Dentists

3. Police officers

Suicide accounted for 1.3 percent of all deaths worldwide, making it the seventeenth leading cause of death in 2019 and all mostly preventable. Loneliness, which gives rise to mental-health issues, is often cited as the No. 1 cause.

Therefore, as we go through life, developing meaningful and lasting friendships is one of the most important aspects of our lives. Where we meet these people is mostly random and mostly lucky. As many fans worldwide as Oprah Winfrey has, she still relies on Gayle King to be her forever friend. They have a bond based on trust and confidence. A true friend is someone you can share anything with.

For many people, their only friends are their family members. I find this somewhat sad in one way, but in another way I don't. If they didn't have their tight family unit, they may have no friends at all. My wife is heavily reliant on her two brothers and two sisters. She is shy to begin with, and her siblings provide great comfort and friendship. Every Sunday, the five of them have a Zoom call, and I hear her laughing like a hyena from wherever she may be. She talks to her two sisters every single day. I text or talk to my brothers every single day.

Luck and Friendship

Who are the people you consider friends? Consider how and where you met them, and how random is likely was.

Usually, such a meeting was simply luck-based. But think also about how you enhanced your own luck to make that happen. You probably had to leave your house, join a group, put on some nice clothes, make an effort to be friendly, and put yourself in the way of possible friends.

Even though we meet hundreds and maybe thousands of people in our lifetime, only a few times have I thought, "This person is somebody I could be friends with."

The people I am friends with bring me immeasurable joy, and when I think of each of them, I also know why I wanted to be friends with them. They bring experiences or commonality that tend to bond us together. But the simple fact remains that meeting most of these friends was based on pure luck.

While in high school and college, I performed magic at Walt Disney World, and I also worked as a character. I was Fiddler Pig, King and, Pluto. Our dressing room was called the "Zoo Crew" because of all the costumes. To this day, those work friends from the 1970s are still close to me. One, Mark Miller, another one of the Three Little Pigs and Pluto, won on *Ed McMahon's Star Search* and later had a successful career with his band Sawyer Brown. Mark is still an active member in our Zoo Crew family. We get together sporadically and communicate constantly on Facebook. Had I never had the good fortune of working at Walt Disney World, I would never have had the good fortune of these lifelong friends.

When I take my walk down memory lane, it is amazing where and how I met so many of my good friends. Remember the story of meeting my wife in church? Well, those same types of stories apply to many of my friends. Had I not joined the ATO fraternity, I don't believe I would have known any of those men. If I had not worked at Disney World, I would not be an honorary member of the Zoo Crew and best friends with Mark. Life is very much luck when it comes to making friends. But you can increase your luck by putting yourself on the path to meet such friends in the first place.

The Role of Neighbors

Another random act in the development of friendships is our neighbors. Neighbors play an incredibly important role in our lives. When buying a house, lots of factors go into that decision. Schools. Price of the home. Quality of the neighborhood. Proximity to airports, shopping, and your work.

When we finally move into our new neighborhood, that's when it can become very interesting. It can be a very joyful experience, or something straight out of hell. My parents were both terrible alcoholics. We had a neighbor, a very nice man, who retired to Florida and built his dream house, a small bungalow, right next door to our family. I don't know why my mother targeted this man, but in her drunken rages, she did. All he wanted to do was enjoy retirement and garden. Instead, he moved next door to a drunk woman, married to a drunk man, with five children running helter-skelter, and a German Shepherd that was never leashed. When I think back about his life there, I am mortified. I think he felt sorry for me.

One day, years later, another neighbor who lived directly across the street from us came to my office to visit me. He was a minister. When he came to see me, he told me he just wanted to look me in the eye and understand how we had survived. I have two brothers who are dentists, a sister who is a mental-health psychologist, and my brother, Tim, who was paralyzed and worked with me. He was amazed. He told me that he and his wife used to hold hands and pray for "you five children."

Before he left, I thanked him for his prayers, and I told him that I thought his prayers had worked. The odds of all five of us surviving and thriving was certainly a longshot at best. Other than Tim's tragic accident, all of us did very well in life. Because I believe in the power of prayer, I have thought about that meeting many times since then. The thought of him and his wife across the street from us, understanding the peril we were in, and holding hands and praying—I believe that luck shined on us by having this godly man across the street praying for our survival.

From Neighbors to Lifelong Friends

Some of us have neighbors who have not only have become lifelong friends, but our best friends. There are neighborhoods that function almost as a gigantic social club. A columnist for the *Orlando Sentinel,* Scott Maxwell, recently posted a picture of his neighbors playing pickleball in a court they had designed in their cul-de-sac. It was a communal activity in the middle of the street.

I can't think of how many times I've seen neighborhoods trick-or-treating together and having the time of their lives at regular social gatherings. People go back and forth between houses when they have great neighbors. They become golf and tennis partners. They dine and celebrate together. Some neighborhoods become so important that people don't move, even when they would rather be in a nicer house in a nicer neighborhood. They simply stay because the neighbors and the neighborhood are so important to their mental well-being.

My son, Mike, lives right across the street from me. I'm lucky in the sense that I have my son and three of my grandchildren right there. I have also watched my daughter-in-law build up a tremendous network of friends within this neighborhood. The rest of my children have moved to a city about fifteen minutes away. It is probably a nicer city than the one we live in, but for Mike and his family, this neighborhood is more important than a more expensive home at a better address.

Children are picked up from school at the school bus stop, and the parents stand there and talk before the bus leaves and before the children are dropped off. It is a very important part of their lives. I would be interested to know how many of you reading this book have had similar experiences in neighborhoods.

Years ago, I built a beautiful home in Maui, Hawaii. I look out on the lanai, and during the winter, whales are frolicking in my backyard. But I didn't know anyone when I got there. Luckily for me, I met a neighbor who has become a very good friend. It is unusual to meet good friends late in life.

Chuck Bergson owns twenty-one radio stations in all of Hawaii. He has introduced me to his great circle of friends on Maui. Chuck and I walk three or four times a week together and discuss life and business. His wife, Gail, is friends with my wife, and they go shopping, whale watching, and to Pilates class. This lucky friend for me has made Maui so much nicer. But for meeting Chuck, I don't know what my social life would be out here.

We share happy hours and dinners at each other's homes. We go out to dinner and exercise. In short, this new friend I've met purely by chance has enriched my time on Maui immensely. This same thing happens in neighborhoods all over America.

I have other homes in both Florida and New Hampshire, and we haven't been lucky enough to make close friends with our neighbors. This is how life goes.

Asshole Neighbors

Just as we can have the good fortune of having great friends in our neighborhood, when the converse is true and you live in a neighborhood where you live next door to Freddy Krueger, things can get out of hand and be very bad. The police are called. Vandalism occurs. And by the way, it doesn't matter what the socioeconomic situation is in certain neighborhoods. Things can get nasty. Bill Gross, the great investor from the PIMCO investment firm, has been in a public war with his neighbor over the smallest things, and the war has spilled into the newspapers. When you Google Gross's fight with his neighbor, you will think you are reading about a kindergartener. No, you are reading about a billionaire who made real money for real people for a long time, but he and his neighbor are just two gigantic assholes.

The good luck in having great neighbors who actually become close friends is a wonderful event and provides people with great security and comfort. However, just as good neighbors can provide all of us with incredible benefits, the negative impact of a bad neighbor can be the worst luck possible. After all, not only are you dealing with the nasty neighbor, you are complicated by the fact that it's not so easy just to sell your house, and you may not want to sell your house. Everything could be perfect in your neighborhood but for that one bad apple. The "war of the roses" sometimes spills out into the streets of suburbia and into the cities of high-rise apartments. Bad neighbors do not discriminate.

There are many reasons that we have falling-outs with neighbors. The worst trait a neighbor can have, according to 67 percent of respondents to a Yahoo.com poll, is being disrespectful of property. Being loud came in second and untrustworthiness was third. Being nosy, messy, and unfriendly were also signs of a bad neighbor.

Shockingly, nearly 20 percent of Americans—that's one in five—have moved because of an obnoxious neighbor. The generations Gen Z and Millennials are the most willing to move rather than put up with a toxic neighbor. Twenty-eight percent and 16 percent, respectively.

It has been reported that 42 percent of the population dislikes a neighbor. Problems with animals, whether they are pets or livestock, can be extra annoying. Pets are often at the center of huge disputes. Dog bites happen all the time. An unleashed dog, especially a big dog, can cause lots of disagreements. Uncontrolled barking at all hours can disrupt sleep.

Realtor magazine reported in 2022 that 52 percent of one thousand Americans recently polled said they are annoyed by their neighbors multiple times a year; 35 percent are annoyed by their neighbors at least once a month. And the younger generations appear to be the most irked by the habits of their neighbors.

The same poll showed that 61 percent of people who live in apartments are more likely to move because of their neighbors. Forty-one percent of respondents who lived in a single-family home would move because of a neighbor, the survey showed.

Bad neighbors can be toxic, and this often leads to bad feelings, which can lead to all sorts of mental-health issues. Being forced to live in close proximity to someone you have such animus for takes its toll over time. Perhaps that is the reason so many people are prepared to surrender, even though they may like their neighborhood and their home. The stress of a bad neighbor just isn't worth it.

In another poll by *Realtor* magazine, 23 percent of respondents say they have called the police on their neighbors. That is a staggering statistic. One out of four people have actually called the police to settle a neighborhood score. When you peel back the onion to see what they're fighting about, it will seem like nothing at all. But over time, anger builds, animosity grows, and a personal dislike for someone takes root. The culmination often comes with the police arriving and then wondering why in the hell they were called.

Just as pets can be a problem, children can be a greater problem. Once, we had a condominium at the beach. I had four young children. There is nothing as interesting as beach condominiums and the association that runs them. In Florida, these residents are known as condo commandos. Many times, the president of that Homeowners Association (HOA) sees the entire structure as their home.

At the condominium we lived in, I was once asked to join the condominium board because I was a lawyer. I informed them quickly that I had four children and would make enough enemies with that alone. The last thing I needed was to be on a board making decisions other neighbors did not like, like an assessment for repairs and maintenance. I respectfully declined, knowing that my children would give me enough enemies in and of itself.

That day finally came when the condominium president and vice president came out to the beach with beach chairs and sat down next to me. I looked to my left and looked to my right. They then informed me they wanted to speak to me about my children jumping over the locked gate to the beach. I politely told them that I could promise that this discussion would not end well for either of them, and I suggested they take their chairs and go back to their units. Luckily the crisis was averted, but I got to feel the full force and effect of a condo commando complaining about my children. I didn't take it well and understand perfectly how it could have gotten really nasty.

Homeowners Associations (HOAs)

Many people see their neighborhood as theirs. And I mean every bit of it. Their house, their yard, your house, your yard, common areas, and rules and regulations concerning shared amenities, overhanging trees and hedges, building-code violations, improper parking, and everything in between. We all know that neighbor, who often wants to become the president of the homeowners association. They are the officious intermeddler. Once they are awarded the presidency of the HOA, problems can quickly arise. With this newfound authority, your neighborhood leader can quickly turn into a tyrant.

HOAs are prevalent everywhere. They can be found in neighborhoods, condominiums, and other multi-tenant environments. These HOAs are set up to make sure the neighborhood stays in good shape and does not become in disrepair, and specifically for condominiums and other multi-tenant environments, they maintain outdoor facilities like siding, roofs, and landscaping. When one home is neglected, it is a blight on the entire street and, of course, the neighbors worry about the value of their own home being dragged down because of the pigpen next door. When the HOA doesn't do its job, the roofs and siding aren't maintained properly, and housing units are damaged by weather.

For most people, the No. 1 expense in their budget is a mortgage payment. One of the primary assets for all Americans are their homes. It is no wonder that if a person believes that the value of his home is being trampled upon, it can give rise to bad feelings and even violent behavior.

It is amazing how many people out there simply can't stay in their own lane. While something may bother them, it is not necessarily their business. Some types of HOA members make it their business and have all types of rationales for their interference.

Friends at Work

We also meet lifelong friends, by chance, at work. My law firm, Morgan & Morgan, has 1,000 lawyers employed and 6,000 coworkers. I have been in business a long time and have watched many people come and go. I have also had the pleasure of watching many of these coworkers become great friends with each other. It warms my heart when I see these people outside of work socializing together. Even though I had nothing to do with them becoming friends, other than forming the company where they met, it makes me happy to know that this type of joy emanated from work. I love seeing some of my retired coworkers and partners socializing with each other still on Facebook. When you work at a place and don't have friends there, that can make for some long workdays.

In life, where we live and where we work gives us the best opportunity to make new and lasting friends. These new and lasting friends are important to our mental health.

As we age, we start to distinguish between friends and acquaintances. Most of our lives, we have included acquaintances when we list our friends. As time goes on, we become more aware of what a true friend is as compared to a mere acquaintance. More and more people tell me, "I am lucky if I have enough friends that I can count them on one hand."

Romances at Work

Thirty-one percent of office romances lead to marriage. Marriage, of course, is the ultimate friendship. A survey showed that most employees had formed some office romance; 58 percent had been involved with a colleague; and 72 percent of those over age fifty have had romantic relationships with workmates. A more troubling statistic in workplace romance reveals that 85 percent of affairs outside of marriage began at work, according to GoodTherapy.

Late nights at the office, long work trips, mutual hobbies — it's easy to see why so many extramarital relationships start at work. A huge portion of an average person's life is spent at work. It's eight hours a day. Furthermore, nearly half of those involved in a workplace romance are top-level executives. Almost 40 percent of those who had an affair at work were the company's owners or executives. The statistic reveals why there are so many sexual-harassment complaints in America.

How Many Close Friends Do You Have?

Pew Research found that a narrow majority of adults — 53 percent — say they have between one and four close friends, while a significant share — 38 percent — say they have five or more. They may be stretching the truth. Sadly, some 8 percent say they have no close friends.

There is an age divide in the number of close friends people have. About half of adults sixty-five and older — 49 percent — say they have five or more close friends, compared with 40 percent of those fifty to sixty-four, 34 percent of those thirty to forty-nine, and 32 percent of those younger than thirty. In turn, adults under fifty are more likely than their older counterparts to say they have between one and four close friends.

What we don't know is, does the person whom one person identifies as a close friend feel the same way in return? We all want to have more friends than we have, and perhaps these statistics are misleading and more wishful thinking than actual fact.

Think about the number of people you consider close friends and count them. Hopefully, it's more than one hand, but probably not for most of us.

Luck and Friendship

Where we study, work, and live will, for many of us, determine who our friends and spouses become. When you move to an apartment or a neighborhood, or start a new job, you have no idea what type of luck is waiting for you around the corner. For some of us, it's a type of luck that brings us together with friends for a lifetime, or a potential lifelong partner. For others, it brings the most debilitating stress that we may experience. Not only are we miserable, but we're trapped. The only way out is to move or quit. That is truly bad luck.

CHAPTER 23

IN-LAWS AND OUTLAWS

There is nothing as risky in life as the joining of two families and the creation of in-laws. In-laws come in all shapes and sizes and, for the most part, none of us have much control over who they are or what they're like. One thing is for sure: certain in-laws can cause tremendous friction and turmoil inside a family unit.

I have been very fortunate thus far. I have three daughters-in-law whom we love and one son-in-law we wouldn't trade for the world. Statistically, we are batting a thousand, and that's hard to do in anything.

Friends are hard enough to make as is. At least with friends, we get to pick and choose. We don't have to be friends with someone we don't like or have interest in. That is not the case with in-laws. Suddenly, after a marriage, we are celebrating birthdays, special events, and holidays with these former strangers who are now like family, whether we like them or not. In-laws come in all shapes and sizes. Your siblings' in-laws because they're often included. Your children's in-laws and spouses. Going to these life events with some of these folks can become rather taxing.

The first dangerous in-law is the person who marries your son or daughter. Those are the new in-laws that will have the closest proximity to your life and the most likely to cause family dysfunction. Most of the time, it is the mother-in-law and daughter-in-law who have the most probable chance of fights and friction.

The mother-in-law/daughter-in-law syndrome emerges when two female members of the household failed to establish rapport, resulting in tension that detrimentally impacts the overall home atmosphere. It has long been held that where there is tension between mother-in-law and daughter-in-law, it is because women are exceedingly territorial, even more so than men. They lay "sole ownership" claims to people, things, and spaces. If someone else violates their territorial boundaries, there's going to be a fight. To add fuel to that fire, according to psychologists and multiple surveys, the issues that develop between a woman and her mother-in-law result when both start competing subconsciously for the affection of the same man, which causes the most problems in marriages.

The Toxic In-Law

A toxic in-law is someone who has a repeated pattern of negativity toward other family members—usually their child's spouse. This may be exhibited in the form of control, manipulation, or abusive behavior. The toxic in-law's actions are sometimes intentional but may also stem from behaviors learned from their own family of origin. There are many reasons that a mother-in-law or father-in-law could be jealous of the new daughter-in-law or son-in-law that could include feelings of abandonment and loss, feeling like their child stopped talking to them when they met their partner, and lastly, the mother-in-law or father-in-law could even feel intimidated. There is no rhyme or reason for the struggle. Sometimes the relationship becomes so toxic that the couple may consider divorce, due to the interference of their toxic in-law. Oftentimes this results in estrangement from adult children and grandchildren as well. Grandchildren are often used as weapons and hostages in this war of wills.

Research shows that how spouses relate to their in-laws is a strong predictor of marriage longevity. A man who gets along with his wife's parents is wise; his chances of a strong marriage increase by about 20 percent. Women who get along with their in-laws actually have an increased probability of divorce by about 20 percent. That did not seem to make sense to me.

It has been reported that almost a third of those surveyed accepted that issues with in-laws and extended family are often cited as a reason for divorce. All of us are territorial and have our own way of doing things. People with strong and domineering personalities can insist on pushing their agenda down your throat. That is never a good move.

One of the real issues with strife among in-laws is that one party is usually trying to defend the indefensible. Maybe a husband tries to defend his wife to his mother or defend his mother to his wife. Maybe a wife tries to defend her father to her husband. In an effort to bring peace, everyone comes from different points of view. Once people dig in with their emotions, it is very difficult to unring that bell. And once certain things have been said, or done, putting that genie back in that bottle could take some doing.

Heaven and Hell

For anyone getting married, your spouse should always come first. Before you get married, it's okay to take your parents' side and follow their advice and opinions. However, once you get hitched, your spouse automatically becomes your first priority. Your spouse's opinions and input should take precedence. Unfortunately, many times they don't. A parent-and-child bond is deep and has been formed by years and years of nurturing. This competition can sometimes lead to a difficult relationship.

When daughters-in-law and sons-in-law work out, it is a glorious thing. Heavenly. I love all of my children's spouses. And love is a big word. Before we move on to in-laws in general, there is one staggering statistic that jumps out.

One of my favorite Christmas songs is "Merry Christmas from the Family" by Robert Earl Keen. Please do yourself a favor and listen to this song in its entirety. To me, it sums up the possibility of bad in-laws in one long Christmas song.

Just as your children's spouse can become an in-law from hell, your children's spouses' parents and the parents of your siblings' spouses also bring a new dynamic to the family. Again, all of a sudden, we are mixed and matched with strangers who at best we might really bond with, and at worst can't stand. This ongoing dynamic can result in hard feelings and, over time, pure contempt.

According to Cambridge University Psychologist, Terri Apter, three out of four couples "experience significant conflict with their in-laws," with the mother-in-law/daughter-in-law relationship the trickiest.

On a personal level, I have never been very comfortable with many of the in-laws who have been brought to various family functions over the years. Every one of them brings something different to the table. Sometimes they are terribly irritating and rude and sometimes just boring. I have no clue how cars run, but I have been with in-laws who stand out in front of the house with the hood open on the car staring at the engine for seemingly hours on end. What in the hell they're talking about, I have no clue and no desire to know. Psychology books have been written about this topic forever. The simple fact is that in-laws are no different than the craps table in Vegas. We roll the dice and then the numbers come up. Some numbers cause great joy, and some numbers cause great pain.

I'm sure you've had your own experiences and life adventures with your in-laws. Sometimes it's great. Sometimes it isn't. And it has nothing to do with skill. It comes with pure luck. So far, I have been lucky with my children's spouses and we've had the best luck imaginable.

CHAPTER 24

MUSIC

Have you ever asked yourself if you had not gone into your line of work what would have been your fallback profession? And then another question is what would your fantasy occupation have been? As to a realistic occupation, I think I may have chosen to work on Wall Street doing deals. I think my personality would work there. However, for my fantasy occupation, I would love to have been a great musician.

These people, especially the ultra-successful ones, have the best job in the world. I have been to many concerts in my life and have enjoyed all of them immensely.

My whole life, I have been hooked on music. I can't drive a car without music. I can't sit on the beach or by a pool without music. I have music going in my house on a regular basis.

On the other hand, my wife is not a big music person and prefers NPR. They say opposites attract. Music has soothed me most of my life. Even when I had my paper route in Lexington, I had a transistor radio with an earpiece, for one ear, and as I delivered papers, I had different AM stations blaring in my ear as I cycled throughout my territory. After delivering papers on Saturday morning, my ritual was to go get my teaser card, make my order at the Toddle House, and then play four, five, or six songs on the jukebox. I never ate breakfast without playing music.

As much as I love music, I evidently had no aptitude for it, as I failed flutophone and was thus barred from going on to play in the band. Despite my lack of talent, it did not ever disrupt my enthusiasm for music.

And I love all music. I love country. I love rock. I love opera. And I love spiritual. Any type of music is usually good for me.

Because I have such a love for this art form, I have been interested in the artists and their ability to come up with these songs. The songs seem to come to them out of nowhere and from experiences. One of my favorite things to do is watch Howard Stern interview famous musicians. Stern made his money with strippers and fart jokes, but later in life became, who I believe to be, the best interviewer of musicians ever. He knows music so well and knows so much about the artist that his interviews are riveting and compelling.

Luck and Musicians

There are several things that strike me as lucky about these musicians. First, they had the aptitude to learn to play an instrument. Once I held a guitar in my hand and I realized that it was simply an impossibility. All of my fingers seemed like thumbs.

But to these lucky individuals, especially the leaders of the bands, they not only have the talent to play music, but many have the talent to write lyrics as well. Of course, some of these musicians have partnerships that are lucky in and of themselves.

Elton John wrote the music, but Bernie Taupin wrote the lyrics. Taupin would give John his lyrics and then John would write the music. These two friends from youth put together one of the greatest partnerships in the history of music. I often have thought, "What if Bernie and Elton hadn't lived in the same community and known each other?" All those songs written in John's bedroom would never have happened had Taupin not lived close by. Another stroke of pure luck.

Once, when my children and I were playing poker at Willie Nelson's, Paul Simon came to the game. We were discussing music, and I asked him which song he wrote that took the quickest amount of time. He told us "Bridge Over Troubled Water" took thirty minutes. The fact that these words and music just appear in a person's mind is mind-blowing to me. It just seems lucky or divinely inspired.

One of the interesting things I have noticed about musicians is that most of their songs were written in their teens and twenties. You don't see many groups or artists having new hits after thirty. Of course there are exceptions to every rule.

Recently, I was watching Bob Dylan, and he was asked if he thought he had any more songs in him. His response was a firm "no." When you examine the great acts of our lifetime and look at the date they wrote their songs and their age at the time, you will find what I've found, and that is the inspiration comes during youth, but luck runs out as they get close to thirty.

And I wonder why that is. It doesn't make any sense objectively. Now many of these artists wrote these songs high on weed or even more potent psychedelics. When you look at the cover of *Sgt. Pepper's Lonely Hearts Club Band*, you know The Beatles were doing some serious LSD.

When the Luck Runs Out

I have voraciously read books about the great musical artists of our time. Their journey, to me, is such a wonderful experience filled with so many great memories.

But it seems that, for most, their luck runs out at thirty. They are still writing constantly. Jackson Browne is one of my all-time favorites and I listen to him all the time. But as I listen, I wonder to myself how frustrating it had to be for him when the hits just stopped coming to his mind. And it's not that he's not trying.

I believe these people were given one of the greatest pieces of luck in the world: musical ability at a genius level. The songs tell the story of love and the story of despair and really the stories of our lives. It is why we are so riveted by music. It is also why it's one thing to hear it on the radio and quite another to hear it live and in person. Rarely can we have such joy as a concert. Tom Petty was one of my favorites, and I actually saw him play at a bar called Dub's in Gainesville, even before the Heartbreakers. Petty was influenced by Dylan and even sounded like Dylan. While Petty had many top songs, his last top-forty hit was "You Don't Know How It Feels" from his 1994 album *Wildflowers*. The song reached No. 13 on the *Billboard* Hot 100 and spent twenty-two weeks on the charts, making it Petty's longest-charting single. I point this out because Petty was forty-four years old, a very old rock 'n roll roller, to be turning out hits. That was an exception to the rule.

Of course, the music world is littered with one-hit wonders — bands and artists who had one hit and that was it. It's like they had one great vision and then, after searching for the rest of their life, it never came again.

Rolling Stone magazine once had their readers vote on the top ten one-hit wonders: (1) A-ha, "Take On Me" (2) Dexys Midnight Runners, "Come on Eileen" (3) Norman Greenbaum, "Spirit in the Sky" (4) Big Country, "In a Big Country" (5) Soft Cell, "Tainted Love" (6) The Knack, "My Sharona" (7) Blind Melon, "No Rain" (8) Chumbawamba, "Tubthumping" (9) ? and the Mysterians, "96 Tears" (10) The Vapors, "Turning Japanese."

Some of these songs you may recognize and some you may not. One thing is for certain, these groups had to think they were the next big thing, only to find out that their luck had run out after one hit. Think of how demoralizing that must have been to believe that you were on to greatness, and you were really on to nowhere.

The music world is littered with other artists who were a little more successful than the usual one-hit wonder but struggled mightily for the rest of their career. Oftentimes when I'm reading about a musical artist, I will Google their net worth on a site called celebritynetworth.com. I don't know how reliable the net worths are, because how would they know exactly? But I do believe it gives us some insight. I am absolutely shocked at the low net worth of some of these famous artists who would been around forever. Many of them still tour and perform to this day because they have to, not because they want to.

The Rolling Stones are now in their eighties but selling out stadiums routinely. I can't think of anything more invigorating than to be on that stage, playing your music with a hundred thousand people singing along. It's the best job in the whole world. But I believe that most all of it is a result of pure luck bestowed upon them with an ear for music and a talent for playing and writing.

Dylan's writing was so profound that he won a Nobel Prize in Literature in 2016. He didn't attend the ceremony citing "preexisting commitments" as the reason. Instead, he delivered his Nobel lecture, which is a requirement for all Nobel Prize laureates, in June 2017, nearly six months after the prize was awarded. When I listen to Dylan's music from the early days, he was speaking to his generation at that time in life, and the writing and the music was magical. Later in life, my daughter and I went to see Dylan in concert and were highly disappointed because he played almost no old songs and mostly new songs. I walked out early, disgusted. Why these artists sometimes subject us to what we don't want to hear instead of playing for us what we came to hear is beyond me. They must be sick of their own material.

More Than Luck—Grit

One thing is certain for most of the great bands, and that is there was a real struggle to get to where they were going. Not only did these musicians need to have the luck of aptitude for music, they also had to have grit, perseverance, and they had to have a relentless spirit that let them live in the back of cars and shower at YMCAs while they chased their dreams. For most of these success stories, it came with a great deal of struggle. Many who had the same talent did not have the perseverance, grit, or relentless spirit. When I read these biographies, their struggle in the early days is astounding. But their love for music and what they were doing was so powerful that they pushed on. In fact, the struggle was often part of their music and success.

For me, music has been a constant and it has saved me at some of the most difficult times in my life. When I was growing up in Lexington, and both of my parents were not being the best parents and our lives were in turmoil, I often turned to music and particularly to one song. At the peak of my family's struggle in 1969, Neil Diamond released "Sweet Caroline." That song spoke to me and soothed me and encouraged me like nothing else ever had or ever has since. I bought a 45 with an A side and a B side. On the B side was another song titled "Cracklin' Rosie." But I didn't play "Cracklin' Rosie," I played "Sweet Caroline" over and over and over again. Sometimes I would play it twenty or thirty times in a row as the music sunk in.

That song became the anthem for my life. To this day, when I get in a car, I play "Sweet Caroline." There is a version he did live at the Greek Theater in 2012. This is the version I play most times. I turn it up full blast, and I'm taken back to those days in Kentucky when this song became my song of hope and my route to escape.

As I've gotten older and gone to restaurants, many times they have live musicians. In the restaurants that know me, the keyboard player immediately strikes up "Sweet Caroline" when I walk into the restaurant. Everyone in my family knows that this song saved my life.

My daughter, Kate, named her daughter Caroline Grace. I know she did it because of my song. We don't call her Caroline; we call her Gracie. But I bought her a music box when she was born. Guess what song it plays?

For some reason music moves me and inspires me and encourages me like nothing else. It is my medicine for depression and my tonic for good times.

Later, we were forced to move from Kentucky to Florida and I was destroyed. I brought my "Sweet Caroline" record with me and began to play it even more. In 1971, Neil Diamond came up with another song that turned out to be my second anthem: "I Am… I Said." It was written for me. It inspired me to keep reaching and grinding and to one day shed my frog costume and become a king.

That song, coupled with "Sweet Caroline," became the soundtrack of my life. Those songs are what moved me through the most difficult times and still do today. After I play "Sweet Caroline" in my car, I play "I Am… I Said." Many times, I have thought about trying to contact Diamond and thank him for these incredible gifts. He has no idea how his songs changed the course and trajectory of my life. Simply put, they gave me hope. Hope is what we all need most of all, for without hope, all the dreams are dashed and all the visions never are.

I became a Diamond aficionado and listen to all of his music on a regular basis. Diamond was a cantor in the Jewish temple when he was growing up as a boy. I believe that God blessed him with these divinely inspired or creative talents so that he could provide this type of comfort and joy to all of us. His songs are amazing, and the depth of his songs are unparalleled. When my children were small, he came to Orlando, and I took them all to see him in concert. I wanted my children to at least see the man who had changed the course of my life with his music.

I believe the luckiest among us are the musicians who get to write these songs, perform them and then watch as we cheer wildly and demand encore after encore. For me, music has been integral to my success. I do not believe I would have a modicum of the luck I have enjoyed but for my music, and I believe that all these great musicians have been given God's greatest blessing, or luck, with their ability to write music and lyrics.

I am the frog who dreamed of being a king and then became one. From where I was to where I am today, there is no doubt about that. While the word "king" seems a bit lofty, the word "frog" is apropos.

CHAPTER 25

THE HITMAKERS

When we think about musicians and especially the great ones, it is important to realize how lucky the very few are that reach the pinnacle of their profession. Let me start with a few facts. In 2021, the U.S. Bureau of Labor Statistics (BLS) estimated that there were 24,080 professional musicians and singers in the U.S. ALONE. In 2022, there were 103,017 musicians and singers in the workforce, with 39.5 percent being women and 60.5 percent being men.

Obviously, there are many men and women who have the dream of being a famous performer, but the road is very difficult and the competition is fierce. The journey to the top is very, very difficult.

I have devoured books on recording artists for years, but one that gave me great insight to the struggle of getting to the top and the luck involved was Bruce Springsteen's autobiography *Born to Run*. The book is absolutely riveting, and it shows the struggles he had in breaking out.

Making little money, sleeping on couches, and playing for basically peanuts was all part and parcel of his rise to fame. This book helps you understand why many of these struggling artists eventually are forced to drop out. Lack of money and lack of prospects can do that to you. At some point, you have to make an exit on the offramp.

The Numbers Don't Lie

Obviously, there are many people out there who have no business being out there. Nothing is worse than the performer who has little or no talent but thinks they do. On the other hand, it is a belief in oneself that powers people like Springsteen on. I believe Springsteen would still be out there playing if the venues were much smaller. It is simply in his blood.

With all of the competition out there, only a very few rise to superstar status and serious riches. The wealthiest performers are in a very rare group.

When *Forbes 400 Richest Americans* debuted in 1982, Yoko Ono was the only musician listed, with a net worth of $150 million (equivalent to $475 million in today's money), largely due to the music royalties of her late husband's band, The Beatles. In 1991, *Forbes* estimated Michael Jackson's net worth at $230 million, equivalent to $500 million today.

As of 2024, five music artists have reached the billionaire status on the *Forbes* report. Jay-Z leads the list with $2.5 billion, and that includes $500 million to his talented wife Beyoncé. Taylor Swift is close behind and rising fast at $1.6 billion, followed by Rihanna at $1.4 billion.

According to *Forbes*, the other two in the top five are Bruce Springsteen with $1.1 billion, and Jimmy Buffett at $1 billion.

Madonna is closing in at $850 million. As I write this book, Sean Combs had a net worth reportedly at $820 million, but I predict by the time this book is published, he may be in serious financial trouble.

Other notable megastars are Julio Iglesias at $600 million, Celine Dion at $550 million, Barbra Streisand at $460 million, and Dolly Parton at $450 million.

Many of these artists have branched out outside of music, particularly people like Dr. Dre and Dolly Parton. Jay-Z has many interests outside of music, which puts him at the top of the heap. Obviously, these numbers are speculative at best, as many of these artists have elaborate lifestyles that bleed their net worth.

When it comes to the greatest bands or artists of all time, that is largely in the eye of the beholder; but as the old adage goes: "The numbers don't lie." We are able to see who sells the most records and the most albums historically. Many different publications list the greatest acts of all time, but again, it is subjective. Your top ten are probably much different than my top ten. It's much like naming the top-five NBA basketball players of all time. The only thing I know for certain is Michael Jordan is one of them.

Rolling Stone is the Bible for music, so for our purposes here, let's take a look at their top-ten music acts of all time.

The list was first published in two issues in 2004 and 2005 and later updated in 2011. It was selected based on the choices of a panel of fifty-five musicians, writers, and industry figures. As the editors explain, the artists were selected by "their peers," and the list aims to be a "broad survey of rock history," encompassing rock 'n roll, blues, hard rock, heavy metal, indie rock, rap, and contemporary pop. (1) The Beatles. (2) Bob Dylan. (3) Elvis Presley. (4) The Rolling Stones. (5) Chuck Berry. (6) Jimi Hendrix. (7) James Brown. (8) Little Richard. (9) Aretha Franklin. (10) Ray Charles.

Now I can hear many of you howling right now, just as I did. For me, where are Billy Joel, Bruce Springsteen, Tom Petty, and Paul Simon? That is the beautiful thing about music. Jimi Hendrix to some of us is just loud screeching noise, but to others, he is one of the greats. Likewise, Janis Joplin. I never understood Joplin, but others adore her.

Masters of Their Craft

The one thing all these artists had in common is they were tremendous at their craft. Being tremendous at the craft is much different than record sales. To me, the real proof in the pudding is the sale of albums and records, and there the numbers don't lie.

According to *Business Insider*, the top-fifteen-selling artists of all time are as follows, and I don't think you'll be surprised: (1) The Beatles, 183 million units (2) Garth Brooks, 162 million units (3) Elvis Presley, 146 million units (4) Eagles, 120 million units (5) Led Zeppelin, 112 million units (6) Michael Jackson, 89 million units (7) Billy Joel, 86 million units (8) AC/DC, 83 million units (9) Elton John, 80 million units (10) Mariah Carey, 75 million units (11) Pink Floyd, 75 million units (12) Bruce Springsteen, 71 million units (13) Aerosmith, 69 million units (14) George Strait, 69 million units (15) Barbra Streisand, 68 million units.

By and large, those numbers did not surprise me, and you would not be surprised at the next fifteen after them. All groups and artists we know and love.

Enduring to the End

The thing most of these artists have in common is that they endured. Many of these artists are now performing in their seventies and eighties and still filling stadiums and arenas. The power of music and the memory of our best days keeps drawing us back to these concerts.

Music is often not a profitable business. Many musicians have to work other jobs to make ends meet, or they may have to spend any money they make back into the band. Another obstacle is that the music industry is so saturated with competition, especially now with the rise of streaming platforms. It's a fact that musicians experience high rates of depression, anxiety, and alcohol abuse. A 2016 study found that poor mental health is common among professional musicians. Many musicians, in the beginning, work other jobs to make ends meet while they're making music full-time. And another factor that sometimes enters into the equation is that the type of music falls out of favor. Remember the 1970s and disco? It was everywhere, and then all of a sudden, it was very unpopular to be dancing to disco, much less dressing in disco dancewear. The Bee Gees were at the very top of the game briefly, and then it became "uncool" to go to a discothèque. The fickle nature of music makes it all that much more daunting.

Rap snuck up on us, and before we knew it, that was the most popular music in America. Today all you have to do is look at the Super Bowl performers to see who is the most popular in this day and time.

Luck in the Music Business

All this to say that luck plays an incredible role. Who your bandmates are may be the luckiest break of all. Even though Paul Simon seemed to be the musical genius in Simon & Garfunkel, I don't know if he would've had that early success without Garfunkel's magical voice. Unfortunately for Garfunkel, he became full of himself, started doing movies, and pissed off Simon, who threw him overboard and never looked back. It seems that Garfunkel, while having a beautiful voice, was not the straw that stirred that drink. For me, Simon's music is magical. I've never known Garfunkel to write a song.

The management of artists can be determinative. For example, if you were lucky enough to get a David Geffen as your manager, you had hit the lucky lotto. Geffen was relentless and a true advocate for his clients. You should never underestimate the power of the agent and the team behind the artist. Your manager, your lawyer, and your bandmates all play a role in your ultimate success. But when it comes to music, it's that stream of consciousness that allows you to write these unbelievable songs that seem to come out of nowhere. What's interesting to me is that there are only a very few chords in the musical world.

There are eight different chord types, all of which have twelve unique chords within the group that represent the different notes on the musical scale. But when you ask how many guitar chords are there? While it may seem infinite, the answer is actually quite mathematical. The estimates vary, but considering only one octave, we can have 4,083 possible chords! That's ten chords across twelve musical notes, with different combinations of notes.

When you start to read and learn about what goes into music, it is quite amazing. But these relatively few basic chords turn out music that is different over and over and over again.

While it is essential that the person be born with a brain for music and a knack for songwriting, it seems to me that is not necessarily learned as much as you are born with these talents. I'm always amazed at watching some savants who are hardly able to function in society, but when they play a piano, they become Mozart-like. The music and the talent are outstanding. These savants are littered throughout the world playing the piano, guitar, violin, and other instruments. My belief is that this strain in the savant's brain is the same strain a person like Tom Petty or Stevie Nicks may possess. It has always been amazing to me the number of blind artists like Ray Charles, Ronnie Millsap, and Stevie Wonder, who have this savant-like talent. Perhaps that savant-like talent is luckily placed in the brains of many of our greatest artists. That's called pure luck.

The Luck of the Draw – Bandmates and Collaborators

While having that gift of music is lucky, no doubt, who you are paired with can be just as determinative as that innate talent.

Think for a minute about The Beatles—four lads from Liverpool who basically lived in a very close geographic range. Paul McCartney, John Lennon, George Harrison, and Ringo Starr were all born in Liverpool, England. Think of that lucky strike. The group began with the pairing of McCartney and Lennon in 1956; Harrison joined in 1957, and Stu Sutcliffe and Pete Best later. In 1960, they adopted the name The Beatles. In 1962, they signed a recording contract and replaced Best with Starr (Sutcliffe had left the group in 1961).

The release in 1962 of such songs as "Please Please Me" and "I Want to Hold Your Hand" made them England's most popular rock group, and in 1964 Beatlemania struck the U.S. Originally inspired by Chuck Berry, Elvis Presley, Little Richard, and Buddy Holly, among others, their direct, energetic songs kept them at the top of the pop charts. As time went on, these guys from Liverpool became the most prolific musical group of all time. But think of the luck of all four being born and living so close to each other in Liverpool. I have often thought it was like Mozart, Bach, Beethoven, and Schubert all being born at the same time and in the same city and starting a band. How can you go wrong?

Yet, this is what The Beatles had. Obviously, both Lennon and McCartney were exquisite musicians and songwriters. Harrison, the quiet Beatle, was not as prolific but did write many of the great songs, had a great voice, and enjoyed a solo career after he left The Beatles and also with the Traveling Wilburys.

Many times, Starr, who wrote a few songs, was described as the lucky Beatle. But when you talk to musical experts, they will tell you that Starr is one of the greatest drummers ever.

So there you have it. One of the luckiest assemblies of musicians in the history of the world. Four boys, with incredible musical skills, all living in a very short distance from each other in a town in England. That is like hitting the ultimate Powerball.

This collaboration made them the greatest-selling band of all time. But it didn't last long. The Beatles worked together as a band for seven years, seven months, and twenty-four days.

What broke up the group remains murky at best. There were financial issues, disagreements between its members, but the best reason seems to be Ono's relationship with Lennon. She was sitting in on sessions, and when you watch these sessions later, the tension is palpable. The main reason seems to be the growing tension between Lennon and McCartney, who had been the primary songwriting duo in the band. The band had different musical artistic visions, and they struggled to collaborate effectively as their personal lives and interests diverged.

One of the songs McCartney wrote when he started his band, Wings, was a song called "Silly Love Songs." In the song, he asked the question, "What's wrong with silly love songs?" Evidently, Lennon did not like that type of music and that was McCartney's message to him.

However, after the split, Lennon wrote some masterpieces of his own, much different than silly love songs. For me, The Beatles are the greatest of all time. Mainly because there were two musical geniuses, one excellent drummer, and a fourth member who was a star in his own right. Collectively, The Beatles have never been rivaled before or since. I've been lucky enough to meet McCartney at the White House, twice. Once for Michelle Obama's fiftieth birthday party, and the second one, when Barack was having his farewell party. At the birthday party, my son, Daniel, actually danced with McCartney's wife and then later with Beyoncé. It was a night Daniel and I will never forget. McCartney was so nice and kind to us that he will remain in our hearts forever, not just for his music, but for his sweetness.

It is interesting to go through the history of music and try to imagine some of these bands and groups being what they were without each other. For example, I can't imagine the Eagles without both Glenn Frey and Don Henley; Led Zeppelin without Robert Plant, Jimmy Page, John Bonham, and John Paul Jones; The Rolling Stones without Mick Jagger, Keith Richards, Ronnie Wood, and Charlie Watts. The chemistry in these bands and the chance meetings that brought bands like them together can only be defined as luck.

And once these members collided their collective musical genius, they then transported all of us into a special place and time. When you go to your own favorite groups, you may find striking similarities. One of the problems that affects many of these supergroups is a case of bad luck, and that bad luck is usually called ego, drug abuse, alcohol abuse, and women—or any combination of all four.

Think about how many bands have broken up over the years over ego, substance abuse, and women. Usually, there is one real superstar, and he or she knows it and begins to resent the other members' financial success thanks to him or her. The Eagles have had many different members over the years as those disagreements bubbled up.

Breaking the Band – Egos and Women

The musical graveyard is littered with ego-centered disputes about who was the true leader and the true talent and who was not. It is always interesting to look at the earnings of the band members to see the hierarchy and structure in that band. One band that seemed to share almost equally was U2. Estimates put the members' wealth at about $300–$400 million each, and Bono about $700–$800 million net worth due to investments, making him the second-wealthiest rockstar today behind McCartney. The band as a total is worth an estimated $1.7 billion. The lack of ego seems to have enabled their longevity. The same can be said for the Rolling Stones and, for that matter, the Eagles.

When trouble starts to bubble over is when you have the one member who believes that the entire success of the band rests with him or her. And by the way, it may be true.

These bands get together as kids and scribble together agreements as eighteen-year-olds. As time goes on, the cream rises, and the leader becomes self-evident. That leader begins to resent the financial windfall the less talented members have. However, the less talented members believe they are equally as important, bring a great deal to the band, but most importantly argue that they were there from the beginning and should be treated the same as when they entered into the agreement at age eighteen.

Lionel Richie left the Commodores in 1982 to pursue a solo career. As time would tell, Richie made the right decision. The Commodores should have just paid him what he wanted. Van Halen has been through multiple lead-singer swaps over the years, but David Lee Roth was the first to leave in 1985. He was replaced with vocalist Sammy Hagar, who left the group in 1996 after a dispute related to recording a song for the *Twister* movie soundtrack, according to *Rolling Stone*.

I've had the great pleasure of meeting Sammy Hagar several times at Shep Gordon's home in Maui on New Year's. A nicer guy you will never meet. Steve Perry, an amazing voice, left Journey in 1987, but Perry's solo career never took off.

Bands break up over women too. Many of these bandmembers swap out girlfriends and wives the way people swap out cars. I still can't get it straight who all was with whom in Fleetwood Mac. I've also had the great honor of meeting Mick Fleetwood at that same party in Maui. What a drummer and what a presence. Mick owned a restaurant on Front Street that was destroyed in the Maui fires.

The Great Micheal Jackson

We can't leave this chapter without mentioning Michael Jackson. The Jackson 5 are one of the most iconic groups in the history of the world. Their father was demanding and reportedly brutal. During the reign of the Jackson 5, members branching out to drop solo records wasn't uncommon; both Michael and Jermaine unleashed full-lengths of their own in 1972, but the Michael Jackson that conquered the 1980s and 1990s wasn't really the Michael we knew until we heard 1979's disco slick *Off the Wall*, an album that was created hot off the heels from his appearance in the sensational movie musical *The Wiz* one year prior. Much later, Michael had the *Thriller* album, which sold more copies than any other album in the history of music. Michael was a talented yet troubled star who was basically killed at the hands of negligent doctors. My next-door neighbor in Maui, Brian Panish, represented Michael's estate in that wrongful death action.

Turning Good Luck into Something Special

These great musical talents, I believe, are born with the innate musical talent. It seems to magically appear, but I am sure they will argue that years of practice also was the reason. Adding to their good luck of the talent and perseverance was meeting fellow band members that elevated and complemented their talents. Staying sober and off drugs helped but was not a prerequisite. In reading all of the biographies that I have churned through, it seems that booze and drugs actually added to their prolific abilities.

All this to say that for me, being Bruce Springsteen or Billy Joel would be the greatest job in the world. Walking out like Whitney Houston did night after night and belting out historic and memorable songs has to be more thrilling than anything I could possibly dream or imagine.

The current phenomenal musical sensation today is Taylor Swift. Swift has had twelve jaw-dropping No. 1 songs. And as the female musician with the most charted songs, 263; most top-forty songs, 164; most top-twenty songs, 100; most top-ten songs, 59; most top-ten debuts, 48; most top-five songs, 36; and most number-one debuts, 7. All totaled, she has 610 singles.

Swift is not only a musical savant, she is a business genius. She knows her audience, knows what they want, and gives the performance like no other. A ticket to her show is one of the hardest to score in all of America. And she is young.

Luck has undoubtedly played a huge role in all of these artists' careers. They took their good luck and turned it into something very special. Unfortunately for me, as much as I wanted to be a musician, failing my flutophone tryout in the fourth grade doomed me to be a spectator for life. But what an enthusiastic spectator I have been!

CHAPTER 26

MUSICAL GENIUSES – JIMMY BUFFETT

While there are many great musical artists and bands, and we all have personal favorites, I was lucky enough to get to know one of these musical geniuses: Jimmy Buffett. I first met Buffett at the University of Florida. I was putting on concerts for the Interfraternity Council and we had three concerts a year. In the winter, I had brought in The Spinners, and for the spring, I booked Buffett.

Buffett had never played inside at the University of Florida; his appearances were for free on the lawn. But I was fascinated by him, his lifestyle, and his music. In 1974, he released a song titled "Come Monday." Later in my life, that very song became the song my wife and I called "our song." It had a lot of meanings to us, and we were separated by distance, as she had graduated and moved Orlando and I was still in Gainesville.

I caught a lot of grief for booking Buffett in the gymnasium, which was known as ALLIGATOR ALLEY. The gym sat about 3,500 people.

In any event, the concert was a great success, and people praised my risk-taking on bringing Buffett to our spring frolics. While he was in Gainesville, he met a beautiful co-ed whom he dated for several months.

Later in life, we became reacquainted over Florida politics. Alex Sink was the university's CFO and running for governor. We decided to have a fundraiser at my home in Florida and Buffett agreed to come and play three or four songs. The tickets sold for $10,000 each, and I sold out the event.

Buffett played in my backyard, I served cheeseburgers and margaritas, and a good time was had by all. We actually had to stop selling tickets because of the size of the crowd. Unfortunately, Alex lost that election, but just barely. She would have been Florida's first female governor. We are still anxiously waiting for one.

Chilling With Barack Obama

Years later, a fresh U.S. senator by the name of Barack Obama decided to run for president. Once again, I swung into action and offered to help raise money for him. Never had I seen a candidate with such potential. It was like he was created on a movie set. I had met him in my home when he was a U.S. senator and he asked, after his first election as president, to come back for a visit.

Having the president of the United States visit your home is an ordeal. Helicopters fly over the house with infrared cameras. Dogs sweep through the house. The Secret Service asked my wife if we had any guns, and she said "no." During the sweep of the house, they found a pellet gun and a bottle of vodka in my wife's closet. Evidently, years before, my wife confiscated the pellet gun and she claims the vodka.

When the president pulls up in front of your house, it is surreal. He was running for his second term against Mitt Romney, and the election promised to be close. That night, we raised a ton of money and, fortunately, from my perspective, President Obama was reelected to a second term.

After the second event at my home with Obama, the campaign called and asked if I could do another event. I informed them that I had probably tapped out my friends and family and would not be as successful this cycle. That's not what they had in mind. They informed me that they had heard about the Buffett concert at my home and wondered if we could do that once again for Barack. I said, "Let me check with Jimmy and get back to you." A lobbyist in Florida, Jeff Sharkey, was instrumental in helping pull it all together, and Buffett came back to the house for his second concert.

We raised so much money in one evening that it was absolutely stunning. Buffett only plays a few songs when he visits homes, and I asked him if one of the songs was going to be "Come Monday." He had brought Mac McAnally who had the playlist with him. Mac informed me that no, that song was not on the agenda.

I told Buffett that song was my wife's and my marital song, and if he could see fit, we would appreciate it. It was the last song of his set, and my wife was, as they say, over the moon.

Before Buffett came to the house, he had given us the name of his preferred tequila and rosé, but before beginning his mini concert, he wanted to know where we could smoke a joint together. We decided to smoke where the air-conditioners were stationed, and then after our brief toke, we were ready for a great time. He put on a great show. At the end of his set, I took the microphone and thanked everyone for coming, and told them that I hoped they could make it next week, as we were having McCartney come and do the same.

Some people laughed, but most didn't. The people at the party believed that if I had Buffett there, it was certainly possible that McCartney was also achievable. That dawned on me much later. It was a testament to how revered Buffett was, especially in Florida.

From Fundraising to Business

Over time, our paths crossed, and we actually got to do some business together. We built a brand of marijuana called Coral Reefer and placed the product inside medical marijuana dispensaries that I was a part owner. Buffett was a voracious user of marijuana and had no problems with it. His songs reference reefer throughout.

Later, I got to meet Buffett's partner, John Cohlan, who is the CEO of Margaritaville and a brilliant guy. Cohlan went to Princeton undergrad and Georgetown Law School. Cohlan's wife was friendly with Jimmy's wife, Jane, and the two were introduced and started the company Margaritaville. Lifestyle brands and restaurants are fraught with problems, but Margaritaville has thrived. I credit most of it to the popularity of Buffett and the marketing genius of Cohlan.

As time went on and we all got to know each other better, there was a moment when Margaritaville, the company, was taking out a big investor and replacing them with another investor. At that moment in time, I asked Cohlan and Buffett if they would slice off a nice-sized piece of the company for me and allow me to buy-in pro rata. Luckily for me, they said yes. So today, I'm a proud partner in the Margaritaville company. Talk about life is luck!

What Buffett and Cohlan did was amazing. The restaurants were sold off to an operating company, and Margaritaville became more of a licensing company. Today we have hotels, cruise ships, food products, restaurants, RV parks, beer, and residential communities for fifty-plus. Jimmy and John built a real empire. Every time I see Cohlan, I thank him.

The Loss of a Legend

Sadly, Buffett was diagnosed with a rare cancer and fought it for four years. During the pandemic, he visited Maui while I was there. It was at a time where restaurants were opening, but you still were careful. We decided to go have lunch at a place called Kimo's. During our lunch, a couple walked over the table and asked if I was John Morgan. I told them I was, and they informed me that they saw me all the time in Philadelphia and wondered if they could get a picture of me with them. I agreed and took the picture.

When we finished taking the picture, I told them that they were going to feel silly when they got back to Philadelphia, and they asked me why. I pointed to Buffett and said, "When your friends ask you why you didn't ask Buffett for a picture, you will know that you blew it." Buffett was sitting at the table with a Coral Reefer hat on, a slight beard, and a mask pulled down around his neck grinning from ear to ear. Of course, the people were stunned and asked Buffett for his picture too!

Even though we knew death was imminent, when it came, it was stunning. We lost a true musical legend. To me, his music and lyrics make him the Mark Twain of the music industry. His great manager, Irving Azoff, brilliantly steered him through his career.

After he passed, several important things happened. Frank Marshall, the great Hollywood producer gave me a blow-by-blow of Buffett's last days. Marshall was one of Buffett's best friends. He told me that before he died at his home in Sag Harbor, Paul McCartney came to the house and played "Let It Be." Some of Buffett's last words, according to Frank, were "No funeral, no wake, party on." And isn't that exactly what you would think his last words would be?

Frank also sent me a song titled "Bubbles Up." I believe it was the last song Buffett wrote, and I may be mistaken, but I think it was with some help from McCartney. If you haven't heard it, it's a must. When Frank sent me the song, his message was simple: "Jimmy saved the best for last."

Buffett's music has been part of my life since high school. But I always took it for granted. Buffett's music was the backdrop to our happiest times. Vacations, concerts, the beach—you name it. When you heard one of Buffett's songs, you knew you were having a good time. That's why that brand has done so well. In the recesses of our minds, when we hear that music, we know all is well.

But since his death, I have listened to his music a lot more and much more intently. They are all different and they are all genius and those songs kept coming for a long, long time. He was a definite exception to no more songs after age thirty I mentioned earlier. He had a fascination with boats and planes and water. His songs were about his life and his friends and his lifestyle. I believe Buffett's music is going to be like the great masters in painting. After some of them died, there was an even greater appreciation for their paintings. Likewise, I believe that, as time goes on, Buffett's music will become more and more popular.

My children know the music by heart because they rode with me in my car. We didn't have the same experience with our parents because all we had was AM radio and some albums at home. The constant playing of music in cars gives our children a window into our era and us.

The Luckiest of Lives

Buffett had one of the luckiest lives I can imagine—maybe the luckiest life that I have ever been close to. Imagine going around the world enjoying yourself, entertaining stadiums, then getting into your plane and going to your boat, and everywhere you go you are loved. I saw him interact with people bunches of times, and it was almost as if he was running for a political office, he was so kind and generous.

The great thing about music is it never dies. Today, here in Florida, when I was out back by my pool, I had Buffett on blaring away. He will never die, because his music lives forever.

Bubbles up!

CHAPTER 27

HOLLYWOOD AND THE BEAUTIFUL PEOPLE

While some of us would love to be a famous singer, rocking arenas and stadiums, others may prefer being a movie star if the choice were theirs. Now for me, I can say clearly that I would much rather be Bruce Springsteen than Tom Cruise. Don't get me wrong, there would be nothing wrong with being Tom Cruise. However, in my professional life, I have spent a lot of times in studios filming commercials, and there is absolutely nothing enjoyable about that. To the contrary, just the opposite.

Movie stars enjoy an incredible status in society. It is almost like they are worshiped. The one thing I have noticed about movie stars is that, by and large, to become a movie star, you must be incredibly beautiful or related to a beautiful movie star who happened to be your parents.

Now there is an exception to all these rules. I know many of you may be thinking about certain movie stars who are not beautiful. Danny DeVito immediately came to my mind. There are all sorts of actors and actresses who are relegated to playing supporting roles. Kathy Bates is the actress that comes immediately to my mind.

The Luck of Being Born "Beautiful"

Unless you are being cast as Quasimodo of *The Hunchback of Notre-Dame*, *The Elephant Man*, or any villain in a horror movie, the prerequisite is usually that you are drop-dead gorgeous. I think acting follows looks when it comes to casting in Hollywood.

When you do a deep dive as to what makes Hollywood tick, you discover very quickly that the famous stars were either beautiful people, related to beautiful people, or willing to sleep with the Hollywood moguls on the so-called casting couch. Yes, in Hollywood, some people fuck their way to stardom.

One of the most lucky happenstances in this world of ours is when someone is born beautiful. Now remember this, no beautiful person had anything to do with how they were going to look. It is simply the genetic lottery. And there is no guarantee that two beautiful people will, in turn, have a beautiful child. Believe me, I have seen some of the most beautiful people with the ugliest children imaginable. The genetic lottery can play great favors but also great tricks.

Have you ever thought about how unfair it is for people to be born good-looking, while you are totally dissatisfied with your looks. I have never liked the way I look. My cheeks always seem too fat, and I was always too short. I also had a propensity later in life to add weight. Of course, drinking gobs of Maker's Mark and then eating at Waffle House at two in the morning certainly didn't help my diet.

My brother, Mike, was very slender and had a slender face. As a child, I was always envious of how he looked. On top of it all, he had this beautiful blonde hair and tanned a golden brown. Meanwhile, I was over there with a fat face and freckles on my shoulders and, God forbid, freckles on my face. Boy did I hate those freckles. The good thing is that with age, the freckles fade away. Thank God for small favors.

Beautiful people seem to have an unfair advantage just because of the way they look. Think of all the beauty pageants you have witnessed. How many times did you see someone and say to yourself, "She shouldn't be there"? The luck of being born beautiful not only works in Hollywood, but it works in the workplace.

Luck, Beauty, and the Halo Effect

Every study done on the subject has concluded that for both men and women, attractive people have an advantage—in getting jobs, career advancement, salary, tips, etc. And, of course, dating. People respond more positively to attractive people, and that impacts many facets of life. According to similar research, people perceived as being more attractive are more likely to be perceived as trustworthy and friendly. This is a cognitive bias known as the "halo effect." Physically attractive people attract more attention and have more opportunities in their lives, whether it's a job or a relationship.

This so-called halo effect basically means that attractive people are viewed as automatically better people than unattractive people. It's a huge factor that underlies a lot of life that often goes unnoticed.

As it turns out, an attractive appearance leads to more risky behavior among young people. The more attractive a teenager is, the greater the likelihood that they will party and drink more alcohol than others. Interestingly, people overall tend to rate themselves more physically attractive than strangers rate them. I may be the exception to that rule.

It is no secret that physical attractiveness can positively influence the way people are judged. Studies have shown that attractive individuals are often perceived as more competent, sociable, and trustworthy, leading to an increased likelihood of landing job offers. Studies also found that those considered attractive were also rated more highly on intelligence, conscientiousness, and academic achievement, even though there was no statistical relationship between attractiveness and academic achievement.

Female servers wearing something in their hair, such as a flower or barrette, often receive higher tips as well! One reason for this may be the simple fact that more attractive women tend to get more tips, and both men and women, interestingly enough, find women with ornaments in their hair more attractive. Some friends of mine founded the wing-chain Hooters years ago. The concept was very simple: make inferior fattening food, put a lot of beer on the table, and basically have scantily-clad women with large breasts serving the patrons. My friends made a fortune. Since that revelation, there have been many copycat wing joints that have followed that model. I don't know why it is that wings seem to be the food of choice, but it must be a food that men love. Wings, fries, and beer.

Forbes magazine referenced a study that followed the career progression of 752 economists between 2002 and 2006, finding that those perceived as more physically attractive not only fared better in job hunts post-graduation, but also enjoyed sustained career success and higher research-paper citations up to fifteen years later, suggesting a strong link between attractiveness and professional achievement.

Attractiveness can influence career trajectories starting from the interview process, where presentation can impact first impressions. In professional settings, attractive individuals may benefit from positive perceptions of confidence, competence, and efficiency, enhancing interpersonal relationships and performance over time. While not the only factor, physical appeal complemented by lifestyle habits, skill development, and networking can serve as an advantage in maximizing professional opportunities.

When you boil it all down, it looks like this: Attractive people have more self-confidence, and the halo effect that surrounds them gives them advantages the rest of us don't have. All this to say it's really not fair, because it is just pure luck.

All the Beautiful People

Think of people in your own life that have risen to the top of the professional food chain. Now Silicon Valley is not going to bear that out. Why? Because most of those in Silicon Valley were the nerds that were laughed at in high school, but those nerds are now having the last laugh while dating the high school cheerleaders and having the high school quarterback as their pool boy. What goes around comes around.

But when you look at the Fortune 500 companies and the pictures of those leaders who were not founders but who simply joined the company, by and large, these are very attractive men and women. Many of them are stunningly handsome and beautiful. You don't see many DeVitos as the chairman of a major bank. You do see Jamie Dimon, who looks straight out of Hollywood. And speaking of Hollywood, when you get to Hollywood and look at the executives in the studios and in the management field, they all tend to be beautiful people. The luck of good looks cannot be overstated.

And while good looks are very important in climbing the corporate ladder, it is absolutely mandatory in the movie-star world. George Clooney, Brad Pitt, and Tom Cruise are not movie stars unless they look just like they do. And likewise, Julia Roberts, Angelina Jolie, and Jennifer Aniston would not be where they are unless they had the physical package that nature blessed them with. It certainly doesn't seem fair, but it's been going on from the beginning. In the golden days, we had Warren Beatty, Jack Nicholson, and Marlon Brando. The general rule is if you're not good-looking, don't apply.

I have often thought of those with great talents but not great looks. It must be terribly frustrating for them knowing that they are better than the others but having to play a supporting role to make the star look great. In the award shows, I have always been much more interested in the supporting actors and actresses, because many times, those are the performances that lifted the movie.

Will we ever forget Joe Pesci for his performances and particularly his performance in *Goodfellas*? Or Philip Seymour Hoffman in so many movies. And, of course, Steve Buscemi, who has had great success not only as a supporting actor but as a lead. His looks did not propel him to the top; his believability as an actor did. Hollywood is a very shallow city. When I visit my offices in Los Angeles, I always go to the Beverly Hills Hotel and to the Polo Lounge to gawk at movie stars and all of the beautiful people surrounding them. Interestingly enough, they are usually not as good-looking in person and invariably much shorter. The great action heroes Arnold Schwarzenegger (6'2"), Sylvester Stallone (5'10"), Bruce Willis (6'), Paul Newman (5'10"), Tom Cruise (5'7"), and Johnny Depp (5'9"), were all surprisingly short, or much shorter than they appeared on film.

Once, at Planet Hollywood, when I had dinner with Sylvester Stallone, I was most surprised at his height. I was expecting a muscular giant to tower over me. Instead, I found myself looking eyeball to eyeball.

Now there is no question that these beautiful people must develop some acting skills to really fulfill their stardom potential. But how much acting is more important than great looks? For me, the great actors of our day, or my day, are Robert De Niro and Meryl Streep. While Streep is pretty, she is not Elizabeth Taylor- or Grace Kelly-pretty. Her acting skills propelled her way above the rest. Same for Marlon Brando. Especially in later years when he became fatter than Elvis.

Stage Parents and Nepotism

Because Hollywood is such a shallow town, actors and especially actresses are constantly dreading the aging process. At certain ages, these former stars just are cycled out. Many make comebacks in period pieces like *Downton Abbey*. These older actresses are magnificent in those roles.

All of this to say that in the business world and in Hollywood, the good fortune of good looks cannot be understated. And while some actors and actresses came to it on their own, many were driven by parents or stage mothers. There are so many parents trying to live their lives through their children. You see it all the time in youth sports. But we don't see it as much in the acting business, because we were just not around it. Macaulay Culkin's family were hell-bent on their children being stars. The Jackson 5 had a demanding father. The Osmonds had the same deal. Whether it's good luck or bad luck to have these parents trying to live their dreams through their children is yet to be determined but the fact is most of these people driven by stage parents would not be who they are without the good — or bad — luck of their parents. Now, just as looks has a lot to do with success in Hollywood, nepotism is alive and well. So many actors' and actresses' children became stars simply because they were the child of a star. More good luck.

I remember, and I don't intend to be mean, when I first saw *E.T.*, and I wondered to myself during the movie how Drew Barrymore was cast to play her role. Not that she was ugly, but just that she was unremarkable. I was so taken aback by her in that role that I researched later everything about her. Surprise, surprise, I found out why she most likely got the role.

It was the first time it had dawned on me that nepotism was at play in Hollywood. As it turned out, Drew is the daughter of American actor John Drew Barrymore and aspiring actress Jaid Barrymore.

Gwyneth Paltrow was born in Los Angeles, the daughter of a noted producer and director Bruce Paltrow and Tony Award-winning actress, Blythe Danner. Jon Voight is the father of Angelina Jolie. Interestingly enough, despite the boost in her career from her father, Jolie despises Voight. Martin Sheen, the great Emmy and Golden Globe winner, is also the father of Charlie Sheen and his brother Emilio Estevez. There are other Estevezes also in the Hollywood business.

Lloyd Bridges was a great actor back in the day, and miraculously, his two sons, Jeff and Beau, got a big break in Hollywood. James Caan, the great actor from *The Godfather*, sired Scott Caan, who went on to work in television. Quincy Jones married Peggy Lipton and they had a daughter, Rashida Jones, who became an actress, producer, and now podcast host in Hollywood. Zoé Kravitz is the daughter of Lenny

Kravitz. Jamie Lee Curtis is the daughter of Tony Curtis. Nicholas Cage is the nephew of Francis Ford Coppola. And Freddie Prinze Jr. is the son of Freddie Prinze.

Mia Farrow, who was married to Frank Sinatra, is the daughter of the director John Farrow and the actress and *Tarzan* girl Maureen O'Sullivan.

The central point of all this is that Hollywood is filled with nepotism and nepo babies. If you ever have a free minute, just Google the subject, and you will be amazed at all of the different connections with stars and former stars to their parents. It must be tremendously frustrating to those actors who have no pedigree, no parents, and no path. Especially when, in their minds, they know they are better for the role. But when Steven Spielberg's child auditions for a position, I give them good odds in being successful. Good luck and good parents cannot be overstated in Hollywood or in business.

The Casting Couch—A Sad and Notable Exception to Luck

Now the one advantage some have in Hollywood that has absolutely nothing to do with luck is the casting couch. Both men and women are willing to fuck their way onto the big screen. Up until the "#MeToo" movement, people spoke of the casting couch as if it were just the way business was done. It was always shocking to me that it was said with such ease.

When somebody would tell me or when I would read that someone got ahead on the casting couch, I immediately thought they had to screw some ugly slob to get the role. In the old days, the owners of the studios were the worst. Just lecherous old men having their way with young girls from everywhere.

The casting couch was first revealed in 1956 in a fan magazine that published the first chapter of an explosive four-part exposé about the casting couch that is simultaneously revelatory and depressing. That article so many years ago reveals the playbook for Harvey Weinstein's alleged abuse of women much later. It sadly reveals how little some things have changed from the old days until today. By using euphemisms such as the casting couch, they've been used to normalize abuse for too long.

It was widely known that Marilyn Monroe was the victim of many casting-couch episodes. After Weinstein was exposed, many women came forward to talk about unwanted advances and propositions that were made. What we will never know is the number of stars, both men and women, both homosexual and heterosexual, who became stars after agreeing to a few sessions on the casting couch. The decision to acquiesce to the casting couch has nothing to do with luck and everything to do with choice. However, to these struggling young people, nothing from nothing seemed to be nothing. Hopefully, those days are behind us.

A Final Appendage

While the pornography industry is not the same as Hollywood, luck is also vital in that industry. The famous porn star Ron Jeremy was gifted with a large male member. For those men who aspire to be pornography actors, the good luck of a large penis likely came in handy.

When it comes to Hollywood, as talented and as smart as one might be, there is no greater advantage than being born with good looks and the right family lineage. And that is all luck.

CHAPTER 28

FIRST PRINCIPLES THINKING

Recently I gave a speech and decided to make it on a new topic. I was speaking to about 500 people in Santa Monica, California, and I asked a question: "How many of you have ever heard of the term 'first principles thinking'?" I was blown away because not one person raised their hand. Based on that response, I am assuming this may be new to you as well.

It's important for a lot of reasons, but mainly so that you can have another arrow in your quiver. Once it is explained to you, you may even say to yourself that you already are a first principles thinker. Let us begin.

In layman's terms, first principles thinking is basically the practice of actively questioning every assumption you think you "know" about a given problem or scenario, then creating new knowledge and solutions from scratch. It is brand-new thinking.

The opposite of this thinking is reasoning by analogy. That is building knowledge and solving problems based on prior assumptions, beliefs, and widely held "best practices" approved by the majority of people.

Essentially, first principles thinking helps you develop a unique worldview to innovate and solve difficult problems in a way that you and everyone else may have never thought about.

The idea behind first principles thinking is to break down something into its most basic elements to get at a core truth of what is known. In essence, it's a process where you deconstruct something and then build it up again just the way you want it. But as you're building it up, you are now questioning long-held assumptions that have guided you for many years. You are swimming upstream. First principles thinking is one of the best ways to reverse-engineer complicated problems and then unleash new and creative possibilities. It is one of the best ways to learn to think for yourself and to unlock your own creative potential.

A first principle is a foundational proposition, or assumption, that stands alone. We cannot deduce first principles from any other proposition or assumption. It is, in essence, brand new. Years ago, Aristotle wrote about first principles and said:

> "In every systematic inquiry where there are first principles, or causes, or elements, knowledge, and science result from acquiring knowledge of these, for we think we know something just in case we acquire knowledge of the primary causes, the primary first principles, all the way to the elements."

Later, he connected the idea to knowledge, defining first principles as "the first basis from which a thing is known." First principles thinking is not unique to philosophy. Through the history of time all great thinkers have employed it.

The Wide Appeal of First Principles Thinking

First principles thinking is used in philosophy, business, and sports. In professional football, for example, every play we watch in the NFL was at some point dreamed up by a coach who thought, "What would happen if the player did this?" After that thought, they went out and ran the play. These coaches assess what's physically possible, along with the weaknesses of the other teams and the capabilities of their own players, then create plays that are designed to give their teams a winning advantage.

In doing so, the coach reasons from first principles. The rules of football are the first principles. These rules tell us what you can and cannot do. Everything is possible, as long as it's not against the rules.

First principles coaches dreamed up plays such as the flea flicker, the end-around and, of course, the famous FSU play years ago, the "fumblerooski." All of these new plays are first principles thinking.

Coaches who just copy plays are not first principles thinkers. They are not coaching geniuses. They may add a tweak here or there, but for the most part, they simply copy something someone else created. And in most aspects of life, sports, and business, people rely on stealing plays rather than creating plays from scratch.

The coach who steals plays would be identified as a person who reasons by analogy. If I owned a team, I would want a first principles thinker as my coach and not just a play stealer.

Another way to think about first principles thinking is the cook and the chef. The chef is a creative person who invents recipes. They are familiar with the ingredients and have spent lots of time in the kitchen experimenting with raw ingredients and combining them. Once they have perfected their masterpiece, it becomes a staple on the menu. The cook, who reasons by analogy, simply uses someone else's recipe. They might create something with slight variations that has already been created. They may add some celery here and some mustard there, but it is in no way close to first unique combination of ingredients.

Elon Musk

I first became aware of first principles thinking in reading about Elon Musk and his management philosophy. Musk is a direct disciple of Aristotle and his crew. He has taken first principles thinking to new heights. Musk is obviously a genius and has built many first principles companies. SpaceX and Tesla are prime examples.

When Musk set out to build SpaceX, he discarded the conventional wisdom at the time that rockets couldn't be efficiently reused. He and the engineers at his company deconstructed the old way of building rockets, discarded former assumptions, then built rockets to be efficiently reused. They gambled that reaching outer space could be more affordable based on the fundamental math of how rockets worked and the economics of their raw materials. Musk basically took years of assumptions and dogma used by NASA and deconstructed their entire way of thinking. He then focused on what he believed was possible, even though decades of scientists had disagreed.

Similarly, at Tesla he did the same thing. The big three automakers shared a common assumption that electric cars were not possible because they could not be affordable. The prevailing convention at the time was that vehicle batteries were just too expensive to make them practical. Had Elon Musk reasoned by analogy and lived in the past, he would have agreed that batteries were too expensive and thus electric cars impossible. He didn't think that way. Instead, he thought with first principles thinking. Musk believes that reasoning by analogy is a mental shortcut. For many things in life, that works. But Musk does not believe that approach can work when it comes to discovering or doing something new. In his own words, Musk says, "Boil things down to the most fundamental truths and say, okay, what are we sure is true? or as sure as possible is true?" and "then reason up from there."

Musk is so tied to this way of thinking that he built a school, the Ad Astra school, in 2014, built around the philosophy of first principles thinking. The school served children ages eight through fourteen at SpaceX headquarters until 2020.

First principles thinking is in fact a superpower. It involves envisioning what ultimate success looks like and then being open to any path that leads there.

As Musk has continued to shock us with his thinking, he continues to innovate both his car company and rocket company with first principles thinking. It applies to every aspect of the vehicles he's building.

The Advantages of First Principles Thinking

In its simplest form, first principles thinking takes a problem and breaks it into its parts. After you have identified all the unique pieces of the puzzle, you then begin to put it together to make sense. One of the advantages of first principles thinking is that it allows you to see the world differently. And this is extremely helpful when you are faced with what seems to be impossible. By breaking it down into smaller pieces, you can find a solution that you may not have otherwise considered.

Another advantage to first principles thinking is that it can help you avoid making assumptions. When you're trying to solve a problem, it's easy to make assumptions about what you think is causing the problem. However, any basic assumption may not be accurate. By looking at the problem from the first principles, you can avoid making these inaccurate assumptions.

Five Steps to First Principles Thinking

There are five steps to first principles thinking:

1. **CHALLENGE YOUR ASSUMPTIONS.** When you challenge your assumptions and consider ALL possibilities, you may find a better solution.

2. **BREAK DOWN THE PROBLEM INTO ITS SMALLEST ELEMENTS.** Some people try to solve the wrong problem because they don't understand it at a deep enough level. By breaking it down into its smallest elements, the possibility for new and better ways emerges.

3. **IDENTIFY THE CORE PROBLEM.** Even if you have identified the problem, it can still be challenging to find a solution if you don't know what the core problem is. The core problem is the most important part of any problem that needs to be solved.

Only once you identify the core problem can you start to look for a solution.

4. **GENERATE WORKABLE SOLUTIONS.** This is where the creative mind comes in. This is where brainstorming with a group can be extremely helpful as you bounce ideas off each other. First, you need to come up with actionable ideas, but then you need to make sure your solutions are workable and will solve problems. And you need to consider risks and challenges.

5. **IMPLEMENT THE SOLUTION.** This is the exciting part. Once you have deconstructed your past thinking and have reconstructed a new way of doing things, you are then ready to implement the solution. Of course, you have to consider everything that can and will go wrong, but then it's time for the rocket to take off.

My Own First Principles Thinking

I have used first principles thinking in many different businesses I'm involved in. Because I am an entrepreneur at heart, I need to try things out and see how they work. In addition to my law firm, I'm in the attraction business, hotels, real estate development, and lots of side hustles. The aspect of my life that has been the most lucrative for me is my law firm. As I write this book, I have embarked on a very aggressive first principles thinking project. I am hesitant to write about it, but I will, because the jury is still out. I still worry about failing.

My business is that of a trial lawyer. I started with one office in Orlando, and then grew throughout Florida and the southeast. I then had a thought. Forever and ever, law firms practiced in one city and that was it. Especially trial firms or personal injury firms. There were very few multi-offices. About fifteen years ago, I had a thought that was a first principles thought. My thought was simple: "What if Google were a law firm? What would it do and how would it do it?" I became obsessed with that thought and with that possibility. In essence, it was the idea of consolidating a very fragmented industry and nationalizing that business through the consolidation—a national trial lawyers' firm.

I am several years into this experiment, and it has come with great exhilaration and lots of work. I have now expanded through the Northeast, the Midwest, and even into California. As I mentioned, I dread talking about it because my fear of failure is something that lives with me every day. But so far, so good. I certainly hope I don't end up like Icarus flying too close to the sun.

My first principles thinking goes like this: my law firm is not a law firm but a tech firm whose services is law. The law work is handled by my firm, but we refer many of the cases out to other great law firms, much like Uber. What I have set out to do is something that has never been done before and relies totally on first principles thinking and scares the living daylights out of me.

On the other hand, my entrepreneurial bent would not be satisfied if I did not take this calculated, and most likely, last big risk of my life. When I tell people I am building the Google law firm, they look at me like I have horns and a tail. They just don't get it, and I don't expect them to. As time goes by, we will see if my great experiment is a boom or a bust. But for me, it's one I have to try.

Other First Principles Thinkers

While first principles thinking was first popularized by Aristotle, many great minds have used it. Isaac Newton used it to develop his famous laws of motion. First principles thinking is also credited with helping Albert Einstein develop his theory of relativity. In more recent, times people like Thomas Edison, Richard Feynman, and Nikola Tesla used first principles ideas to allow them to solve some of the most intractable problems.

When you look at Bill Gates, Steve Jobs, and Jeffrey Bezos, you are looking at the epitomes of first principles thinkers. Because I have studied first principles thinking at such great length, I have also come to study the great minds who utilized it. In doing so, I have asked myself a question that may not be politically correct or even woke. When I examine most of these people, many are clearly geniuses. But some of these geniuses seem to be on the autism spectrum.

Many people on the autism spectrum are incredibly brilliant. But they do have difficulty with social interactions and social language. Many do not emote in a normal way. Things can be black and white to them. And many have limited conversational skills and either undershare or overshare. They can be obsessively focused on one topic, which can be an unusual one. They often make little to no eye contact, and don't understand typical nonverbal behaviors.

When you look at Jobs, Gates, Edison, Einstein, and Newton, all were geniuses, and possibly on the autism spectrum.

The question I have wrestled with forever is, "Is it good luck or bad luck?" For the world at large, some parts of the autism spectrum seem to be very good luck. These men and women have changed the course of the world and mostly for the better. For some, their amazing minds never turn off. Edison rarely even slept. He took a series of catnaps during the day.

Many people are walking among us with different forms of autism. How that came to be will be debated forever. Some people with autism are totally non-communicative and need twenty-four-hour care. Others are simply very, very bright with unusual habits and idiosyncrasies. That part of the autism spectrum seems to come with a beautiful mind and a great potential for doing great things. Whether these people are lucky or not depends on their circumstances and life trajectory. One thing is for certain: The human race has benefited greatly from these geniuses who live among us and often are not afraid to challenge long-held assumptions, but rather deconstruct, reconstruct, and build better mousetraps for all of us. Whether they were lucky or not depends on them. But for you and for me, we are all very lucky they live among us.

CHAPTER 29

HOPE IS NOT A PLAN

One of the things I want to be clear about is that while luck is seemingly identified with coin tosses, the truth of the matter is that there are many things all of us can do to enhance our luck. I know that many people may be bothered with the idea that luck had something to do with their success. As previously mentioned, successful people are usually hell-bent on being self-made. And the reason for this is real.

There is no doubt that for most successful people, they have spent an unbelievable amount of time and effort in achieving their success. In my own life, I know that is true. I can tell you flat out that I have worked like a dog since I was a child.

In my life, I have never *not* been working. When I was in college, I worked several jobs because I didn't want to have student debt. The business I started was very successful for a college and law student, and it also enabled me to avoid student loans.

So if someone were to question my work ethic, I would be highly offended. I put those hours in, and it was not easy. If somebody said that my success was all based on luck, I can certainly see how I could be offended, especially when I know all the time and effort that I put in.

The point of this book is not to diminish anyone's success — yours or mine. The thing I am most proud of is the work that I put in. When

I was a young lawyer starting out, I used to spend every Friday asking for new business. I would schedule a lunch in a town with someone I already knew. But from nine o'clock until lunch, I would canvass local law firms, walk in the door, and ask to meet the main person.

Once I was in their office, I would engage in small talk and then ask them the big question: "Who do you send your personal-injury work to?" Many times, these lawyers were taken aback. I don't know if anyone else ever came in off the street and asked that question, but I did.

Before going to law school, when I sold Yellow Pages, I developed lots of skills that were helpful in this endeavor. Basically, I learned how to cold-call strangers. It was hard, but I didn't mind because I knew the payoff could be great. When other people, and even my family, would hear what I was doing, their mouths fell open. The thought of cold-calling another lawyer and asking for business seemed foreign to them. To me, it seemed a natural fit. I did this for many years. It was very effective, and I developed a tremendous referral network from my Friday meet-and-greets. To this day, those lawyers still refer cases to my firm. The first lawyer who referred me my first case from a cold call was a fellow named Jim Perry, with offices in Sanford, Florida. We became great friends.

Later in life, I was honored to recommend him to my good friend, Governor Charlie Crist, who appointed him to the Florida Supreme Court. When Jim was sworn in, Governor Crist told him, "You have a very good friend in John Morgan."

Those cold calls were not as easy as I make them seem. Many times, I had to steel myself for the reactions that would come my way. Lots of times, I had a pit in my stomach before walking in. But I knew something: if you don't ask, you don't get. This simple exercise on Fridays was one way I went looking for luck. Had I stayed in my office working by myself, these referrals and relationships would never have become reality. If you're not willing to look for luck, you will never find it.

More Swings of the Bat = More Luck

Some of my God-given gifts included the gift for gab and a genuine affection for people. I enjoy people. Because of these traits, it made my visits easier and much more productive. However, without using some of my other gifts, like being relentless, being hungry, having grit, and not minding work, I was able to build a very big business in a very short period of time.

One of the easiest ways to enhance your luck is to get more swings of the bat. The more times you swing, the more times you have a chance of hitting that ball. It is the law of averages. There are real estate agents who understand the law of averages. They may host an open house all day on Saturday for three consecutive weekends and not one buyer shows up to visit. However, had they not had those open houses, they would have had zero chance of selling that house. But on that fourth weekend, they do sell the house, and at a price way above asking. It is easy to become discouraged. That's why people who are lucky enough to be born with grit and determination have been given a great gift by nature.

The more lottery balls you draw out of the jar, the better chance you have of winning the lottery. We see it all the time in sports. Professional teams are usually given many more lottery balls for the first draft pick if they have lost the most games of any other team in the league. That's why we see teams throwing games at the end of the year to get more lottery balls for the next year's draft. It is a mathematical formula.

How Athletes Enhance Their Luck

For much of the year, I live in Orlando. Shaquille O'Neal was the first overall pick in the 1992 NBA draft as a result of lucky ping-pong balls. In 1993, the ping-pong balls were once again good to the Orlando

Magic, and they got the No. 1 pick again and chose the draft rights to Penny Hardaway.

When teams draft players like O'Neal or Michael Jordan, that team has just improved its odds in doing very well. This whole lottery-ball phenomenon also plays out in life. The more times you take a shot, the better odds you have of making a shot, at least one. Wayne Gretzky, the Great One, famously said, "You miss 100 percent of the shots you don't take." And boy is that true. You won't have the opportunity to be considered lucky if you never take a shot. Taking shots enhances luck.

As I've written about in earlier chapters, great athletes were very fortunate to have the genetic makeup and size and strength that allowed them to be professional athletes. Then they took their God-given genetics and parlayed it into a very meaningful career. But even with their physical prowess, they won't have the careers the great ones have unless they are constantly looking to enhance luck.

How does an athlete enhance luck?

- They condition relentlessly.
- They live in a weight room.
- They watch tape endlessly.
- They listen to their coaches and are respectful.
- They work out, even when the workouts are not mandatory.
- They train in the off-season when others are drinking and having a good time.

They are taking all of their gifts that they were given by nature and making moves to enhance luck. Without all of that extra effort, Gretzky would never have become the Great One.

Ways to Enhance Luck

There are many ways that we enhance luck.

BE BOLD AND MAKE BIG DECISIONS

Lucky people are more likely to take calculated risks and make the most of those opportunities. Taking risks can lead to some of life's most meaningful moments, such as learning a new skill, going on a first date, or applying for a job. However, it's important to be able to tolerate uncertainty and show yourself compassion if you fail.

Taking small risks, showing appreciation, and staying open to all ideas, even the crazy ones, builds the foundation to catch luck when it comes. Luck is created by how we approach opportunities and life.

BE OPEN-MINDED

Lucky people are open to new experiences and opportunities, and they are curious about the world. Being open-minded means being receptive to new ideas, information, and opportunities. It also means being objective, listening to other points of view, and being willing to admit what you don't know. To me, the most dangerous person in the world is the person who does not know what they don't know.

Open-mindedness can be a valuable trait in many areas of life, including:

- IN THE WORKPLACE. Open-minded people can embrace change, learn new things, and work well with others. They can also be more respectful of others' cultures, boundaries, and opinions.

- IN BUILDING KNOWLEDGE. Open-minded people can build knowledge about specific issues or points of view. They can also provide sound recommendations and advice.

- IN RELATING TO OTHERS. Open-minded people can relate to people from different backgrounds and cultures.

There are certain characteristics of open-minded people:

- They don't jump to conclusions.

- They seek out and examine all available evidence before forming an opinion.
- They are objective when they approach new things.
- They are willing to admit what they don't know.

Most people who describe themselves as lucky tend to be extroverted, optimistic and, most importantly, open-minded. They keep a sense of curiosity alive at all times, and they see things that others might miss.

BE OPTIMISTIC

An optimistic mindset can help you believe good things will happen, which can lead to taking actions that make those good things a reality. There are tips for being optimistic:

- LOOK FOR OPPORTUNITIES. Lucky people are good at noticing and taking advantage of opportunities.
- EXPECT GOOD THINGS. Have an optimistic outlook and expect good things to happen.
- FIND WAYS TO TURN BAD LUCK INTO GOOD LUCK.
- PAY ATTENTION TO UNSEEN LUCK. Many times, luck is staring us right in the face and we miss it.

Psychologist Susan Albers with the Cleveland Clinic believes you can drum up good fortune. "Research indicates lucky people have two things in common: they are more optimistic, and they think in positive ways," Dr. Albers said. "They don't believe magic makes good things happen. Instead, they believe it is an attribute or a characteristic they have. In turn, this leads to positive thinking." According to Dr. Albers, having an optimistic mindset and believing you are lucky will make it more likely that good things will happen.

BE SELF-CONFIDENT

Recently I was talking to a longtime friend of mine, Jay Colling. I met Jay when I moved to Florida in the ninth grade. When we were talking, I explained how because of my crummy home life and alcoholic parents, I tried to hide all of that from my friends. I would never let anyone even come into my house because I was so embarrassed about our surroundings. I told Jay that I thought I had pulled it off pretty well. His response shocked me.

Jay said, "You didn't fool any of us. We all knew what was going on inside your house and inside your life. What we didn't understand is how you were so confident." That exchange blew me away. All of this time I had been certain that by compartmentalizing my life at home and my life outside of home, that I had fooled everybody. In reality, I had only fooled myself.

But I had something going for me: my self-confidence. I believe that was just part of my luck in life. I had no reason to be self-confident—economically, academically, or for any other reason. However, when I walked out of that house, I felt that I had left all my troubles behind and all of those troubles were now invisible. After talking to Jay, I know they were not invisible.

BE SOCIAL

Lucky people have a wide network of friends and professional contacts. They smile more and make eye contact, which can lead to new opportunities.

Putting Yourself into a Lucky State

Professor Richard Wiseman of the University of Hertfordshire is the leading academic researcher studying luck. He spent his career seeking to understand the difference between lucky people and unlucky people and discovered that there are very specific things lucky people do to increase their good fortune. Most importantly, he also discovered that we can create more luck for ourselves through changing the way we think and behave. Increasing your luck isn't about manifesting a vision or staying relentlessly positive or repeating what you want over and over until it magically shows up. Just like we can consciously choose to put ourselves into a flow state, into a meditative state, or into a loving state, we can also put ourselves into a lucky state that then impacts our behaviors and thus, some outcomes.

Wiseman took these four principles and turned them into "luck school," teaching unlucky people how to turn their fortunes around. In total, 80 percent of the people who attended said their luck had increased, and on average, they estimated their luck had increased by over 40 percent. Here are his rules:

1. LOOK FOR AND JUMP ON OPPORTUNITIES. One of Wiseman's studies found that lucky people smile twice as much and engage in more contact than unlucky people. That social interaction often leads to new opportunities for them.

   - One quick way to do this is to change up your daily routine and put yourself in new environments or new experiences.

   - Another is to say yes to things that you would normally decline. As we get older, we tend to accumulate wisdom, which is what makes us feel as though we have all the answers to life and that we know how things will unfold. By consciously adopting open-mindedness, we can try to stay more open to surprises and moments where our luck could change.

2. FOLLOW YOUR GUT. Lucky people listen to their gut feelings and act upon what they hear.

3. EXPECT GOOD THINGS. Lucky people expect that life will be full of good things. Because of that belief, they tend to put themselves out there more, as they believe they will get what they want and aren't ashamed to ask for it. This translates into raising your hand for opportunities, asking for things you want, and advocating for yourself, all of which have very positive outcomes.

4. FIND WAYS TO TURN BAD LUCK INTO GOOD LUCK.

5. SET CLEAR GOALS. When you set these goals, make sure that they are specific, measurable, achievable, relevant, and time-bound—SMART. It's important to write your goals down,

which makes them more tangible and helps you stay committed.

Also, make your goals relevant. Make sure your goals are aligned with your values and aspirations in life. While you are at it, make them measurable. Set goals that you can track so that you can measure your progress and at the same time, set goals that are achievable, realistic, and attainable.

In setting these goals, it is very important to set a time frame. If you don't have this time frame, there is no urgency in achieving your goals. And once you have your goals, share them with someone who will hold you accountable and provide support. It's also important to regularly review your goals to ensure they stay relevant.

6. BE CURIOUS. Keep a sense of curiosity alive so you can see things that others might miss.

7. HAVE A CONTINGENCY PLAN. To "improve luck" with a contingency plan, focus on maximizing opportunities by proactively identifying potential risks and taking steps to mitigate them, actively seeking out new possibilities, and ensuring you are prepared to capitalize on unexpected situations when they arise, essentially "making your own luck" through planning and readiness.

There are many ways and strategies to improve your luck through contingency planning:

A. IDENTIFY POTENTIAL RISKS AND OPPORTUNITIES. It's important to conduct a comprehensive analysis to identify all possible risks and potential opportunities that could impact your goals, both positive and negative.

B. PRIORITIZE RISK BASED ON SEVERITY. Evaluate the likelihood and potential impact of each risk to determine which ones require the most attention in your contingency plan.

C. DEVELOP PROACTIVE MEASURES. For each identified risk, create specific actions and strategies to minimize its impact or even turn it into an opportunity.

D. BUILD A FLEXIBLE NETWORK. Network with individuals and organizations across different industries to access diverse perspectives and potentially identify new opportunities that might not be readily apparent.

E. STAY INFORMED AND ADAPTABLE. Continuously monitor your environment for changing conditions.

F. PRACTICE SCENARIO PLANNING. Regularly run through hypothetical scenarios to test your contingency plan and identify areas for improvement.

G. DELEGATE ROLES AND RESPONSIBILITIES. Clearly define who is responsible for executing each part of the contingency plan in case of emergency.

H. REVIEW AND UPDATE REGULARLY. Periodically revisit your contingency plan to reflect changing circumstances and incorporate new insights.

Having a Plan

Luck is often about being prepared. By actively managing potential risks and opportunities, you increase your chances of being in the right place at the right time. But don't just focus on immediate concerns, look for opportunities beyond your typical scope. And don't wait for problems to surface—plan ahead to ameliorate their impact.

While there are many different scenarios to enhance luck, it all really boils down to this: *hope is not a plan.* Many people go through life just hoping something good is going to happen to them. Just hoping that they may one day catch lightning in a bottle. Hoping one day that luck may shine on them for no apparent reason.

And we know people are like this because we see it in betting on lotteries, sports, horse racing, and any other form of gambling that can take them out of their current situation. Gambling and lotteries are not a plan. They are simply hope. And while hope is important, it certainly will not lead you to opportunities. A plan is like a map that guides you from where you are to your own personal pot of gold. Without that map, you don't know what roads to take, what mountains to cross, or what bodies of water lie in front of you. Without a plan, you are flying an airplane in the dark and you are not instrument-rated. When this happens, you will find your aircraft turned upside down and crashing into the ocean.

Much of the luck you receive in life, like your parents and your physical makeup, is totally out of your control. But much of the luck you can experience is totally within your control if you have a plan.

The great football coach, Darrell Royal at the University of Texas, once said, "Luck is when hard work and preparation collide." Believe me, Royal had a plan, and it wasn't based on hope. It was a game plan that he had prepared for over and over again in practice. When that trick play worked, it only worked because of the preparation and planning that had gone into that razzle-dazzle play that shocked the stadium.

Never forget: *hope is not a plan.*

CHAPTER 30

SETTING GOALS AND LOOKING FOR OPPORTUNITIES

It's important to talk about goals and searching for opportunities as we go forth looking for luck. Every year, I have three goals that I write down and refer to the rest of the year. They are goals I need to meet during that calendar year. There are some important aspects goals should have so that you are not wasting your time and going in the wrong direction.

Most of us have some type of goal in all parts of our life — making good grades, making a sports team, getting married, getting divorced. Goals come in all shapes and sizes, but there must be a method to your madness to make sure that the goals give you your best chance of finding favor.

In the last chapter, we talked about SMART goals: specific, measurable, achievable, relevant, and time-bound. This way of looking at goals forms a roadmap for how you should go about setting your goals.

Goal-Setting Best Practices

After you have set your SMART goals, it's important that you then write down your goals. People with goals do better than people without goals. People with written goals do better than people with unwritten goals. Writing down your goals makes them feel more tangible.

Once you write down your goals, it is vital that you create an action plan. An action plan can help you identify a plan to reach your goal and make it easier to stay motivated and monitor your progress. Without an action plan, you have no idea how well or poorly you are doing.

It's also preferable, in my mind, to prioritize your goals. Consider what resources are available, including your own personal abilities and energies. By prioritizing your goals, you take care of the big ones first; and even if you fail to get all of them completed, at least the major goals are behind you.

I also believe strongly in setting short-term goals. By setting short-term goals, it enables more frequent opportunities to review and acknowledge the achievement of goals. If you're trying to pole-vault 17 feet, your first go at it would not be 17 feet. It would be much lower. Each and every day, you can increase that short-term goal.

Once upon a time, running a four-minute mile was thought to be impossible. Then Roger Bannister broke the record. That record has been broken over and over again, and the times have gotten faster and faster. That's because in the beginning, runners working on this set short-term goals. It may have been five minutes, and it may have been four minutes thirty seconds. Each time a runner achieved one of these goals, they set a new one.

By having your goals written down and prioritized, it allows you to do something very important: check your progress regularly. By checking your progress, you will stay motivated. When people try to lose weight, it is important to step on the scale every single morning. That's the same way we deal with goals. Sometimes we wake up and have inexplicably gained two or three pounds. It causes us much consternation because we don't think we ate that much. However, whatever the reason for the weight gain, I can promise you by checking in the morning, your food intake for that day will be totally different than had you not stepped on the scale. When we are checking our progress regularly, we are stepping on our business and life scale. The more you see your weight, the better chance you have of reaching your goal.

And finally, once you have mastered those goals, you can switch goals. Switching goals can encourage you to pursue something bigger and even more challenging. But first, you must clear the lower bar before you can try the high bar.

How I Set Goals

Setting a budget for expenses and income is my ultimate goal. In all of my businesses, I have very specific goals for overhead and income, which gives me my net profit. I track those goals every single day. Every day, money is deposited into my businesses, and I keep a very strict watch over expenses. When I start in January, I get my first month's net profit. I then multiply that by twelve and that will show me my trend for the year. Of course, January can be tricky, but it's important to me, nonetheless. It's an exercise I do at the end of each month. At the end of March, I see what my net profit is for the first quarter and then multiply that by four to give me my trend for the year.

Of course, that doesn't work well with the attractions I own, because the bulk of my profit comes in the summer months. However, I watch very closely year-over-year income and expenses to make sure I am on goal. I am obsessed with setting goals, I am obsessed with monitoring goals, and I am obsessed with tracking goals all the way until the very last day of the year. It is simply how I operate and how I look for luck.

Years ago, I used to take one week a year and just think. I kept articles and ideas in a folder that I would review during my week of thinking. It was during this week of thinking that I would set my three goals for the new year. By the way, I have many different businesses, so I set many different sets of goals. I have goals for my attractions, goals for my law firms, and goals for my real estate and other assorted businesses. Each business needs goals. Without goals and the focus on goals, I have no chance of winning. At the end of the day, goals are set so that we can win.

The BHAG (Big Hairy Audacious Goal)

While at the same time that we are setting these goals, it is also important to know there is another type of goal that only can be attempted every so often. It is called the BHAG—Big Hairy Audacious Goal. It is a goal that is so aggressive and so ambitious that it can only be described as a *moonshot*. It is not your normal three-pronged goal for the year. I'll spend a little bit more time on the BHAG in a future chapter, but it is important that you have this particular goal in your arsenal for your own personal moonshot.

Rockefeller and the Art of Looking for Opportunities

While it is very important that we have goals, it is also important you understand that you can enhance your luck when you are aggressively looking for opportunities. Opportunities are everywhere and come in all shapes and sizes. The best book I have ever read on this particular subject was *The 38 Letters from J.D. Rockefeller to his Son* by J.D. Rockefeller. I really cannot urge you strongly enough to read this brilliant book. They are letters that were meant to be private from the elder Rockefeller to his son, John. These nuggets of life lessons will change everything about your search for luck and the success that comes with it.

Rockefeller was always looking for new business opportunities and ways to expand his profits. By age twenty-five, Rockefeller controlled one of the largest oil refineries in the nation. By age thirty-one, he had become the world's largest oil refiner. By age thirty-eight, he commanded 90 percent of the oil refined in the U.S. By the time of his retirement at age fifty-eight, he was the richest man in the country. By the time he died, he had become the richest man in the world. The Rockefeller key to success was "Be your own tyrant." He stated, "I would rather be my own tyrant than have someone else tyrannize me." Rockefeller's most striking quality was what his biographer, Ron Chernow, calls his almost "eerie self-control." He relentlessly honed his will, training himself to be master of his emotions, desires, and schedule so that he could direct all his impulses toward his aims. He set big goals for himself, then attacked them with a disciplined, workday ethic. Rockefeller understood that if you wish to be your own boss, you have to learn how to boss yourself. Many fail to learn this lesson, and it is a major mistake.

"Many of us who fail to achieve big things… fail because we lack concentration — the art of concentrating the mind on the thing to be done at the proper time and to the exclusion of everything else." – John D. Rockefeller

As a boy, Rockefeller's mother taught him, "Control of self wins the battle, for it means control of others." He took the maxim to heart, adopting a far different leadership style than the stereotypical corporate tycoon, cultivating a power that relied not on loud, blustering displays and a belligerent table pounding, but quiet authority and a sphinxlike demeanor. He had a temper as a teenager and struggled with it. But he trained himself to control it and moved through the rest of his life with exceptional equanimity and was unruffled, no matter the circumstances. The more agitated others became, the calmer he grew. In looking for opportunity, Rockefeller believed that there was strength in silence. He listened far more than he talked in his meetings with the men at the top as well, and this air of almost supernatural calm only heightened his influence in the boardroom. As Chernow explains, "The quieter he was, the more forceful his presence seemed, and he played on his mystique as the resident genius immune to petty concerns." His long silences while negotiating deals often threw members of the other party off their game, tying them up in self-defeating knots.

Rockefeller loved to tell the story of the time an irate contractor burst into his office and laid into him with an angry tirade. Rockefeller sat with back turned, hunched over a writing desk until the tongue lashing ran its course. Then he spun around in his swivel chair and coolly asked, "I didn't catch what you were saying, would you mind repeating that?"

While I believe it's important that you read all of Rockefeller's thirty-eight letters, there are key points from these letters that he used to be in search of opportunities.

- CONSTANT VIGILANCE. Rockefeller encouraged his son to always be on the lookout for new markets, emerging technologies, and potential areas of growth to stay ahead of the competition.

- COST-EFFICIENCY FOCUS. He stressed the importance of minimizing costs through careful management and operational optimization, often by seeking out cheaper production methods. Rockefeller was consumed with being focused. Without keen focus, opportunities can be missed or simply squandered.

- STRATEGIC PARTNERSHIPS. Rockefeller advised his son to consider collaborations with other businesses where it can benefit both parties and create a stronger market presence. Rockefeller, like Warren Buffett, would buy entire companies and leave able management in charge. This enabled him to scale much more quickly and for his opportunities to be crystallized and fast-tracked.

- ETHICAL CONDUCT. While prioritizing success, Rockefeller emphasized the importance of maintaining integrity and a positive public image, avoiding practices that could damage the company's reputation.

As we try to enhance our luck, goal setting and searching for opportunities are at the forefront of our endeavors. Simply going through life hoping and wishing is a folly. You can't find your way to a destination without a map and a plan and incredible focus. Goal setting allows for this focus, and searching for opportunities, in many cases, leads to one.

CHAPTER 31

NEVER EAT ALONE

In our search for luck, there are many different ways that good fortune comes our way. One thing is for certain: you can't win in bingo unless you decide to go into a bingo hall. And the more bingo cards you have, the greater chance you have of winning. It is simply the law of numbers.

Networking

Networking is the action or process of interacting with others to exchange information and develop professional or social contacts. Networking is the process of making connections and building relationships. Networking occurs at every stage in our lives. When we were in high school, there was a certain caste system. There was always a table where the cool kids sat—the jocks and the cheerleaders. As you went through the cafeteria, there were many other tables with different people all spread out in that caste system. Unfortunately, for some, they either sat alone or sat at a table that was not desirable by them. When you looked at the cool table, you could only dream of sitting there one day.

That same social climbing and networking goes on throughout life and in business. When I went to the University of Florida and joined the ATO fraternity, I had an immediate network of friends. It proved to be invaluable, and many of those friends remain my closest friends today. I have often thought what my four years would have been like without the fraternity. Of course, there are those who detest the Greek system and everything it stands for. But those people are okay. They set up their own network in totally different ways. The engineering students had special fraternities where they socialized and traded notes. Networks come in all shapes and sizes. The bottom line for enhancing luck is that you must get out from behind your desk, or out of your house, and venture into the world. You have to ask for business or develop relationships that will enhance your business. You don't ask, you don't get.

This is particularly difficult for introverts and shy people. Some people break out into a cold sweat at the thought of networking. They have some sort of social anxiety that freezes them up like a board. They just can't do it. Unfortunately for them, that is bad news for their luck.

Build and Maintain a Professional Network

I have been guided in my life by many books. Another I would recommend is called *Never Eat Alone* by Keith Ferrazzi. The book is a very short but necessary read. It really talks about how networking presents so many opportunities. Remember, the luckiest people are constantly looking for opportunities. Unlucky people rarely look for opportunities. The book gives tips on building and maintaining a professional network. You will learn how to network with people who can help you achieve your goals; how to use conferences to network; and how to use social media to get new contacts to come to you. Remember, earlier we talked about looking for opportunities and setting goals. Those two action items are vital in the hunt for good luck.

Ferrazzi states, "Success in any field, but especially in business, is about working with people, not against them." Back in 2005, over half of all jobs were found through personal contacts, with only 20 percent resulting from applying to advertisements and just 10 percent going to people as a result of unsolicited applications. By now, over 80 percent of jobs are landed through networking, so some tutoring in the subject that you never had in school should come in handy.

There are three lessons to help you become a better networker.

1. Relationships aren't like cake; they are like muscles.

2. You must build your network long before you need it.

3. How you spend time with people is much more important than how much time you spend with them.

Relationships have a lot in common with muscles. The more you use them, the stronger they get, because they grow each time you exercise them. Cake, on the other hand, disappears over time, because it gets smaller with every slice you take.

But just like muscles, building relationships takes time. If you go to the gym for a short-term investment of working out once until you collapse and then expect to look like Arnold Schwarzenegger or Simone Biles the next day, you are in for a rude awakening. Instead, constant generosity and loyalty will get you where you want to go. Sticking with the muscle example, if you show up to the gym twice a week for a year, you'll reap the rewards of a good body.

Your network needs to be built long before you need it. It's sort of like a boat and life vests. We have the life vests, but we don't use them until we need them. The same principle applies for networking.

Quality Time — It's Not a Sprint

A good networker establishes relationships like a long-distance runner, not a sprinter. When Bill Clinton was twenty-two years old, he started writing down the names of everyone he met that day in order to remember them better. When he ultimately ran for president, he started calling all those people because they had known him as genuinely nice and were interested in him long before he ran for president.

Finally, lots of people get discouraged with networking because they think it's about how much time you spend, not how much *quality time* you spend. A good network doesn't consist of fleeting acquaintances.

It's a web of real and trusted friends. Ferrazzi calls these relationships "relationship glue"—the stuff that turns acquaintances to friends. Don't look at how much time you spend with people, just how you spend it with them. Get to know them in a setting where it is fun and relaxed and not where they feel they have to make small talk just to have conversation. The best small talk isn't small talk at all.

I can tell you firsthand that much of my success has happened outside of my office and outside of my city. I have often said there are not many people who make $1 million a year who don't live on airplanes. During the years, I have often been asked to speak as a keynote speaker for different organizations. Each time I am asked, I remember saying yes before, and when the day came close, I was sorry I had said yes. But once I went, I was always happy I had gone. The thought of getting on a plane, going to a strange city, and sleeping in a hotel is not really appealing. The older you get, the less appealing it is. I try my very best to sleep in my own bed as many nights as possible.

The speeches I have given have turned into gold for me. I've met people that I've developed long-lasting professional relationships with. People I spoke to have referred me business and opportunities over the years. And even more importantly, it has been in these networking environments where new opportunities presented themselves to me that changed the course of my life. Had I decided to sleep at home and not take those trips, much of my success would have been less than what it is. As a personal injury lawyer, I have spent countless hours in union halls and in union bars drinking with the powers that be. Those early days of shooting pool with the business manager were invaluable. And by the way, I had a load of fun. I'd rather be in a dive bar than in any country club I've ever walked into. I don't like country clubs. I think it's because I don't feel like I belong. When you grow up in a certain economic circumstance, there is a lot of scarring that goes on about whether you even should walk into a country club. Being poor takes a toll throughout life, regardless of how much you have as an adult. But being poor, while bad luck, often turns into good luck by providing an incredible drive never to feel that economic insecurity again.

So get out and get busy.

Saying Yes to "Why Bother?"

There is one more action point I would like to tell you about that I use constantly. If I'm presented with an idea or an opportunity, I will say to myself, "Why bother?" And when you ask, "Why bother?" you'll often answer, "I won't."

It is very easy to say no when the question to yourself is "Why bother?" Just the words alone make your effort seem pointless. But if you say yes to "Why bother?" one thousand times, the cumulative effect is incredible. One grain of sand is nothing. But millions and millions of grains of sand form a beautiful beach.

Going forward, I challenge you to think differently. If you have an idea of doing a podcast, don't tell yourself, "There are too many podcasts out there, so why bother?" Instead, say something like, "There are many podcasts out there—should I bother? Yes. There's obvious opportunity and a market out there."

As you go forward you will have times in your personal life and business to say, "Why bother?" Remember this chapter and *do* bother. Over time, all of the yeses to "Why bother?" will add up in a very big way.

And one last thing. If you don't bother, you have no chance of building that cumulative amount of goodwill and networking. If you don't bother, what will you be doing anyway? If you don't appear on someone's podcast, what activity will you be doing that will enhance your business? Usually when we say no to "Why bother?" we waste our time doing nothing. The more you do, the more chances you have to do better. As you go through life, try not to eat alone. And when you ask yourself, "Why bother?" go ahead and bother. For me, it has made all the difference in the world.

CHAPTER 32

BUSINESS PARTNERS

In our hunt for good fortune, one of our most important and sometimes fatal decisions is whom we choose to partner with. As we discussed earlier, 50 percent of marriages—the ultimate partnership—end in the divorce. And only 17 percent of all marriages are happy ones. The punchline is very simple: partnerships are iffy, tenuous, and sometimes not meant to last.

Many business partnerships are formed because we know each other as young people. Often we met in college or high school. Those friends that we met when we were nothing tend to be our best friends throughout life. We loved each other for each other and nothing more and nothing less.

In business, there have been many great partnerships that began with two young people dreaming the dream, and later, that venture grew into a magnificent business. The first business partnership I think of is Hewlett and Packard. Hewlett-Packard was founded in a one-car garage in Palo Alto by Bill Hewlett and David Packard in 1939. Initially, they produced a line of electronic test and measurement equipment. The HP garage at 367 Addison Avenue is now designated as an official California Historical Landmark and is marked with a plaque calling it the "Birthplace of Silicon Valley."

Hewlett and Packard graduated with degrees in electrical engineering from Stanford University in 1935. The company started in the garage during a fellowship they had with their past professor, Frederick Terman, at Stanford during the Great Depression, whom they considered a mentor in forming the company. In 1938, Packard and Hewlett began part-time work in a rented garage with an initial capital investment of $538—equivalent to $12,000 in 2023. In 1939, Hewlett and Packard decided to formalize their partnership. They tossed a coin to decide whether the company they founded would be called Hewlett-Packard (HP) or Packard-Hewlett. Obviously, Hewlett won the toss. Over the years, the company earned global respect for a variety of products. They introduced the world's first handheld scientific electronic calculator in 1972 (the HP-35), the first handheld programmable pocket calculator in 1974 (the HP-65), the first alphanumeric, programmable, expandable calculator in 1979 (the HP-41C), and the first symbolic and graphing calculator (the HP-28C). On March 3, 1986, HP registered the HP.com domain name, making it the ninth internet dotcom domain to be registered. This partnership is a prime example of one that was extremely successful. Hewlett and Packard were lifelong friends and partners who remained friends and partners their entire life.

A similar partnership was formed between Bill Gates and Paul Allen; their company, of course, is Microsoft. Gates and Allen were childhood friends and business partners who founded Microsoft in 1975. They met in the late 1960s at Lakeside School in Seattle, where they bonded over their shared interest in computers. They first worked together when they exploited a bug in a rare and expensive computer terminal to get free computer time. Allen convinced Gates to drop out of Harvard and start Microsoft. Allen was a creative thinker who helped Microsoft succeed in the early years.

Their relationship was often contentious, with Allen claiming that Gates was headstrong, aggressive, and competitive. Allen left Microsoft in 1982 after being diagnosed with Hodgkin's lymphoma but remained on the board of directors. Gates and Allen eventually repaired their relationship and remained friends until Allen's death. In 1986, they donated $2.2 million to Lakeside School. Gates called Allen "one of my oldest and dearest friends." Allen's creative thinking and ability to solve difficult problems were important to Microsoft's early success.

Now while I know nothing about the inner workings of Microsoft, I have often felt that Gates' other partner, Steve Ballmer, was the luckiest guy on the face of the earth. Gates and Ballmer were once close friends and colleagues at Microsoft, but their relationship reportedly "drifted apart" in later years.

Ballmer joined Microsoft early on as an employee and was considered a close confidante of Gates. When Gates stepped down as CEO, he handpicked Ballmer as his successor. A major point of contention emerged when Ballmer was CEO—primarily from disagreements about the company's direction, particularly regarding the shift to mobile technology. Ballmer felt Microsoft should have invested more heavily in mobile. They often describe their bond as "brotherly" but with significant strain in later years.

Once Ballmer left Microsoft, Ballmer's and Gates's relationship became less close. When Ballmer ran the company, it did poorly and the stock plummeted. Interestingly enough, Ballmer is richer than Gates. How? More than 90 percent of Ballmer's $157 billion net worth is in Microsoft shares, according to the Bloomberg Billionaires Index. Gates, meanwhile, has diversified his $156 billion fortune. About half of his wealth is held through Cascade Investment, which was created with proceeds of Microsoft stocks sales and dividends. One other interesting point is that had Gates never sold a share of Microsoft, he would now be a trillionaire.

The stories of Hewlett, Packard, Gates, and Allen are rare. Usually, these geniuses are lone wolves who need to have complete and unfettered control. Steve Jobs immediately comes to my mind. And he had difficulty with his business partner, Steve Wozniak.

Jobs and Wozniak were cofounders of Apple. Jobs primarily focused on marketing and business strategy, while Wozniak was a technical genius behind the hardware. They created a strong partnership despite occasional tensions. Tensions were particularly high when Jobs became more demanding and focused on new projects, sometimes neglecting the Apple II, which was crucial to the company's early success. Overall, they maintained a respectful relationship throughout their careers, even after Wozniak left Apple.

They met in high school, and while they respected each other, Jobs' demanding personality sometimes caused friction, especially when Wozniak felt his contributions were not fully appreciated. The Apple II, largely designed by Wozniak, is considered a key turning point in the personal-computer industry and solidified Apple's early success. Although their working relationship evolved over time, Wozniak has consistently expressed respect for Jobs and maintained a friendly connection until Jobs' death.

Wozniak left Apple in 1985 after he recovered from a plane crash that almost killed him. He wanted to go back to college and finish his degree in electrical engineering and computer science. He did that and then started doing all sorts of odds and ends. Obviously, going back to college was a dreadful financial mistake for Wozniak.

The Rarity of Successful, Long-Term Partnerships

As we go through the annals of companies and strong-lasting partnerships, we find very few. Of course, these titans of business had people around them that they relied on, but rarely do we see two partners who are able to' stay together for the long term or even begin their company in the short term.

Think of these names: Einstein. Edison. Tesla. Ford. Carnegie. Rockefeller. Mellon. The list goes on. It seems to me that when we look back in time, partnerships that were effective and lucrative were few and far between. I believe the answer is an easy one.

First, some of these geniuses want full and utter control, and feel that anyone who has a say can only slow them down. Control is everything.

Second, over time, one of these partners usually emerges as the straw that stirs the drink. We can meet when we're young, but we have no idea of the other's work ethic or intrinsic value that they may or may not bring to the enterprise. We basically go in blind.

Third, I believe the overriding reason partnerships break up is that one partner feels they are clearly the leader and are bringing the real value to the business. One thing is for certain, we all believe we are more than we are. Every single one of us.

So we have these situations where a partnership began, but over time, one partner feels that they are carrying the burden of the business while the other partner is sitting in the back whistling. I have always described it is as "oars in the water." When you get in the boat to row, you expect your partner to be rowing with you. Sometimes in partnerships, you find yourself rowing at a breakneck speed only to turn around and see your partner not rowing but eating out of a picnic basket. That partnership is terminal.

Deciding to Dissolve a Partnership

Many times, people partner up with those who seem to have incredible potential. Unfortunately, potential does not always translate into action. Probably the worst attribute of all is unrealized potential—the person who seems to have it all. Looks. Charm. Wit. Tremendous personality. But they lack one thing, and one thing that matters most. Work ethic. They are lazy.

The real point of this chapter is that when you go looking for luck and opportunities, often it is the partnership you are in that is doomed. We usually realize when we are in a wrong or an unfair partnership. We realize that we may have started down a road with the wrong teammates. The most important thing to learn is that the further that you go down the road with the wrong team, the harder it is to come back up that road and start all over. One way to enhance our luck is to do today what we know we must do some day.

The longer you stay in a partnership that you know is doomed, the longer the unwinding of that partnership will take, and the longer it will take you to get back on the right track.

Partnerships are delicate matters. The most delicate of all partnerships is the egos that are involved. All of us believe that we are more than we are. Unfortunately, there are people who are not only less than they think they are, but they are a total waste. These people often are the ones who believe in themselves the most, which makes the unwinding difficult but in many ways easier.

Before entering a partnership, ask yourself a simple question: "Are my partners the type of people who can take me to heights and success that I dream of, or are these people going to hold me back because I'm the only person rowing the boat?"

Unproductive partners do not usually walk into your office and say, "Hey, it really seems that you are doing the lion's share of work here. I think you should be paid substantially more." That never happens. Ever.

Is the Partnership Worth Repairing?

An important question to ask yourself is: "Is the partnership worth repairing?" The most pressing issue is always the share of profits, and that discussion is very painful.

Years ago, after being in a partnership for several years, I realized that one of my partners, twenty-five years my senior, was not pulling his weight. He had 10 percent more stock than me but was worth far less. Finally, I had enough and addressed it head-on. He met me with cold silence. Five minutes of no talk.

When he finally asked me what I proposed, I told him that I should receive 50 percent of the profits, and he and the other three partners should split the other 50 percent any way they wanted. Once again, there was a long silence. Our partnership never lasted past that day. He was simply unable to admit that his time had come and gone. I left him and one other partner, and the two of them did not do well in the ensuing years. I am so grateful that I asked for what I wanted that night. It took me months and lots of tossing and turning at night to finally pull that trigger.

Before you dissolve a partnership, you might suggest rearranging the sharing of profits. However, in some cases, that step is not enough if you know you are with the wrong person. Machiavelli taught us in *The Prince* that you can tell the most about a person by the people he surrounds himself with. Many times, when I meet someone's business partner, it tells me all I need to know about that other person.

If you want to enhance your luck in business, you have to do what I call "lion's shit." Everyone wants to be a lion until it's time to do lion's shit. Lion's shit is messy, bloody, and contentious. But if you want to be a lion, you have to act like a lion. You have to be ready and able to not only go for the kill but to make the kill. Sometimes the opportunities you are searching for will never come your way with your current partners. As you reflect, you have to make one of the great decisions of your life. Do I stay or do I go? Or do I say goodbye to certain partners and keep others?

These decisions are extremely difficult, because in many cases, you and your business partner probably started out as great friends. Money can strain friendships like nothing else, especially if you have a lazy partner who is taking and not giving. The best way to have bad luck is to let bad luck continue. The best way to have good luck is to get rid of people who were bad choices. Jeff Bezos says, "Sometimes you pay people just to go away." And I have done that many times in my life.

Your partner is an extension of you. They represent you professionally. In some cases, we spend more time with our business partners than with our spouses. Especially when we are building our business. However, I would much rather build a business with partners than build alone. I love the joy of sharing wins and successes, and I hate the burden of losses alone. I was built to partner with people; though, over the years, I have had to say goodbye to partners at certain times in our relationships. Time changes everything. Time changes work ethic. Time changes personalities. Time changes priorities. Partnerships are fluid. Some last forever and some last only for a while.

The main thing to remember out of all of this is that our partners will have more impact and influence over our success than almost anything else we do. Failure to address a partnership that may be past its prime is being an ostrich with its head in the sand.

To find luck, you have search for opportunities. As I've written earlier, hope is not a plan. But a plan with a bad partner is almost as bad as no plan at all.

CHAPTER 33

LOCATION, LOCATION, LOCATION

I wrote previously that one of the games I like to play with myself when riding down a road is called *Will They Make It?* When I see a new business going in, I ask myself, "Will it make it or not?" Often the location alone is enough to let me know there is no way in hell that business will make it. Other times, the business itself just screams failure before it even opens the door, regardless of location.

The Two Prevalent Reasons Businesses Fail

The two most prevalent causes of business failure are bad location and inadequate capital. One of the best ways to find luck is to stay away from bad locations or open a business short on cash. Luck has nothing to do with a bad location or inadequate capital. So when I see certain businesses fail, it's not because of bad luck or good luck, it's because that person decided to take an outsized risk that was 99 percent bound for failure. It's their own damn fault.

While there are many reasons businesses fail, none are as prevalent as a bad location or lack of money—sometimes both.

Once upon a time, I owned Shell gasoline stations across central Florida. It was at a time where the old gas stations with mechanics were being torn down to build gas stations with convenience stores and car washes. It was a wonderful opportunity for me (remember, to find luck you need to be looking for opportunities) because these mechanic-station owners had no interest in selling beer and cigarettes. Shell tore the old stations down and built the new convenience-store model. I was able to buy quite a few. I did not own the real estate, Shell did. However, I got to see a lot of stations across Florida fail and usually for one good reason: a bad location.

There are many real estate brokers who specialize just in gas stations and convenience stores. Ingress and egress are critical. If you can't get in easy or get out easy, the business can be a bust. What I noticed were older gas stations that were also convenience stores sitting dormant, usually at a corner location. Just because the station is on the corner doesn't mean it has good ingress and egress. The way the traffic lights are configured, and the curb cuts, and the median cuts also play into it.

But I would see huge stations with a full car wash shut down in a matter of months, because the approach and exit were difficult. When a station is in a bad location, there is no fixing it. Station owners can't start making curb cuts or median cuts once they are open for business. Dealing with local transportation departments may be the most frustrating endeavor in the world.

There are very few misses in the convenience-store area. These brokers usually get it right the very first time. But when they miss, they miss spectacularly.

Don't Forget About the Parking

I once opened a very small amusement park with multilevel go-kart tracks. The location was fantastic, but there was a problem. There was inadequate parking. Because it was located in a great tourist destination that was accessible by foot, I foolishly thought that I would not need the parking. To make a long story short, my business did okay but never great. My location was great, but I never had enough parking. I had assumed, wrongly, that people would walk from their hotels and that would be enough. Mercifully, because of the thrill ride and the location, I was able to sell the business at a small loss, but a loss, nonetheless. When you take a loss, you also have to figure in all the time you spent planning, building, and operating until you pulled the plug. Location is important. A great location with bad parking is the same as a bad location.

The Lack of Cash, Knowledge, and a Plan

Most businesses fail not only because of a bad location but because they ran out of money due to insufficient capital, poor financial planning, or cash-flow problems. Many people assume they will have cash flowing from Day One, and that is a terrible assumption. If you don't have at least six months of burn already in your bank account or on your line of credit, you are playing Russian roulette. But because people want to be in business so badly, they take this risk. That is absolutely the wrong play. To enhance luck, you need to be properly capitalized. Without capital, your chances for disaster are huge.

Businesses fail for other reasons too. Lots of people go into a business they know nothing about. For example, just because you're a good cook doesn't mean you should own a restaurant. Many of us like the idea of owning a bar or nightclub. It seems glamorous. It is not. I have owned a nightclub in Orlando, and all I can say is that at best, it was a break-even proposition. On the other hand, I had a ball. I don't regret it. If you are going to open a bar or a restaurant, you better plan on not being an absentee owner. If you are, they will steal you blind.

Many people rush into new businesses without a well-defined business plan or failing to properly research the market. If you're not financially well-capitalized, you will not have the ability to pivot or adapt to change as market conditions require to avoid making a business obsolete.

Just so you have some data going forward, remember this: According to data from the Bureau of Labor Statistics, around 20 percent of small businesses fail within their first year, with approximately 50 percent failing within five years, and 65 percent failing within ten years.

What does that tell us? It tells us that probably only 35 percent of business owners are going to have a business that is sustainable. The rest will lose their shirts and potentially their futures.

The Blinding Desire to Be Your Own Boss

Many people want to be their own boss, and that is understandable. That is the American dream. However, this desire can be blinding and cause us to make mistakes. The desire to say, as Johnny Paycheck said, "Take this job and shove it," is a great one. The desire to be the captain of our own ship is understandable. But that desire can lead us into opportunities that are really opportunities to fail.

Years ago, my children were friends with two boys. Their father had a business idea and came to see me about it. He worked for Igloo, the maker of coolers and such. He had a great job and money in the bank. However, he had a desire to be his own boss. When he came to see me, he presented his idea.

There was an ice cream franchise called Mickey Moo. He showed me the materials and he showed me the location. I had never heard of the franchise, and his location was close to a movie theater but hidden from the street. I immediately told him that I thought this was a bad idea. Ice cream is a tough business. I once owned a Ben & Jerry's franchise in a high-traffic area, and it struggled. Here this guy was, planning to open a franchise I had never heard of. In addition to the lack of name recognition, his location was hidden from traffic and nestled in next to a theater. He was counting on all the moviegoers to be ice cream buyers.

The story is a sad one. He quit his job and his wife quit hers. They opened up and it was an unmitigated disaster from the beginning. Within six months, they closed the business, depleted their life savings, had bank loans to pay, and were financially ruined.

The desire to be their own bosses ended up costing them what would have been a great retirement and happy life ever after. Making bad plays is the same as making bad bets in Vegas. There are certain things we can do to enhance our luck, and there are certain things we can do to cause bad luck.

This is not rocket science. Location, location, location. Coupled with a good business plan, a good business mind, and adequate capital, you have a chance. But you still only have a 35 percent chance of even making it, not to mention how much you may earn or how little.

The moral of this story is, go in with your eyes wide open.

CHAPTER 34

SUCCESSION PLANNING

As difficult as luck is to come across, luck is also difficult to hold onto. Making money is hard, keeping money is harder. This chapter is mainly for the person who has already found their luck by building a successful business, or they know it is within reach. By the time we are between the ages of thirty-five and forty-five, our future is pretty well determined. It is just question of how high our rocket will fly.

One of the most common ways that good fortune is demolished is when the succession of a business is not handled in a business-like manner. For many, the psychology of parents who coach little league and Pop Warner football creeps in. The parents still want their son to be the pitcher or the quarterback, even though he has no business playing either. The love we have for our children causes many blind spots along the road.

The Declining Odds of Success

According to the Family Business Institute, about 30 percent of family-owned businesses survive into the second generation, 12 percent into the third generation, and only about 3 percent into the fourth generation and beyond. These statistics reveal a daunting challenge for those at the helm of family enterprises.

This story plays out time and again in the annals of business history. There was a family in our town that my children grew up with. The father was very hard-working and built an incredible business. The family seemed picture-perfect. They were close-knit, very well received in our community, and pillars in our faith community. They were the perfect family.

Over the years, we continued to see our friend's business grow, and over time, he kept buying bigger and bigger houses, which demonstrated his great good fortune. At a certain point, he brought his son into the business. The son, it turns out, was a know-it-all who had contempt for his dad's abilities, even though his dad had built an incredible business. But at the time, we were all happy for the family, because nothing could be better than handing off a successful business to one of their children.

In a few short years, the wonder kid son had ruined, or almost ruined, the family's business. The business relied on futures, the type that requires skillful investing in the commodities market. Commodities can be anything, but are commonly fruits, vegetables, and livestock. The futures market is very important in areas such as oil, because if you bet right, you buy oil at an incredibly low price, but if you bet wrong, you can bankrupt the entire company.

In this case, the know-it-all son made a huge and terrible bet, which caused the family business to suffer a loss like no other. It was as if he had gone to Las Vegas and hit on 16 hoping to draw a 5. This spoiled boy broke every rule in the commodities book.

Unfortunately, this business decision caused a tremendous strain on this once-close family. After being given everything, this son destroyed the business. Then he took the low road, blamed everyone but himself, and moved to a new state, devastating his parents because now he and his children — their grandchildren — were far away. There is no question that his shame caused the move. Unfortunately, there were very few options for the family. They, of course, could have sued their son for damages, but they weren't going to do that, because they didn't want to be estranged from their son and grandchildren. They simply had to grin and bear it.

Planning for the Future

A family business is fraught with possible fissures and heartbreak. Recently, my son, Matt, was meeting with a prominent wealth manager in Boston. He asked Matt a series of questions.

Are your parents still married? Yes.

How long have your parents been married? Forty-three years.

How many siblings are there? Four.

Are all of you still speaking? Yes.

With those answers, the wealth manager then had his own statement to make. "You have no idea how rare this is. Most people in your financial strata have serious disagreements and most are not talking."

It was such a stunning statement that Matt called me immediately. We could never imagine something like that happening in our family. However, what happens over time is that money and ego change the dynamics. Those small children who we once worshipped may grow up to be totally different than what we had hoped for. That sweet little girl who gave you so much joy is suddenly an older woman suing you over the business, inheritance, or another ancillary issue that might cause her grievance. Obviously, it is heartbreaking. From the time our children are born, we begin to devise a plan for their inheritance. If our children marry and have their own children, we might start to plan for our grandchildren's inheritances as well. There is no other place that we would rather see our money go than to our children. However, in many cases, these children might grow up to be someone we don't recognize.

Having adult children not become the humans we would have wanted is the ultimate heartbreak. Coupled with the heartbreak, adult children may start withholding grandchildren's visits, love, and affection as a way to punish their parents. Or grandparents may attempt to be too controlling in their adult children's lives.

The Allure of Success

According to research by Karl Pillemer at Cornell University, around 27 percent of Americans report being estranged from a family member, meaning they are not speaking to them. This data is based on a large-scale survey of American adults. This means roughly one in four Americans are not speaking to a family member. Family issues are complicated enough as they are, but when we add the dynamics of a family business and money, we have now poured kerosene on an already-flaming fire.

A business founder, while anxious to turn the reins over to their children, in the back of their mind may think that only they are truly capable of taking this company where it needs to go. They're the founder after all.

At the same time, many adult children have dreamed of being their parents for their entire lives. Imprinting is real. We see it clearly in ducks. Our children are no different — the same imprinting occurs. The only difference is, these baby ducks stay around for a long time. They might not fly off and build their own nests; sometimes they have known the nest they are going to for their entire lives.

Even when we don't think we are teaching or imprinting, our children are in the back seat. They are listening and watching our every move. As life has gone on and I've heard my children repeat some of my sayings, I am dumbfounded. They were listening all along. The more successful your business, the more drawn your children will be to it.

Many of us watched the HBO show *Succession*. It was a drama based on Rupert Murdoch and his dysfunctional life and dysfunctional children. That TV show illustrated everything that was possible in a family business. Even one as big and convoluted as Fox.

The truth of the matter is that at the end of the day, we evolved from monkeys, and much of our behavior is monkeylike. A Netflix series that I watched with great wonder was titled *Chimp Empire*. If you haven't seen it, watch it. It is fascinating. This tribe of chimps has the same issues and desires that we have as people. There is a pecking order. There is a leader. There are fights for dominance throughout the chimp's life.

In *Chimp Empire*, if we didn't know better, we would be watching ourselves. Ultimately, one of these baby chimps had long seen himself as the leader of the clan. When and for how long is anyone's guess. But these chimps behave like we do, except they do it in the jungle and not in cities throughout the world.

Avoiding Tomorrow's Bad Luck Today

One of the things I have witnessed with my own children and their friends is that much of their bad luck that comes later in life could have been avoided by the parents early on. I was always aghast when I would see children drive up to high school in a brand-new Mercedes or BMW. First of all, most early drivers are going to have a wreck or two. Most importantly, you are fulfilling an unwanted prophecy, and that is, the children of affluent people become entitled. I think parents ruin their children by giving them new cars. It is also my feeling that, yes, they do it to feel good about what they can do for their children. However, I think the real reason they do it is so they can show their friends and colleagues how well they are doing and that they can afford a new BMW or Mercedes for their sixteen-year-old child. It is a surefire way to start looking for bad luck in the future.

None of my children ever had a new car in the beginning. They all drove old SUV clunkers. I know that most cars are wrecked by first-time drivers. My thought was, "Let's let these big tanks take the licks until they're prepared." None of my children had a new car in high school. The first new car we bought for them was when they went to college, and that was for the warranty, primarily. I told my children that I would buy them one final new car once they graduated from grad school, if that was their life's path. They each had a new car to last them seven years.

Once at Christmastime, our family was sitting around the table discussing the Christmas break. I asked my two older boys, who were sixteen and fourteen at the time, when they planned to go to work. Fortunately for them, or unfortunately, I owned an attraction, WonderWorks, that needed young people all day long as attendants and ticket takers. When I asked my boys when they planned to go work, my oldest son, Mike, stated, "Nobody at our school is working this Christmas." Immediately my second son, Matthew, said Mike was absolutely correct. No one at their school was working. I told them that I knew that not to be true. They both bellowed at once that it was true, and my response was: "I know some people are working who go to your school because you two m-effers will be working. And the good news for you is that you can work eight-to-five, twelve-to-nine, or five-to-two. But you boys are working forty hours a week during Christmas." They were very unhappy, but they worked their forty hours.

It is my personal belief that many parents ruin their children by coddling them early and never stopping for the rest of their lives. We have all heard of helicopter parents. There has been a proliferation of helicopter parents. I can't tell you how many times a parent has called me for their adult child asking for a job in one of my businesses. Hotels, attractions, ad agency, real estate endeavors, and law firms. Here is what I want everyone to know: as soon as a parent calls me asking me for a job for their child, that child will not be hired. I do not want any children working for me who were raised by helicopter parents—children who can't make their own phone calls. The parent's call to me tells me all I need to know about that candidate.

Not Everyone Should Be a Pitcher

On the other hand, I have written thousands of letters of recommendation for my friends' children. A letter of recommendation gives a young person a leg up in a competition for a job—it's not asking for the job itself. Similarly, I have made calls to college deans and admission officers for my friends' children. I will do anything to help young adults be more marketable and more self-sufficient. But what I won't do is hand them jobs they didn't earn. This is destructive behavior, which is a constant with the helicopter parent.

So whatever your business may be, we are all faced with that huge decision as to what to do with our children and our own business. Our love for our children and our plan throughout life is overwhelming. But here's the simple truth: some children should not pitch for their little league team. Some children should not be quarterback for their Pop Warner team. They should not get any position they didn't earn. Yet, time and time again, these baseball and football dads make the same mistake. They put their kid in a position that they have no business being in. The same thing happens in business, and that is when their good luck starts to turn into bad luck. That unqualified child can sink a company, destroy a family and, like our friends' son mentioned in this chapter, leave and is never to be heard from again.

Before I conclude this chapter let me give you some eye-opening statistics.

The Key Reasons Family Succession Fails

Adult children can ruin family businesses when they lack the work ethic, commitment, or necessary skills to manage the company effectively. All these factors often lead to poor decision making, financial mismanagement, internal conflicts, and a decline in business performance. This is especially true if they feel entitled to the inheritance without putting in the necessary effort. These difficulties can be exasperated by lack of clear succession planning or poor communication within the family regarding business expectations.

There are key reasons why adult children might damage a family business:

1. LACK OF BUSINESS ACUMEN. Not having the required business knowledge or experience to make sound decisions, leading to strategic errors and missed opportunities.

2. ENTITLED ATTITUDE. Feeling that they are automatically entitled to a leadership role without proving their competence, leading to complacency and poor work ethic.

3. INTERNAL CONFLICTS. These can include sibling rivalry or disagreements over business direction, which can create tension and undermine collaboration.

4. POOR FINANCIAL MANAGEMENT. Mismanaging finances, excessive spending, or neglecting important financial controls.

5. LACK OF PASSION FOR THE BUSINESS. Not being genuinely invested in the family business, prioritizing personal interests over company goals, or being interested in different career choices that the parent business owner did not approve of or support.

6. FAILURE TO ADAPT TO CHANGE. Resistance to updating business practices or adopting new technologies, leading to stagnation and a loss of market share.

7. UNREALIZED EXPECTATIONS. Having unrealistic expectations about the ease of running a business, leading to disappointment and frustration when faced with challenges.

Those are all factors, but the one I have seen the most is entitlement. It's that kid that grows up, like Spaulding in the movie *Caddyshack*, and is just a spoiled rotten piece of shit. This kind of person is the most dangerous heir to take control. They have never understood what it took to get the business to be successful and have lived a luxurious life along the way.

One of the things that I have known about myself for a long time is that I am not that smart. But I am smart enough to know it, and most importantly, smart enough to find people who are smarter than me. I surround myself with smart people and I run my businesses by consensus. I want to hear what everybody has to say. Then I want a digest it, remember who said what and why, then make my final decision.

My Succession Story

My children had no interest in my attractions, businesses, real estate, or any other business endeavors other than the law. All three of my sons decided to go to law school. I took that as a great compliment to me and their mother, because they had seen our life and it must have looked good to them. The danger was how to assimilate them into the firm.

I have been very lucky that my children are very, very smart and very, very different. While I'm not academically smart, my wife is. She was a National Merit Finalist, Phi Beta Kappa, and basically made straight A's her whole life. I, on the other hand, have been hanging on for dear life. Fortunately, those brain genetics were passed to my three sons and my daughter. My sons and daughter are extremely capable.

Inside my firm though, I first appointed a COO who did remarkable things in his tenure with the firm. He built everything I dreamed of building. He built systems and structures that I had no chance of building, because I was not that type of smart. I just knew what I wanted, and he built it. We are forever grateful.

Today my children have big roles in the firm, but they are not necessarily the titular leaders. I have a CEO who has been with me for almost thirty years. I appointed two COOs who run different parts of the law firm. The law firm is big business. In 2024, we did $2 billion in total fees and settled or resolved $5 billion worth of matters.

Inside of my firm, each one of my children has a very specific and vital role.

- The engine of our firm is run by our personal injury practice, and that is our son, Matt's, domain. Like his mother, he has OCD and is constantly looking to get better and better.
- Our son, Mike, is a critical thinker and heads up our mass tort, class-action, and products liability sections. These cases are very complicated and very expensive.

- Our son, Daniel, is a connector. He is a combination of Matt and Mike. He may be most like me of all our four children. In his role, he establishes relationships with law firms all over the country and is heavily involved in our social media presence and the making of ads.
- Our daughter owns a structured settlement company, which does great work for our firm.

Each one of my children has a vital role in the firm, which keeps them extremely busy. Fortunately for me, the two COOs I chose are very good friends with my children. While I must admit there have been rough patches along the way, as I write this book, the rough seas are now calm seas. For now, my family business is sailing along smoothly.

I am very fortunate in many ways because I get to work with these four people, whom I love the most in the world, every single day for the rest of my life. I am at a point in life where most people are retiring or thinking about retiring. I certainly think about retiring all the time. The way I look at it now is I am fighting the war at 36,000 feet instead of in the trenches in Afghanistan. Luckily for me, I have spent years on succession planning, and I have layers of leaders who are responsible, specifically, for many different things. If everyone is accountable, no one is accountable.

My law firm has over 6,000 employees and 1,000 lawyers who rely on their jobs. I could have played favorites with my children and potentially destroyed my business in the process. Instead, I decided to be direct and forthright and to plan like hell for succession. Failure to do so could result in a total loss of business.

And one final thought. While second generations can prove to be the death of your business, problems of succession can become even worse for the third generation. Now please understand, there is no person in this world that loves their grandchildren more than Ultima and I love our six and counting. They are all we think about. But I am also a realist, I look at statistics, and I believe that the past is the best predictor of the future. It makes me sad to think that these grandchildren could one day be a real source of problems for our family and family business. Whatever might happen, I won't be here to see it, but their parents will.

There is no magic formula or magic wand for succession, or the failure or success of business. There are things we can do to improve our chances of good luck and even continue our family's business long after we have left this world.

CHAPTER 35

WHEN TO SELL OR CLOSE

Of all of Kenny Rogers's songs, I believe the most memorable one was "The Gambler." It speaks to all of us but in different ways. It can be about love, business, life, or any other situation where you find yourself at a crossroads.

The money line in the song is one I'm sure you know by heart. "You've got to know when to hold 'em… Know when to fold 'em… Know when to walk away… And know when to run…" It is a perfect song to give thought to your own succession, and that succession may well be the sale of your business.

My brother, Mike, is a dentist and a very good dentist, I might add. Mike worked his ass off. He would get up and go to the jail on many mornings to do extractions and made an extra $100,000 a year. Then he would go to work. Most dentists make good money, but Mike made great money for a dentist. Around $800,000 a year.

Like many people, Mike had the No. 1 net-worth slasher come his way: divorce. The easiest way to see your net worth plummet is when you get divorced and have to pay alimony. It is a wealth destroyer.

Mike chose poorly when he got married—his wife was a spender. She had drawers full of watches and eyeglasses. She would wake up and buy a car on a whim. She had an addictive personality and was in and out of AA. She replaced her alcohol addiction with a shopping addiction. She just blew money.

Later, when she and Mike divorced, she was awarded $15,000 a month in alimony and child support. She remained unmarried for quite a few years, but finally an older guy came along and married her. Mike was ecstatic. He had just saved himself $180,000 a year. Mike was so grateful to the old man that he did his teeth for free and has no trouble playing golf with him. It was one of the great business deals of Mike's life.

So as Mike approached retirement age, he had fought off a free-spending wife and years of alimony, but he was still basically okay, but not totally. He sold his practice to get his final number. And it worked out great for Mike, but not as well as it could have if he'd chosen his spouse more carefully.

The reason I bring the story of Mike up is because there are so many successful businesspeople in the world who ultimately finish their career and run of good luck with a whimper. They simply close the door and walk away with nothing in their pocket. A lifetime of building a great business and they get nothing for it. So let's talk about how you get your final piece of luck and perhaps the cherry on top of a life of good fortune.

Bring in a Trainee for Yourself

This first solution—bring in a young trainee to teach—seems simple, but it's not. The founder at some point needs to bring in young blood who can learn the business, run the business and, ultimately, buy the business. That is the perfect way to do it. The problem comes when the founder really doesn't want to sell anytime soon and drags their young buck along until the young buck just leaves. I've seen two or three young potential trainees/buyers dragged through businesses only to leave later.

If you're not serious about this plan, don't try it. You will have bad feelings from your young trainee/buyer who will feel, rightfully, used. However, if you're serious and dealing in good faith, bringing in someone early to time your retirement is the perfect way to do it. This training and sales period shouldn't be too long. People who are ready to buy a business are ready to run a business… yesterday. Don't do one of these "In ten years, it will all be yours." It needs to be a window of two or three years. And it needs to be in writing so that you can't string someone along. You need to go when it's time to go. Greed stops us from doing the right thing and usually costs us money in the long run.

Sell Your Business

The other solution is the solution my brother Mike used, and that is just to sell your business straight out. However, you need to sell it while it's on top. When people look at businesses, they are looking at trends. If your revenue and profit are declining year over year, that is a bad sign. You have to go out on top. I tell people all the time, when you tell a funny joke at a party, and everyone is dying laughing, get the fuck out right then and there. Leave them laughing and they will remember you. If you stay too long, they will remember you for totally different reasons.

Biology dictates our energy. When we were young, we believed we could work forever. Biology tells us we can't. Many times, the drive dies, even if you never thought it would. But it does. Most retirement is focused around the age of sixty-five, and that's a good number to plan around. If you decide that you are going to sell your practice or your business, think in advance and have your timing down pat. Remember, hope is not a plan. A plan is a plan.

According to the U.S. Chamber of Commerce, around 600,000 businesses close every year in America. However, the data doesn't specify whether they were sold or not. Sixty-five percent of all small businesses close within ten years. That means that 35 percent are in business for the long haul.

If you multiplied 30 percent times 600,000 that would come out to 180,000 businesses closed every year, without the owner receiving one red cent for their lifetime of work.

Preparation and Strategic Positioning

Many business owners face a critical issue when it's time to sell. The stark reality that 80 percent of businesses listed never find a buyer is a sobering statistic, highlighting the importance of preparation and strategic positioning. What most likely happens is people wait too long, they become tired, and their business is in a decline.

Doctors, lawyers, and CPAs often go out of business with a whimper. And it's such a waste, because had they planned properly, they would have received a final payday for a life of hard work and success.

If you don't start thinking about selling your business in your mid-fifties, your retirement age can sneak up on you in a second. Whether you find an industrious young person who wants to learn your business and then buy it from you, or you just sell it straight out, either option is fine. What option is not fine is to simply close your doors and get nothing for your life's work. Can you imagine if, at the end of your life, your house had no value? That is what is happening to your business. Except your business was probably worth more than your house at a certain point in time.

If you own a business, and you've had a successful run, start thinking and planning by age fifty-five. Here at the end, I would just like to put a few cherries on top of your sundae.

"You've got to know when to hold 'em… know when to fold 'em… know when to walk away…"

The amazing part about entrepreneurs is that we are all gamblers in many ways. We want to be the boss, and we don't want to work for others. When that is your mindset, you are a different breed.

To understand the gambler's mentality, let me give you some fun facts. According to Gallup data, roughly 64.2 percent of American workers work entirely for someone else, meaning they are employed by a company and are not the owner. Only 2.4 percent of working adults in the U.S. are considered "owner-employers" with their own business and employees. This indicates that the vast majority of Americans work for someone else rather than owning their own company. A large percentage of people in America work for federal, state, and local governments. Another slice of workers are self-employed, but they are the only employee. Very few of us own and operate our own businesses with employees, payroll and all that goes with it. Those are the gamblers with that gambler's mentality. But like all gamblers, some are reckless, some are cautious, and some are somewhere in between. But they are all gamblers, nonetheless.

The Shopify-Gallup Entrepreneurship study finds that most Americans share the desire to be their own boss. More than six in ten U.S. adults (62 percent) say that they would prefer to be their own boss, while 35 percent would prefer to work as an employee for someone else. While 62 percent want to be their own boss, it appears that, not counting the self-employed with no employees, only 2.4 percent of us are true entrepreneurs, true gamblers.

Hopefully, you will use this chapter as your final bridge to your final piece of good luck. And you will hire someone to train and ultimately buy your business, or you will plan far in advance to sell your business at the right time and not before it is deteriorating and on its way down.

If you're not going up, you're going down.

CHAPTER 36

FAILURE IS YOUR FRIEND

There is nothing more discouraging than to have a business fail or perform poorly. In my life, I have had a few failures of my own. The small amusement park that I built, Magical Midway, performed poorly because while I had a great location, I made the mistake of not paying attention to parking. That's a mistake I will never make again. The bars and restaurants I have been involved in have taught me one valuable lesson: being successful with food and beverage is next to impossible unless you are a gigantic chain or an owner who never leaves the shop.

My Second-Time Story

Because I am an entrepreneurial junkie, I have dipped my toe back into the food and beverage business. But I only did so understanding everything I learned in my past failed endeavors.

- I learned that location was everything.
- I learned that competition was fierce.
- I learned that labor was next to impossible to find.
- I learned that turnover in labor was rampant.
- I learned so much that I'm surprised I ever did get back in the food-and-beverage business. But I did.

Learning From the Past

I have a friend by the name of George Miliotis. George has been in the restaurant business his entire life. His father had great restaurants all over Orlando and a location in a mall called Mr. Dunderbak's, which was a fantastic delicatessen. George had a lot of successes along the way.

He converted the Top of the World Lounge at the Contemporary Resort in Walt Disney World into the California Grill. It became one of the best restaurants in America. After his success there, Darden Restaurants recruited him to build a concept for them. He did so, and it was called Seasons 52. George also became the wine expert for all of Darden.

There are very few grand sommeliers in the world with his level of expertise. He is one of ten. Because of his success at Disney and then at Darden, years later, Disney approached George about building a concept at Disney Springs in Orlando. Disney Springs sees about 32 million people on foot every year. It has a parking structure that can hold as many cars as you need. From my past failures, I was particularly interested in foot traffic and parking. This was not just a good location—this was a great location. Our rent was based on a percentage of our sales. So Disney took the ride with us. All the lessons I learned from my past failures came into play in my decision making here.

It had a great location. Great parking. And one of the best operators in the business. To make it even better, George was going to be putting the lion's share of the money in and I was placing a minority share with him.

I'm happy to report that, at this writing, I have recouped all my money, made a nice return on it, and I have an operating restaurant in one of the best locations in the entire world. George was so successful that we opened another spot in the Orlando International Airport. In case you are ever in Orlando and want to have one of the greatest wine experiences of your life, visit Wine Bar George located at Disney

Springs. If you're passing through in the airport, have a glass of wine. Toast me, and I'll toast you back. One of the ways that I look to have an edge in finding luck is to partner with the right person. As I say all the time when I go to the horse races to see my horses run, "I never bet on the horse, I always bet on the jockey." George Miliotis turned out to be an even better jockey than I dreamed of.

Because I am in the entertainment business, I get to meet a lot of people in that same space. Remember the concept of "Never eat alone?" Well, as I'm out and about, I have met many different people along the way. One such person lured me back into the food business, despite my grave reservations. Bucky Mabe is a young man whose business and family business has been in arcades. He knows more about arcades than anyone I know. Throughout my time, I got to know him and picked his brain for the small arcades I kept in my attractions. Because I never eat alone and because I spent time with Bucky, one day he came to me with his grand idea.

He pointed out that Dave & Buster's is a company that does very well. Dave & Buster's has virtually no competition and recently bought out their only competitor—a chain called Main Event. They have a monopoly on that entertainment concept. Bucky's idea was simple. Let's build a huge food-and-entertainment venue, but instead of having mediocre food, let's have great food. Let's get a great food person the world knows about.

As a result of Bucky's vision, I was introduced to Guy Fieri from the Food Channel and the show *Diners, Drive-Ins, and Dives*. The concept was basically this: Dave & Buster's meets Guy Fieri, who meets the arcade guru, who meets me, a person involved in the entertainment business. The end result was our concept that is known as Downtown Flavortown.

It is 60,000 square feet and located in one of the great locations in Pigeon Forge, Tennessee (home of Dolly Parton's Dollywood). I already had two attractions in Pigeon Forge, so I knew the area. Parking was unlimited right next to a great location known as The Island.

Even though I had those failures and some not-so-great bars, those past failures taught me what I didn't want to do and what I definitely wanted to do. I had two jockeys that I decided to bet on: Guy Fieri and Bucky Mabe. We had a great location with great parking found in a tourist town that stays busy virtually all year long. Our location is far superior to Dave & Buster's.

The short story is, that concept has done very well. In 2024, we grossed $18 million, which is huge for a restaurant. Our margins are great because we have a lot of booze and arcade revenue. Those two revenue sources are almost pure profit.

With this concept launched and validated, we have now decided to start rolling these out in a big way. Recently, Bucky and I bought an old mall in Myrtle Beach, South Carolina, and are in the process of turning it into an entertainment complex, as well as our second Downtown Flavortown. As I write this book, we are converting an old JCPenney into our second flagship store. Myrtle Beach is a tremendous tourist town, and I have one of the top-producing Bass Pro Shops in America as one of my out-parcels (a building lot separated from a commercial development). The location is a 10. And it just got better because of the roads that have been diverted toward my mall.

The success I have so far enjoyed with Wine Bar George and Downtown Flavortown came on the heels of some minor losses and some minor ventures. The lessons I learned before were helpful today.

My family recently bought an interest in a bar concept in Key West known as Hog's Breath. My good friend, Jim Gissy, the CEO of Westgate Resorts, was kind enough to offer me a piece of that deal. Hog's Breath is iconic in Key West, and we believe the intellectual property has value as well. It has the greatest location you can imagine on Duval Street, the main street through Key West. And here's the truth: people go to Key West to get drunk and have a good time. You have to go right through Hog's Breath to do that.

What to Do With Business Failure

Failure for most business owners is the end of the line for many reasons. The most obvious reason is that they shot their wad on business No. 1 and don't have the capital to do it again. The other reason is, it's traumatic to have a business fail. You thought you had the greatest idea in the world and were going to be building something that was going to be great, and it turned out that all of your instincts and decisions were dead wrong. *You lost your ass!* That experience is devastating. Have you ever been dating someone, and they dropped you out of the blue? Or have you ever been fired from your job, and you never saw it coming? It is that feeling. It's helplessness that you have never experienced before, and it comes with a lot of baggage. Bank debt. Loss of investment capital. Humiliation. And a real wake-up call to yourself, which is, "Am I just a failure?"

Because of those issues, most people never use failure as a friend to rebuild and start anew. If this is you, rebuilding and starting again, you can use the most valuable asset you have—your own experience—which is a roadmap to success. When you set off on your first business, you have no roadmap. You are blindly running and driving through a dense forest. Left turns. Right turns. U-turns. The good thing about that exercise is when you decide to go back through that forest for a second time, you know where you are going. You know where the ditches are. You know where the cliffs are. You know where the dangerous animals live. Every single mistake and turn you made last time, you now understand and know by heart. You have tied yellow ribbons on all the trees, which will guide you on your second venture.

However, the searing memory of failure and all it brought to you and your family is hard to forget. I was recently having lunch with a high school friend who has taken a chance on a business that disinfects airplanes and emergency vehicles. I think he is really onto something. But he's been struggling for the last fourteen years. Every time he almost fails, somehow he finds a lifeline. He told me at lunch that his wife once said after losing their house, "We are never going to risk our house again." Think of that. Losing your home for your grand plan. You have to be a real gambler to do that, and you really have to believe in yourself.

I believe that, ultimately, he is going to be successful, and I believe that his family is going to benefit from all of his efforts. There is no quit in my high school friend.

But his business is different, he's still alive and in business. The question for all of us is, how do we handle failure when we are looking at it square in the face? It's really hard to start anew.

You have probably heard it said that "Failure is the mother of success." It is a proverb that means setbacks and mistakes can be valuable learning experiences, providing crucial insights to eventually achieving success. Essentially, failure is a necessary step on the path to achievement, allowing us to adapt and improve from our mistakes.

This proverb is often attributed to ancient Chinese culture. By embracing failure as a teacher, we can analyze what went wrong and use that knowledge to make better decisions in the future. This phrase encourages perseverance and a resilient attitude toward challenges, viewing setbacks as opportunities for growth. Remember, you can only have luck if you are looking for opportunities. Nothing in the rulebook says you can't look for opportunities in the rubble of a failed business. That's where some of the best opportunities live.

There is not one successful person who at some time in their life has not experienced failure. Successful people learn from their mistakes. It's part of what makes them successful. The least successful person is the one who doesn't recognize when they have failed.

There are many ways that we find success through failure.

1. LEARNING FROM MISTAKES. Analyzing what went wrong in a failure helps identify areas for improvement and allows us to make better decisions in the future.

2. DEVELOPING RESILIENCE. Overcoming failure builds mental toughness and the ability to bounce back from setbacks, which is crucial for achieving long-term success.

3. **PROMOTING ADAPTATION.** When faced with failure, we are often forced to adapt our strategies and try new approaches, leading to more creative solutions.

4. **SHARPER CRITICAL THINKING.** Reflecting on failures encourages deeper analysis and critical-thinking skills, allowing for better decision making in the future.

5. **INCREASED MOTIVATION.** The desire to avoid repeating past mistakes and full motivation to work harder and strive for better outcomes.

6. **IDENTIFYING POTENTIAL WEAKNESSES.** Failure can expose areas where improvement is needed, allowing us to focus on developing necessary skills.

7. **BUILDING CONFIDENCE THROUGH PERSEVERANCE.** Successfully overcoming challenges after experiencing failure can boost self-confidence and belief in our abilities.

FAMOUS EXAMPLES

Some people who famously experienced setbacks are as follows, but these are only a few. The list is endless.

- Thomas Edison famously failed thousands of times before successfully developing the incandescent light bulb, using each failed attempt to learn and improve his design.

- J.K. Rowling's first *Harry Potter* manuscript was rejected by multiple publishers before finally finding a home, demonstrating the power of perseverance in the face of rejection.

- Despite numerous missed shots and setbacks, Michael Jordan is considered one of the greatest basketball players due to his dedication to learning from failures and improving his game. He was cut from his varsity team early in his career.

The real lesson here is that when you are looking for luck, you are looking for opportunities. The best opportunities that may be staring you right in the face are the ideas and ventures you once traveled into but hit a brick wall, for a variety of reasons. The good news now is that you know how not to hit that brick wall. You know when to turn left, when to turn right, and when to turn around. The lessons in failure give us the best chance of not only good luck but great luck.

Applying the Lessons of Loss

In my home state of Florida, I made the decision to conduct a ballot initiative to legalize medical marijuana in Florida. I spent a small fortune, but the ballot initiative failed. You need 60 percent of the vote to win. I got like 58 percent.

When that effort was over, I was upset because I had spent tens of millions of my own money; but most importantly, I had lost. The taste of that loss would not leave me. Then I decided to start looking at my failure and the reasons why. I learned a lot in that failure.

From my loss I learned these things:

- I should've done it during a presidential election when voter turnout was greater.
- I should've been more forceful in pushing back against the opposition.
- I understood that on the second go-round, I really needed to barnstorm the state to make this happen.

I took all those mistakes and lessons and did it again. The second time around, it was successful, garnering 72 percent of the vote, which was a landslide.

Had I decided to stop, there would not be medical marijuana in Florida today. If I had decided to stop, one million Floridians would not have access to this miracle herb that my brother, Tim, swore by. For me, I called it political philanthropy. Yes, I was spending millions of dollars of my own money; but if it passed, I would have done so much good for so many people in ways I could never have afforded myself. So today Florida has medical marijuana for all who need it.

The cherry on top was when I decided that after I'd learned so much in the medical-marijuana fight, I had one final gift to give Florida. The minimum wage was $8 an hour. I took my playbook from medical marijuana and launched my third ballot initiative to raise the minimum wage to $15 an hour. Everyone said I was crazy. Everyone said I would fail. But with those lessons from before, I prevailed and won. Today the minimum wage in Florida is $15 an hour. It came courtesy of my failures in my first attempt at medical marijuana. Failure was not only my friend, but the friend to millions of Floridians who benefited from this political philanthropy.

In the next chapter I'll explain my greatest risk that rose from the ashes of failure.

CHAPTER 37

MOONSHOTS

Much of this book thus far has dealt with the act of looking for opportunities, where luck resides, and finding ways to enhance our luck along the way. Certain games and certain businesses have a better chance of winning. We discussed that in our section on casinos and lotteries. However, there are certain businesses that are what I call "moonshots"—dreams so big that they actually seem impossible.

I remember as a little boy listening to the soundtrack of *Man of La Mancha*. The theme song was titled "The Impossible Dream." For some reason I loved that song then and I love that song now. Whenever you are dreaming, play it on your iPhone. It is inspiring.

Most of our visions and dreams actually seem possible. A restaurant seems possible. Certain retail stores seem possible. Other businesses seem to some of us doomed to fail before they open. Remember Mickey Moo?

The "Bullets Before Bombs" Rule

My rule of thumb in all businesses has been *bullets before bombs*. In other words, start small. If the bullets seem to be hitting the target, then and only then do you unleash the bombs. Before you open up multiple concepts, do one. Proof of concept will tell you a lot about going forward. The first thing it tells you is whether you have a bust on your hands or not. With a bad business, you'll know fairly quickly that you have had a miss.

Before we open our business, we do a lot of back-and-forth, worrying, and wringing of hands before going forward. One thing is certain about any business you may start: If you need to be 100 percent sure that you have a surefire winner, then you will never open up any business. It is impossible to be 100 percent. If you are 100 percent, you are bound to fail, because you are delusional, have no fear, and have no guardrails. Being 100 percent certain is a guaranteed recipe for disaster. No matter what, all of us who go into business have to take the leap, and usually with some trepidation. The saddest business owners are the ones who go broke quick but thought they had the next best thing. Often I will see new restaurants pop up in old fast-food locations, and rarely have I ever seen it work. When those folks were opening up though, they believed they had the next McDonald's. Dreaming is part of who we are as human beings.

As we go out looking for our next great thing, there are many obstacles in the way and many hurdles to clear.

- Plan on bullets before bombs — start small.
- Work on your proof of concept first.
- Are you properly capitalized?
- Location, location, location.
- Is your business partner one who adds or subtracts from the venture?

Take all of these factors into consideration before you launch that business. When you do launch that business, it is your firm belief that you are going to be successful, even though you know statistically that most will fail. Just like there are 50 percent divorces in first marriages, 65 percent of all small businesses fail within ten years. But that entrepreneurial spirit and that desire and hope pushes you onward. Those businesses that I'm talking about above are just regular run-of-the-mill businesses. Dentists. Pharmacies. Real estate brokerages. Food and lodging. Repair. Retail. And so on. Basically, the type of businesses that run America.

The Moonshot

And then there comes another type of business. It's a business that I call *the moonshot*. A moonshot is so risky and so bold that you really don't have the opportunity to do things like bullets before bombs or rely on your own past failures. While past failures may help a little, a moonshot is one for the ages.

Many times, I hear people say, "The sky's the limit." Every time I hear that, I think they are wrong. The sky is not the limit. The sky is just the beginning. Once the rocket pierces through the sky and into the galaxy, it becomes unlimited. The planets, the sun, the moon, and all of the stars are still waiting to be explored. The sky is not the limit. The sky is the beginning of a shot to the moon.

Moonshots are not hard to define. A moonshot is when you go all in, and in a big way—pushing all your chips and investors' chips into one spin, on red. If you win, the win is staggering. If you lose, you lose quickly. When a rocket heading to the moon bursts into flames, there is no saving it.

I was having lunch the day the *Challenger* broke apart. We were inside a tavern having a sandwich and watching it on TV. I was with my friend, Jim Robinson, whom I had sold Yellow Pages with years before. When the rocket ship cracked up on TV, we stepped outside into the parking lot. In Florida, you can be standing in Orlando and see the rocket ships take off. It is a glorious sight and makes you so proud to be an American.

Just a few minutes before, we stood in the parking lot and watched the rocket take off, and we went inside as it was disappearing. A few short minutes later, we were back in the parking lot watching the rocket fall to the ground. When a moonshot fails, it is not forgiving. There are usually no survivors in a moonshot failure.

The Problem With Sexy

With that said, there are entrepreneurs who take moonshots on a regular basis—some with their own money and some with other people's money—but moonshots, nonetheless. Recently both Kevin Costner and Francis Ford Coppola each risked $100 million of their own money to make movies. Two separate movies and two separate disasters. These two icons, who seem to never miss, missed badly in the twilight of their careers.

Now the good thing about failing at this age is neither will be missing any meals or evicted from their homes. I don't care who you are, losing $100 million hurts. You have to make $150 million to keep $100 million. At least they may get some tax breaks with the write-off.

In the business world, people take moonshots every day. There may not be a more risky business in the world than making movies and producing Broadway plays. Graveyards are full of these disasters.

Schuyler Moore, in *Forbes* magazine, wrote:

> *Most films lose money. Indeed, 80 percent do. The fundamental reason for this phenomenon is simple. If you were trying to impress someone at a cocktail party, what would you rather say: 'I make movies' or 'I make widgets'? Face it, the film industry is sexy. Even if not of the direct ilk (a non-infrequent motivation), most people who produce films are driven by the conscious or subconscious sexiness of the industry. The law of supply and demand takes it from there. For example, there is a wild oversupply of film productions—approximately 600 to 700 per year—while only 200 or so obtain even a decent release, permitting any return at all, much less a profit.*

So why do people make movies? It's sexy and their ego drives them there. Remember one of my golden rules is, "You can't eat ego."

Broadway plays aren't much better.

According to most industry reports, only 20 percent of Broadway shows recoup their investment, meaning that the "success rate" for a

Broadway play is roughly one in five shows. This means that while a few shows can become major hits and run for years, the majority struggle to cover their production costs and turn a profit. Even a moderately successful run might not be enough to recoup expenses.

But there are people who are enamored with the film and Broadway industries, and even though they know full well that their moonshot will likely end in disaster, they climb in, strap in, take off, and go hurling into the galaxy. The results are fairly predictable.

My Own Moonshot

My moonshot came to be in the mid-1990s. I got married in 1982, and by 1995, we had four children. As a result, we were doing everything for our kids. Zoos. Theme parks. Anything to make them smile and learn. Obviously, going to the science center from time to time was also on our agenda.

At the same time, I had been dabbling with an old friend in fair business. He managed some fairs around America, and I helped him get a new fair that we owned together in Lexington — The Bluegrass Fair at the Red Mile. Consequently, I was spending some time on fairgrounds. One of our exhibitors had a huge tent. And in the tent, he had all sorts of interactive games, experiments, and even science projects. They were larger-than-life, and people could not get enough of these simple exhibits.

I made a note to myself that night. At the same time, when I would take my children to any science center, it was just boring as all get-out. Science centers, for the most part, suck. I began to think, what would it be like to have a great science center with interactive exhibits, and build it in a facility that was like a children's nightclub?

I shared that thought with several people, including a guy by the name of Barry Frank. Barry had been involved in *Ripley's Believe It or Not* and had some renderings of ideas from *Ripley's*. One day, Barry came to my office with a huge cardboard painting of a gigantic mansion turned upside down. The idea was to build the house, which looked like the White House, upside down, and have people enter onto the ceiling. It was the most fantastic rendering I had ever seen in my life. I knew when I saw it that I wanted to do it.

I then had to inquire as to how we would go about building it. Remember, I know nothing about construction. Over time, I became convinced, and I don't know why, that I could build this structure. Looking back on it now at my age, I wonder what in the hell I was thinking. I would never do that today. Youth gives us way more courage than we should have, and all of us are a little crazier in our younger days.

Once I became sold on the building, I had to find the location. I looked and I looked, and at the end of the day, there was only one site that I would have taken. A shopping center called The Point was being built on International Drive in Orlando, right next to the convention center. This area of International Drive had not taken off yet, but it was sure to. Or at least, as sure as I could figure.

The problem was that the outparcel the developers wanted to lease was prime real estate, and they had been in heavy negotiations with *Ripley's Believe It or Not* to build a *Guinness Book of Records* there. Jim Pattison is the richest man in Canada, and he owns all of *Ripley's* and *Guinness Book of Records*. So I didn't think I had a chance.

One day, the developers called me and said if I made a deposit for $250,000, the site was mine and that *Ripley's* was moving too slowly. I drove back out to the site one last time. Drove my car up onto the grass and looked both ways. There was nothing there, but I could see what could be. I barely had $250,000 in 1995, but I went home, put the money together, and wired it to their bank in Canada. My moonshot had begun and there was no turning back.

I won't bore you with all the details of what went on into building this, I'll only share a little. I spent about a year traveling the country visiting science centers and finding the latest and greatest. I saw things that were a wow, then I built them two to three times the size because not only did I want the participant to enjoy the experience, I wanted the parents watching to enjoy the experience. I wanted exhibits that adults would enjoy too. At the end of the day, adults are just big kids.

I searched the world over for the exhibits to put in the attraction. I had a great architect design it, but I made a terrible mistake by doing what is known as a design build, which is sure to cost extra money. Why? Because I was at the mercy of the construction company and all the change orders that would soon follow. Change orders are the worst words in my vocabulary. It is a way I got cheated by my builder. In any event, I built WonderWorks and it opened in March 1997. Half of the exhibits didn't work. The earthquake simulator caught on fire the very first night. A lot of my inside theming had not been done. In short, I thought that I might go out of business very quickly because I certainly had no money in reserve.

But a miraculous thing happened. Because I had a great location attached to a parking garage that was done, I wanted to build the building to draw the moths to the flame. While building it, I kept saying, "We cannot flinch on the outside." The outside would make people want to come and pay on the inside. And that first year, I made enough money to pay for my cost overruns and some much-needed theming.

Now for the very short story. Today I have six WonderWorks locations in America and have bought out most of those early partners along the way. Today WonderWorks has an EBITDA (earnings before interest, taxes, depreciation, and amortization) of $33 million a year and no debt. The enterprise is valued at between $250 million and $300 million.

Moonshots Come With Their Share of Luck

This moonshot that I took decades ago turned out to be a winner. When I think of all the problems I've had along the way with that business, I know that I got my share of luck here. People have asked me how I had the time to build these attractions, build these hotels, build these shopping centers, and ad agencies, and billboard companies, and on and on and on. I'll tell you how. I don't fish, hunt, or golf.

I don't see the point in fishing. The only person that seems to be having fun is the guy driving the boat. I sit in the back being splashed and getting ocean water in my cocktail. I also don't like the idea of catching a fish and ripping its mouth open or tearing its eye out and then humanely throwing it back into the water. There is nothing humane about it to me. Don't get me wrong, I eat fish, but I don't want to be part of catching fish.

I don't hunt. Once, in college, I went hunting and they put me in a deer stand. While I was standing up in that deer stand at five in the morning freezing my ass off, I said to myself, "What the fuck am I doing up here? Even if a deer climbs up here, I'm not going to shoot it." To make matters worse, I don't even like the taste of venison. I can taste the fur and smell the fur. Also, I still have post-traumatic stress disorder over Bambi. So hunting is out.

Finally, golf is excluded as well. I played a little in high school and in college, but once my children came along, I didn't have the time and later in life decided against it. Why? When I see Tiger Woods hitting the ball into the water and into the woods, I don't want to play that game. It would be like watching Michael Jordan take a free-throw shot, but have it go off his right hand and into the stands — not under the basket, but at midcourt.

Because I didn't hunt, fish, or golf, my sport was business, making money, and taking the occasional moonshot. So all my endeavors to me were like hobbies. It was not money that drove me, it was the idea of having an idea that the masses would accept, adopt, and pay for. It's an incredible rush.

My Law Firm's Moonshot

I am on another moonshot in my law firm that I call the "Google law firm." The question for myself is, what would Google do if it were a law firm? My answer is that it would be everywhere for everyone and control a large amount of the cases in America. This is a moonshot that has hurled me far into the galaxy, and with lots of the risk associated with it.

However, so far, so good. Morgan & Morgan is the largest injury firm in the history of the world. In 2024, we settled or received verdicts for $5 billion and had fees of $2 billion. The Google law firm is still in its infancy as far as I'm concerned, and as we know about moonshots, the rockets can crack up at any given time without warning.

Forget the Sky— The Galaxy's the Limit

So while we want to do our very darnedest to enhance luck in every opportunity we go after, we also have to know that there are no guarantees in life other than paying taxes and death. (Or, if you own a hedge fund, you don't pay taxes either.)

I described a moonshot as one of my BHAGs (Big Hairy Audacious Goals) that we spoke about early on. There are goals and BHAGs. BHAGs are your moonshots, and you can only take them so often. Failure is more probable than not. But when you win with a moonshot, the sky is not the limit, the galaxy is.

CHAPTER 38

THE DECISION TO RELAUNCH

America is fascinated with crime and punishment. Just think of all the TV shows and movies you have seen involving cops and robbers. Network television is full of true-crime stories. Movies have been made for years about gangsters and the police. With that as my thinking, I had the occasion to visit Alcatraz in California. When I got to the gate, it was sold out for the next three days. When you flash a $100 bill in front of a ticket taker, you are usually able to buy the last two tickets. So we went in.

I was enthralled with Alcatraz and all that went with it. I was most enthralled about the fact that there was a three-day wait just to see an old prison. My mind began to churn.

I had never seen any museum dedicated to crime and punishment, but the world was fascinating. Then I got to work. I started researching artifacts and ideas for my new attraction. I wanted to have some interactive exhibits because they had done well at WonderWorks. But what I most wanted was to produce a class-A museum on the history of crime and punishment.

I started having these thoughts when I was visiting Washington, D.C., on a regular basis. After being a national finance chair for Bill Clinton's campaign and then on Barack Obama's, I had many invitations to parties at the White House and in D.C. I had a bird's-eye view of this incredible tourist town. When I worked at Walt Disney World years ago, one of my supervisors was a fantastic human being by the name of Paul Bosch. Paul was managing the Spy Museum in D.C. By all accounts, it was a great success, but I'd never looked under the hood.

Paul told me that their attendance was 700,000 people a year. My thought was, if I got half of that, I've hit a home run. So D.C. became foremost in my mind. When I said I never really got under the hood, I simply took Paul's word that was his attendance. So I became fixated on opening an attraction in the nation's capital.

However, in D.C., there were so many free attractions, and most guest's stays were far less than in typical tourist towns. I worried about both of those things. Yet the success of the Spy Museum kept coming back to me. Ultimately, I negotiated a lease in a building across the street from the National Portrait Museum, and I went full bore into building what I called the National Museum of Crime and Punishment. I wanted to make it like a D.C. museum.

Shooting for the Moon

This undertaking would be classified as a moonshot. I had no proof concept and really no market studies that were worth a hill of beans. I had my gut instinct, the Spy Museum, and a city brimming with tourists.

I began the process of gathering artifacts and pieces for my museum. I had met John Walsh, the host of *America's Most Wanted*, once on a plane ride to California. We actually bonded over Ambien. I took one on the ride out and gave one to him. We both woke up when we landed at LAX.

Later, I called his executive producer, Lance Heflin, and pitched the idea of filming *America's Most Wanted* in the National Museum of Crime and Punishment. To make a long story short, they loved the idea, and we built a full television studio in the basement. Additionally, I collected my artifacts and built a CSI laboratory. Before it was over, the museum was a masterpiece. I had Ted Bundy's VW, John Dillinger's sedan, the

Bonnie and Clyde death car, and OJ's Bronco. Those were the grand finale, and the time it took to go through museum was about three and a half hours. A true value.

Unlike my other attractions where I built fantastic buildings that lured tourists in, D.C. is impossible to deal with. No theming was allowed on the building, and I couldn't even put footprints on the sidewalk leading into the building. It is not a very friendly city for outside tourism.

Because this was going to be a moonshot, I decided that I would raise money from former investors. With any moonshot, you have to understand that you might lose all of your money, and all of your investors' money. I decided to hedge my bet by including investors in this project. Of course, I put the most money into the deal, because it was important, I felt, for my investors to know that if they lost, I lost the most.

I raised the money, put my money in, and launched my moonshot. We opened up to great fanfare, with the great rooftop party. That was the last fun day for that business.

Failure to Launch

I found out that a lot of my assumptions may have been wrong. To this day, I wonder if the Spy Museum really had 700,000 paid visitors. Madame Tussauds opened up after us and was an abject failure. All the free attractions in D.C. sucked the oxygen out of the paid attractions.

Without theming, we were just an office building in the middle of the city. I had made almost every mistake known to man. However, the attraction itself was a masterpiece. It was the best work I had ever done.

The attraction continued to limp along, paying its rent and very little else. At some point, the building notified me that my attraction was not doing the numbers they had hoped for and that the lease had a provision to terminate my lease should we not reach those thresholds. I was given a notice to vacate. I asked them if they had another tenant, and they said no. As of this writing, I still don't think a tenant has moved in. Some dumbass decided to be the smart guy and kick me out and lose all that rent for all those years. Just because you have an MBA doesn't mean you are smart.

On one hand, I was relieved. It was like running in place all day and going nowhere. I felt like a hamster on a wheel. But I loved the finished product.

I had to give the bad news to all my investors, and it was humiliating. Failure is. As I took the museum apart, it was with a heavy heart. What kept coming back to me was that this failure had taught me so much. If I didn't learn from it, then I was a hypocrite. Don't forget, I'm the one who says, "Failure is your friend."

Back to the Launching Pad

I then started thinking, do I build this again in a tourist town? My wife, who is fairly conservative with money, was enthusiastic about me doing so. So I called all my investors, told them what I was thinking about doing, and gave all of them the opportunity to invest if they wanted to. I informed them that I was looking at new sites and would be back to them shortly.

Subsequently, I found a killer location in Pigeon Forge, Tennessee, gateway to the Great Smoky Mountains. I already had my WonderWorks there and it was kicking ass. The site that I found was adjacent to a very successful venue called The Island. There was plenty of parking and plenty of people. The best part was, I could build the building and theme it the way I wanted, unlike D.C.

Next, I went to all of the investors, showed them the new location, showed them the rendering for the new building, and offered them to invest once again at the same level as before. Only two people took me up on my offer. Failure has a stench to it, and that stench was all over me.

I told my wife that the investors were not interested in taking a second ride with me. To her credit she said, "Then we need to do it ourselves." And she meant all of it. That was a lot of money for us, but it also met the litmus test. If we lost all of it, it would not disrupt our lifestyle.

In earnest, I began building what I called Alcatraz East. I built it like an old prison in the 1800s. You can Google it on your phone to see what it looks like and some of the exhibits inside.

Mission Accomplished

It was not just a great success, it was an incredible success. I got great tax deductions because it's an attraction. My location was a 10. Parking was unlimited. And there were millions of people passing by yearly.

It has become the most profitable attraction in my inventory. The failure and lessons in D.C. turned out to be gold in Pigeon Forge. I must admit that saying, "Failure is your friend," is easy. It's much harder to actually use failure as your friend and go forward. Many times in the process, I had real doubts about what I was doing, with that failure always in the back of my mind.

At the end of the day, my wife's belief in our project and her belief in my vision proved to be invaluable and lucrative. I feel bad that the old investors did not come along with me, but I do understand. I now have enough artifacts to build my second location, which I'm scouting for now.

Going Forward After Failure

My story of failure is one I hope you can learn from. We can all talk theoretically about failure being our friend, but to actually go forward after a failure, and use those experiences, is a whole other kettle of fish. It's different because you can still feel the pain and humiliation of failure. I give my wife credit for pushing me forward. I do not believe I would have done it without her. Especially when she said we would invest all of our own money.

Now I have three great venues in Pigeon Forge: Downtown Flavortown, Alcatraz East, and WonderWorks. If you ever find yourself in the Smoky Mountains, I invite you to visit all three. I promise you the time of your life. And if you don't like it, I'll give you your money back!

CHAPTER 39

DREAMS

I don't know about you, but I've always been fascinated with dreams. Over the years, I have read many parts of the Bible many times. I have never read the Bible from start to finish, but I've read a bunch of it. One of the things I've always wondered in reading the New Testament and Old Testament is whether some of those visions I read about were dreams.

I once had a dream that I was deep in a spring on a very hot day. It was sweltering out, but when I went into the spring and down below, it felt like 65 degrees. Sitting on a rock was Jesus Christ. I sat there and talked to him for hours. When I woke up, I was sorry that I had awoken. That dream was many years ago. However, many times when I'm going to sleep and saying my nightly prayers, I go back to that dream and that same spot. It was so soothing and comforting to me. While I have had many dreams over the years, that is the one that remained with me.

When I was a little boy, I used to have the greatest dream ever. I could fly. And when I flew, all I had to do was scissor my legs and I would go higher and higher. Sometimes I was only 10 feet above people, and they saw me flying. Every time I woke up from those dreams, I was sorry I had. It has been years since I've had a dream about flying.

I know there have been many studies on dreams. They are fascinating to say the least. The question is, do they mean anything, and if not, how and why do they occur?

As I got older, I had other dreams that weren't as fun. One recurring dream goes like this: I'm a lawyer, but I have just discovered that I was actually nine credits short of graduating. But I'm thirty years post-law school. In my dream, I enroll back at the University of Florida to take some classes. I don't mention that I didn't have enough credits, because I'm afraid that they would take my law license away.

In this dream, my law firm is still up and going, but I am surreptitiously in Gainesville going to law school. In all these dreams, the same thing happens. I don't go to class, and I don't study. The week of exams comes, and I am totally unprepared. I don't even know where the classrooms are because I've been too busy having fun while back in college. On the day of the exam, sometimes I find out where the classroom is and sometimes I don't. When I find out where the classroom is, I have no idea what the answers are to the test, and in many of my dreams, I simply give up on finding the test classroom. In every one of these dreams, I make the decision to move back to Orlando and to pretend it never happened and that, hopefully, it is not discovered that I graduated without enough credit hours.

The second recurring dream I have is somewhat similar. I have been successful, but somehow, I've lost it all. I've gone broke. I'm driving around in a twelve-year-old Mercedes that's on its last legs. Every time I wake up from this dream, it is the greatest relief you can imagine.

Common Dreams

I am confident that these dreams emanate from other parts of my life, as well as my insecurities. One dream I used to have is that I was riding on a unicycle ten stories high in downtown New York City. And I was good on it. But in my dream, I didn't know how to get off. Sometimes in that dream I would stop and rest against the building, but I still had no clue how to disembark. There was no net, no landing spot, no safe exit. Luckily, all of my exits occurred when I woke up from my dream, panting in fear. There are many common dreams, and the interpretation is open for debate.

1. You are back in school, taking the test. This is a very common dream, much like my law-school dream. We have all probably had this dream, and for many of us, we were unprepared for our test.

2. You're hanging out with a celebrity—any celebrity. I had a dream once that I was in a house with Brad Pitt shooting the breeze and he was the most fantastic guy in the world. Every time I see Brad Pitt I think about that dream.

3. You are running late to something important. It could mean anything.

4. You are pregnant. Hopefully only women have this dream—but in this new world, who knows?

5. You are standing on a cliff, and suddenly you are falling into nothingness. Being out there in the real world with no real net could be the cause for this. Unfortunately for people with this dream, they do not have the flying powers that I had as a young boy.

6. You are naked in public. These dreams are often accompanied by feelings of embarrassment and shame. They can also be related to feelings of vulnerability and exposure. But if you're in the nude and feel no shame, it could be the total opposite Perhaps this person wants to be seen, acknowledged, admired.

   Just a funny aside for one moment. Twice in his life, my brother, Thad, a dentist in Lake Mary, has woken up nude in two separate hotel lobbies on two separate occasions. Evidently, Thad sleepwalks. As I have told him, it would only happen to me one time. I would stop sleeping nude while in hotels.

7. You have lost your voice, and you are unable to call or shout out for help. Many experts feel that this may not just be a dream but may be the result of sleep paralysis. During REM (rapid eye movement) sleep, the sleep cycle during which we dream, our bodies experience REM atonia, a natural paralysis during the REM cycle.

8. Your teeth are suddenly falling out. This is a dream I have had, and my bet is you have had as well. All of a sudden, I have a handful of teeth and nowhere to put them. Again, mercifully waking up is wonderful.

9. You are being chased. It all depends on who is doing the chasing. Often people are being chased by a monster. The monster may be a manifestation of an indiscretion, an addiction, or a debt, explains experts. If you have the unfortunate dream, or nightmare, of being chased by someone you know, it could differ. Your associations about the person chasing you are often more insightful than focusing on the actual person chasing you, the experts say.

10. You are in a position of power—a CEO, president, queen, or religious figure. The experts believe that the dream turns the unpowerful dreamer in the dream world into the opposite. What looks like grandiosity is actually compensatory. The dream compensates, or covers up, for the feelings of being powerless.

There are many types of dreams, but usually for most of us, it is one of the old standbys. By the way, the people interpreting these dreams seem to have as much knowledge about it as I do. It has to be pure supposition. But it is fun to try and figure out what those dreams may be.

My Dream: Turn Financial Insecurity into Dignity for Others

The funny thing about dreams is that in our real world, we all have dreams. Dreams come in all shapes and sizes. There is something all of us have wanted to do, or to be, at one time or another. For me, my life was defined by financial insecurity. Not having money was a huge issue for me. Being powerless and helpless is the worst feeling of all.

As I've looked back at my life, I don't feel sorry for myself at all. Of course, it seems bad now looking back objectively, but when I was living it, it didn't seem as bad. The reason I don't ever feel sorry for myself or make excuses for myself is because so many people had it so much worse. It is estimated that 25 percent of all girls are sexually molested. No telling how many boys. That alone beats any problems I ever had. So for the people who talk about walking to school with no shoes in the snow, my message is give it a rest. There are some people out there who've had some really difficult days. Way worse than yours and mine.

In December of 2024, *Forbes* magazine, which names billionaires throughout the world, had me on their cover and a huge article. You can read the article itself when you Google "John Morgan net worth." As I write this book, *Forbes* has me ranked 2,104 in the world. It also includes what my family may have. My wife and I have been very careful in making sure that our estate planning was done early and judiciously. The one thing I do not want to do is to leave one penny to the IRS. I want all my pennies to go to my foundation for food, water, clothing, shelter, and medicine — to give dignity to others.

I will tell you that seeing your face on the cover of *Forbes* is jarring and surreal. I think you are a billionaire when you have a billion liquid in stocks, bonds, and cash. The fellow who started Patagonia was making $100 million a year, and *Forbes* said he was a billionaire. His answer resonated with me which was, "I'm not a billionaire until I have a billion in the bank."

Kanye West was a billionaire for like three months, and then he wasn't. Who knows if the Kardashians are billionaires or not. Many of these billionaires are only billionaires because the magazines have extrapolated their income last year and given it a ten-times multiple, making them billionaires. I was just recently looking at Trump's new cabinet and the so-called billionaires. I call bullshit on most of those billionaires. Most of them don't even have $100 million liquid.

Catastrophic Thinking

Now for my confession. Even though I have exceeded my wildest dreams, and even though I probably have generational wealth now, I feel more insecure today than I did when I was climbing. I don't even know if I am as happy today as I was when I was climbing the mountain. Once you get to the top of the mountain, whatever that mountain may be, there is nothing else to do except climb down, or live on the top of the mountain.

As life has gone on and as I have acquired more wealth, property, and things, I have become far more worried than you might expect. In fact, I remain downright panicked about losing it all. And the more success I have had, the more that panic has set in. I believe at any moment the curtain is going to be pulled back and everyone will see that I was a fraud.

It's like I'm living one of my dreams. I have really delved into this worry of mine, and through my research, I have found out what I am experiencing. It is called *catastrophic thinking*, and I am fucking eaten up with it. I believe that this catastrophic thinking was the genesis for my book, because I truly believe that the reason I am where I am is 99 percent luck. Some people say that you could strip them naked and put them in New York City with no money and they would be a millionaire in a year. I don't necessarily feel that way.

Catastrophic thinking, also known as *catastrophizing*, is a cognitive distortion where people exaggerate the potential negative consequences of events or situations. They tend to focus on the worst possible outcomes, even if they are unlikely to occur. Does this resonate with you? There are many characteristics of catastrophic thinking:

1. Exaggerating the severity of threats or problems

2. Assuming the worst-case scenario will happen

3. Focusing on negative possibilities, ignoring positive ones

4. Feeling overwhelmed and helpless

5. Difficulty seeing alternative perspectives

Catastrophic thinking can be caused by many different factors:

1. Anxiety disorders, like a panic disorder

2. Depression

3. Trauma

4. Stressful life events

5. Learned patterns of thinking

I know that my wife gets tired of my catastrophic thinking because she is just the opposite. She walks around as if she doesn't have a care in the world. Meanwhile, she is married to Chicken Little. I know that this is not healthy, and I know that I have enough money to live like a sheikh just on the interest, but it doesn't change the anxiety I feel.

When I further investigated how all of this was impacting me, I found another syndrome that applied to me as well. At the beginning of my life, I felt like I could do anything. As I have gotten more successful over the years, I have started to doubt myself in ways I never thought possible. For example, I have an ongoing fear that all of this is a dream and I'm going to wake up and it never happened. I have become less secure with more success.

Imposter Syndrome

Imposter syndrome, also known as imposter phenomenon, is a behavioral-health experience where individuals doubt their skills, intellect, or accomplishments. It can manifest as a constant inner criticism, or panic-like response to stress. People with imposter syndrome may feel like frauds or failures when they can't answer a question. They may also experience anxiety, depression, and fear of being exposed as a fraud.

They are also more likely to experience low self-esteem, somatic symptoms, and social dysfunctions. Now when people meet me, they would never in a million years think I was a catastrophic thinker, or that I had impostor syndrome. I have been bluffing most of my life.

Life Is Truly Luck

When people say to me, "Did you see all of this happening when you were a young man?" my answer is very simple: "FUCK NO." Not in a million years did I see this happening. And the truth of the matter is, I firmly believe that if I started all over again, it would not happen. I further believe that if I started all over again a thousand times, it would never happen. There are 8.5 billion people in the world, and *Forbes* magazine has me and my family as one of the 2,500 wealthiest families. No way it happens again. I'm not sure how it happened in the first place.

All I do know is that it has happened, and there are black swans that seem to follow me everywhere. I am almost sorry I read the book *The Black Swan*, because I have been obsessed with it ever since.

The one thing that I have been convinced of through it all is that life IS truly luck.

Albert Einstein once said, "Everything that exists in your life, does so because of two things: something you did, or something you didn't do." The problem with my success is I really don't know what I did, and I really don't know what I didn't do. The only thing I know for sure is that I was built to work. I love to work, and I love being paid for my work. Other than that, I have no idea.

CHAPTER 40

A PURPOSE-DRIVEN LIFE

During my life, I have spent lots of time watching ants and bees work. It is an amazing spectacle to behold. These insects work all day at a feverish pitch. Doing what exactly and why? I am not completely sure.

I know the ants work at the pleasure of the queen. They are in a nonstop marching and working mode. Bees are feverishly making honey and storing it in the honeycomb. Why the ants and bees are drawn to this work is baffling to me, but it's very interesting to watch.

When I have watched the ants and bees, I often wonder if there were someone watching humans the way I watch bees and ants, what would they think? What would they believe that our purpose on Earth was for?

Therein lies the great question: what is the purpose of our life? Many people give the rote answer, "To love and serve others." Of course, that is a noble thought, but far too often, that is not what happens with humans.

In almost every civilization, there has been one form of God or another. Even today, many religions have many different versions of who and what God is. Mormons are very secretive about their religion. As I understand it, the end comes when all of them are gathered once again, in their human body, and located on a top-secret planet in the universe. The religion was founded in the late 1800s by Joseph Smith, who was also big on the idea of polygamy and with much younger women. Buddhists believe in reincarnation and that we are all on a journey to hopefully keep getting better and better in each stage of our new lives. Islam and Judaism have many of the same tenets of Christianity. They all look good on paper.

However, it seems like from the beginning of time, most wars have been about whose God is the correct God and, of course, most communist leaders don't even believe in God.

There was a time in my life when I believed in God just as much as I believed in Santa Claus and the Easter Bunny. I will confess, it was a wonderful and hopeful feeling. As a little boy, I often wondered and worried about who from my family might make it to heaven and how could I be happy in heaven if one of my family members was not there. It was a thought that drove me to distraction.

As time went on, I figured out that Santa Claus, the Easter Bunny, and the Tooth Fairy were all made up. As I got older and presumably smarter, I began to have doubts about the existence of God. And that was a terrible feeling that brought with it much dread. I was raised Catholic and was all in, all the way. The pedophile abuse in the Catholic Church was really bad for me and my religion. I would go to Mass and wonder if the priest was a good guy or bad guy. Women were not allowed to be priests, which also rubbed me the wrong way, just as them not being married was an issue for me.

During my children's childhood and through their college years, I could never remember a Sunday that we didn't go to Mass, even on vacation. I read once where children look to church attendance by their father as a bellwether for whether they would go to church every Sunday. I wanted to set that example.

Over time though, doubts and questions crept in. It seemed to me that unscrupulous men and women, primarily men, were making the church what they wanted it to be and not what God intended it to be. Much of what I was witnessing in the past and present seemed to be a lie made up by mostly men for their own sexual and financial pleasures. It has all taken a real toll on my faith. I am not discouraged. At the end of Mother Teresa's life, it was reported that she had real doubts herself. I didn't feel alone.

There are a few things I know for certain that give me hope. Every night and every morning, I pray to God, ask for forgiveness, and ask for certain things for certain people. In my greatest times of need, I really pray hard. They say that there are no atheists in a foxhole. I see why.

I tell myself, the fact that I speak to God so frequently means I must believe in Him. I look at my faith on a scale of 1 to 10 — 10 being an absolute dead-solid perfect and 1 being when I die, I go to sleep forever and don't even dream. Lights out. Total darkness. For me on this day, I give myself a 7. I wish I were a 10, but I must be honest — I have serious doubts. Yet, from time to time, there are breakthroughs in my life and in my spiritual life where I feel myself climbing toward 10. In my own life, I have had several instances where I believe that God heard my prayers and answered my prayers. The results were so spectacular that the events seemed miraculous. I have had days in my life where I was also a 0.

The way that I have come to grips with all of this is that it is okay to have doubts. Judas betrayed Christ for silver. Peter denied him after living with him for years. And even after the resurrection, Thomas insisted on seeing the wounds from his tormentors and placing his hand inside them. And these were the guys who knew him best.

So, for me, here is how it goes. First, I live my life exactly as if there is a God. I'm not taking any chances with eternity. Of course, in my life, I have sinned and repented. Even though it is promised that God forgives us, sometimes I have had trouble forgiving myself.

The next thing I do, on a daily basis, is read scriptures and pray like crazy for faith. I pray that the Holy Spirit will enter my heart and soul and move me closer to full belief.

And finally, I try my best to live my life the way my scriptures, Christianity, instruct me to. Serving and helping others has a lot to offer and is restorative to our mental health.

When I see human suffering and terrible things happening, my heart hurts and I am overcome with emotion, compassion, and empathy.

I thank God all the time for making me this way. But the daily struggle of faith is real.

I read a book once titled *The Purpose Driven Life*. I was knocked out by the book, because most of my life I have asked myself, "What is my purpose here, and what is our purpose here?" I was so taken with the book that I funded an event for the author at the Orlando Magic's arena. A friend of mine by the name of Daryl Carter had asked me if I would help. What I was so taken with was the number of people that filled that arena. All of these people were looking for purpose too.

When I was a young lawyer, my mentor and boss, Jerry Billings, was the chairman of the mayor's prayer breakfast in Orlando. By happenstance, Billy Graham was conducting his crusade in Orlando that week, and Jerry lined him up as the guest speaker. I got to have breakfast with Reverend Graham, and it was a high point in my life. Even though I am Catholic, I decided to go to his crusade in Orlando. He filled the stadium night after night. What struck me then and strikes me now is that many people were in my same boat. They were looking to strengthen their faith and looking for a purpose in life. Religion and faith are the things that give our lives purpose. I was taught at Christ the King in Lexington, Kentucky, that we humans were the only animals or living organisms that had a soul, and that only we are eligible for Heaven or Hell. That upset me a great deal because I have always loved dogs more than people. I really can't imagine heaven without dogs.

We are all looking for a purpose-driven life. Because life can be boring, many people try to fill it with golfing, hunting, fishing, and a wide variety of hobbies. When we are raising our children, our life has lots of purpose. As the baby birds leave the nest, that purpose becomes harder and harder to find.

During my lifetime I have tried my best to be a good person. At work, I have gone out of my way for my employees and their families. Yet, many times when they finally say goodbye to me, I discover that they were never really fond of me in the first place. I was just a means to an end. I had a woman who became my bookkeeper when my firm was very small. She was dumb as a rock, but our business was not complex.

She had a high school education from West Virginia. During her time with me, I can't even count the money I gave her when she was in a jam. I hired both of her children to work at my businesses, and even their friends. When her sister was denied cancer treatments, I stepped in and made the insurance pay. I was paying her crazy money for her expertise and skill level.

At a certain point in time, the job had really outgrown her, but I didn't want to hurt her. It came at a time where she was having serious back trouble and unable to even come to work. I decided to hire a real CPA, but to keep her on at her exact same salary. When I did this, she resigned. I was shocked and hurt, but secretly relieved. She had been a huge anchor around my ankle.

After she left my firm, I began to hear of her hatred for me. I was shocked and stunned. After all I had done, I thought she would be the last person who would be ungrateful. Not only was she ungrateful, but she bad-mouthed me at every single opportunity. I was stunned.

There have been other moments in my life where people I trusted 100 percent betrayed me and turned on me. I simply didn't understand why and was crushed. Betrayal by someone you have trusted may be the biggest gut punch in the world. To realize that you were nothing more than a means to an end, even though you had real love and affection for them — that type of body blow is hard to shake.

Other times, when I have helped some people out financially, and sometimes in big ways, they kept coming back and asking for more. When I finally said no, it was as if I were saying no for the first time, not the tenth time. Their reaction was telling. I had simply been a means to an end, and they had no gratitude for what I had done.

During the pandemic, all businesses had to make drastic decisions. One of mine was pausing the salaries of some people in my firm who were bringing nothing to the table. I had a lawyer who was older and had come to work for me. He turned out to be a huge blowhard who brought nothing to our table. To make matters worse, he had become a real embarrassment to the firm over his ethics in the public sector, and he was constantly a front-page story. I stood with him because it's what I do.

During the pandemic, when I paused his salary until we got our sea legs back, his wife unfriended me on Facebook. When I noticed this, I knew that he had just been using me all along. It hurt like hell. I had been loyal to him, but he wasn't loyal to me.

And speaking of Facebook, that is where life has truly become a lie. Everyone on Facebook looks great and is having the time of their lives. We see them in all the fun places with all the fun people. Life is a cabaret!

Almost everything on Facebook is a lie, and worse, it ignites real resentment from those who have a tough life. Once, a fellow I know called me looking for a bankruptcy lawyer. He told me his story, and he was flat broke. The next week, I saw him on Facebook — in Las Vegas, in a limousine with champagne, and headed to a concert at Caesars Palace. That was the moment I coined the phrase "Life is a lie." The problem with adopting "life is a lie" is that it's very unhealthy for our mental health as well as our spiritual health. We cannot allow a few ingrates or a few disloyal actors to ruin our karma. Yes, we are tempted to withdraw and go into our own little cave. However, when we do that, we are really just hurting ourselves and our own spiritual journey.

Instead, what I focus on is the people who have been with me from day one. When I look at that, it changes everything about my outlook. Ninety-five percent of my key people in all my businesses have been with me from the beginning. I am extremely proud of that, because I believe it means I must be doing something right. It is also helpful in my perspective going forward. It should be for you as well.

Yes, in many respects, life can be a lie. And when those lies come your way, the hurt and pain is often unbearable. Have you ever been dropped by a boyfriend or a girlfriend, or divorced by your spouse? The pain is inexplicable, especially when you never saw it coming. When you never see it coming, life really does seem like a lie and then you wonder, "What is the purpose of all this?"

If we decide to live as if "life is a lie," then we are really damaging ourselves and our soul. We are taking love out of the equation, which damages our faith. Instead, what we should all try to do is not focus on the ingrates, or those who have betrayed us, but focus on the ones who have made our life and our business worthwhile.

In my law business, I basically had three secretaries or personal assistants throughout my career. Two of them, Laurie Morgan and Anna Mills, retired when they reached that golden age. One of them, Darlene Erickson, is actually helping me with this book. Darlene, Laurie, and Anna were very smart people who probably knew the law better than I did. I cannot imagine having the success I've had without these three women. When I think about luck, I think about Darlene, Laurie, and Anna. I also think about all the lawyers in my firm who have been with me for almost thirty years. And when I think of them, I am exceedingly grateful.

Of course, my right arm all these years has been Judy Diaz. She was very young when she began, and I have watched her two sons become fine men. Judy does everything. She knows how I think and can handle most anything. Many times I tell her, "just be me… do what I would do." Having her all these years has made me more productive than I could have ever been. To describe her value would be impossible because it is so far-reaching. Every lucky business person needs a Judy… it frees up so much time. She is 24/7… even when boating with her family on weekends.

The same is true for my attraction businesses. Janine Vaccarella has been with me from day one and is like a sister. My EBITDA is $33 million with no debt. Had I not had Janine and the many great managers in all of my locations, there is no way that I'd have success in that sector.

I have been so lucky that all of these people fell into my lap. There is no question that luck had a huge impact on my success. There were times, however, where I had real cancers in my organization who were not only bad for the organization, but were actually actively trying to undermine my businesses. The real quick answer for this problem is when you know you have a cancer (and believe me you will know it when you see it), you must excise the cancer quickly. If you don't, your luck will disappear and bad luck will fill your organization.

Don't let the ingrates and those who disappoint you ruin you. If you let them and they stop you from being the person you should be, you most certainly will be ruined, and your spiritual journey shortened.

As I have aged, I've noticed that life is moving at warp speed. It seems like yesterday that I was on my Schwinn bicycle delivering my papers in Lexington and today I'm knocking on the door of seventy years old. I ask myself, "How the fuck did that happen?" But it does and it did.

When Billy Graham was on his deathbed, he was asked a question: "What has surprised you most about this life?" His answer was profound: "The brevity of it all."

It seems like every week, I lose somebody. I dread reading the obituaries. At night when I pray, I think about all these lost friends and colleagues, and I realize that my life will one day end soon too. Death is undefeated. While there are pitfalls in this long journey of life, there is also great joy. We cannot allow life to be a lie. If we do, we are destroyed.

No, the answer is that life is love. The purpose of our lives is to love one another because I believe, if there is a God, that he resides in each and every one of us. When we love and serve each other is when we can find joy and purpose in life. Life is not a lie. Life is love. And love will give you a purpose-driven life.

CHAPTER 41

ANSWER THE BELL

I previously wrote about the book *The Black Swan* by Nassim Nicholas Taleb. Reading it transformed my life. My wife believes that book was the beginning of my catastrophic thinking—*only the paranoid survive.* After finishing it, I tried to divine the meaning. It seemed simple: "Be prepared." So today I have my black-swan strategies in place for all of my businesses. I have levers to pull in case of emergencies and even more levers to pull in case the first one doesn't work.

So now that we're at the end, I want to give you the meaning of it all.

The Value of Work

I know that all of us chafe at the thought of telling ourselves that we were lucky in life. Especially if we were very successful. The more successful a person becomes, it has been my experience, the harder they believe they worked. While I believe that they worked very, very hard, there were lucky parts of their life that allowed them to be a worker.

It does not take away from our work. The work was real. When I think about those days on that paper route, I know for a fact I was working hard every day. When I think of my schoolwork in college and law school, the work was very hard, and there was lots of it. When I look at my businesses, I think of all the mornings I rolled out of a warm bed, next to a beautiful woman, and showered and headed to the airport early in the morning to travel to cold cities and stay in strange hotels. That was hard work. The risks I have taken along the way have been bold. I am a risk-taker by nature. We have all worked hard, but we were all lucky in our march. I have met many very rich people. My takeaway is that most of them are not smart. In fact, most of them are dumb, except for the computer crowd. But luck and karma shined on them all.

Bad Luck Can Lead to Good

When I distill this book to the granular level, it is simple. Life begins with unbelievable luck. Us just being here is almost impossible. And through life, different turns and twists will determine our fate just as much as our own efforts. Decisions, good and bad, will make us geniuses or failures.

So in order to find luck, you must be looking for luck. When you stop looking for opportunities, you will never find another opportunity. It is also possible that bad luck can turn into good luck. The girl who broke up with me on my birthday did me the favor of my life. She was a train wreck, and my wife is the greatest.

Bad luck can lead to good luck.

The day my family left Lexington, I cried all the way to Florida. That was the worst luck in my life up to that point. Looking back now, it was the best luck I ever had. While I may have done well in Kentucky, I can't imagine doing as well as I did in Florida. As we go through life looking for opportunities, we have to understand that life has the same type of book that we have in casinos. There are moves and measures we can make to enhance our luck, to increase our luck. And once we have luck, the question is do we double down and triple down to get a better return on luck? That all depends on your risk tolerance and boldness.

If you have been successful in your life, please don't be offended when I say that you are lucky. It is not an insult; it is just a fact of life. Failure to see that makes you a delusional person.

As I have looked back on my life, there is one thing I know. I was not academically a smart person, but I was smart enough to know that I wasn't smart, and I was smart enough to go find people who were smarter than me. My greatest luck was knowing my limitations and realizing when I needed help. And, boy, have I needed help throughout the way. I can think of so many people that had they not been in my life, I wouldn't have the same life I have now. There have been so many close calls along the way that could have undone me. But miraculously, those close calls never came to pass. Those moments also added to my catastrophic thinking.

I hope you take this book as it was meant—as a guide to enhance and improve your luck in life. It was meant to make you better and to make you grateful. It was meant to be a gut check for all of us.

Today, people will wake up in America and it will be their last day on this earth. And they will never see it coming. But in life, we need to be prepared. Being prepared enhances our luck. Being prepared for life after will also prepare us for everlasting life.

Answering the Bell

The greatest fight in the history of boxing was the "Thrilla in Manila" in 1975—Muhammed Ali versus Joe Frazier. This was the rubber match. At the end of the fourteenth round, Ali could not stand up. He told his trainer, Angelo Dundee, to cut his gloves off. In the other corner, Frazier's eye was swollen shut and he couldn't see his trainer Eddie Futch's hand. Futch told Frazier he was going to throw in the towel because he didn't want him to be hurt. Frazier told him, "You better not."

As the bell rang for the fifteenth round, you see Ali's corner pushing him to stand up. Across the ring, Futch saw Ali stand, and threw in the towel. The fight was over. Ali was the greatest.

Then a funny thing happened that is instructive. Ali takes one step and collapses on the mat. There was no way he could have finished that fight. There is no way he could have lasted three seconds. However, had

Frazier simply been allowed to walk to the center ring, he would be the greatest of all time. Instead, Ali is the greatest.

When you ask yourself, "Why?" the answer is simple. Ali answered the bell. To enhance your luck and improve your life, it's important that when things get tough, and things get hard, and you don't think you can walk on or move on, simply answer the bell. The competition on the other side doesn't know you're out of gas, and has no clue how that fight might end. Simply answering the bell will enhance your luck.

Love and Service

In life, I have been surprised at all of our pursuits of peace and material things. I now know that material things don't bring peace. Money does not bring happiness. The happiest I was in my life was when my children were small, and we had no money, and I was climbing the ladder. As I was climbing the ladder, even though I was broke, I bought my grandmother a condominium because she had never owned a home. I bought my brother, Tim, a home, even though money was tight. My wife was very supportive in me helping my family when we didn't have money ourselves. But those days, when the struggle was real and the money was tight, were my best days. I cannot describe in words the peace and happiness I got from helping my brother and grandmother.

As life has gone on, the more money I have made has not moved the needle as far as happiness. Or peace. At the end of the day, we all think we are striving for material things and riches. But that is not what makes us happy in the end. What makes us at peace at the end is love and service to each other.

So I will close my book with a poem from Mother Teresa. It is called "A Simple Path."

The fruit of silence is prayer.

The fruit of prayer is faith.

The fruit of faith is love.

The fruit of love is service.

And the fruit of service is peace.

It is important to remember this prayer and to connect faith, love, and service. When you connect those dots, you will have a peace that you have never enjoyed in your life. The peace of doing something for each other is the greatest peace. I believe this because I believe that God lives in all of us. I believe that service to each other is service to God. Service brings the Holy Spirit into your heart and soul and gives you the peace that so eludes us.

I hope you have enjoyed this book. I wish you and your family, and your business associates, the greatest life, but most importantly, God's ever-loving peace and love.

Life is luck—but more importantly, life is love!

EPILOGUE

It seems like just yesterday I was riding my Schwinn Typhoon bicycle on my paper route. I think I could still remember my customers. When I go back to Lexington, Kentucky, I often walk that route and remember. I'm sure my fellow paper boys have the same fond memories.

Upon that bike is where I dreamed and pretended to be all sorts of people. It's where my imagination allowed me to start dreaming—it's all I did. Here, all these years later, it's hard to believe the life I have led is mine.

I've welcomed sitting presidents to my home, along with dozens of U.S. senators. I've met two popes and traveled the world. I've attended parties with some of the most famous people in the world and even got to hang out with the Dali Lama. The one person who was nicest to me was Paul McCartney, at two parties at the White House.

I live in Maui, Hawaii in the winter and there I met one of the most interesting people in the world: Shep Gordon. The parties at his home are legendary. You never know who you will meet. At some of his New Year's parties I was introduced to Alice Cooper, Adam Sandler, Mick Fleetwood, Richie Sambora, Mike Myers, Owen Wilson, Sammy Hagar, Steven Tyler, and the list goes on. The book and documentary about Shep is called *Supermensch*. I highly recommend it. Shep's first guest at his first New Year's party was George Harrison.

When Shep first left college and came to LA, he made a wrong turn and mistakenly ended up at the Landmark Hotel. He heard a woman in distress by the pool and went to help her. She was not in distress but having sex. Her name was Janis Joplin and they became fast friends. The next morning, she introduced him to Jimi Hendrix who told him he should manage bands. Other soon-to-be famous musicians were also there. Shep met Alice Cooper, whose career had not taken off yet. He became his manager and to this day is still without a contract. Alice lives here on Maui.

That meeting at that hotel launched one of the most successful careers in music and film. Shep also invented the "celebrity chef." What I most admire is that he lived with Sharon Stone for five years. I call Shep the Maui Lama. Every important person stops off at Shep's and he cooks the greatest Chinese food.

The moral of Shep's story is the moral of many stories. Sometimes the wrong turn is the right turn after all.

Mahalo for reading my book. If you're ever in Maui, come by for a joint or some tequila. Until then… aloha. And remember:
LIFE IS LUCK

John Morgan
"for the people"

FAMOUS FORMER PAPERBOYS AND PAPERGIRLS

From the 1950s through the 1970s, the paperboy was a fixture of American neighborhood life—an institution coinciding with the post-war economic boom. Parents encouraged their children to take on delivery routes, viewing it as an opportunity to develop responsibility, time management, financial literacy, and a sense of community.

The paper route was not merely a job. For a staggering number of history's most consequential figures—presidents, Nobel laureates, astronauts, inventors, entertainers, and titans of industry—it was where greatness began.

Legends of History

BENJAMIN FRANKLIN

Statesman, inventor, and Founding Father

The proto-paperboy. Franklin helped deliver his brother James's *New England Courant* in 1721—over a century before the profession even had a name. He went on to help found a nation, invent bifocals and the lightning rod, negotiate the Treaty of Paris, and author the Declaration of Independence. He is sometimes called "America's first newsboy."

THOMAS EDISON
Inventor

Worked as a newsboy hawking papers on trains before accumulating over 1,000 patents. He invented the phonograph, the practical electric lightbulb, and the motion picture camera—essentially lighting, recording, and filming the modern world.

MARK TWAIN
Author

Delivered newspapers before becoming one of the most towering literary voices in American history. *The Adventures of Huckleberry Finn* is still widely regarded as the great American novel, and his wit remains as sharp as ever more than a century later.

MARTIN LUTHER KING JR.
Civil rights leader and Nobel Peace Prize winner

King earned spending money as a paperboy for *The Atlanta Journal-Constitution*. He landed the gig with help from his father and frequently used his newspaper funds to purchase books. At 13, he became the youngest person to assistant manage one of the paper's delivery stations. He became the defining moral voice of the twentieth century.

DWIGHT D. EISENHOWER
34th U.S. President and Supreme Allied Commander

Delivered papers before commanding the largest military operation in history (D-Day) and serving two terms as president. He oversaw the creation of the interstate highway system and issued his famous warning about the military-industrial complex.

HARRY S. TRUMAN
33rd U.S. President

Former newsboy who authorized the end of WWII, launched the Marshall Plan to rebuild Europe, integrated the U.S. armed forces by executive order, and shepherded the founding of the United Nations — all within a single presidency.

HERBERT HOOVER
31st U.S. President and humanitarian

Began as a paperboy, became a self-made millionaire mining engineer, fed millions of starving Europeans after WWI through extraordinary logistics and fundraising, and then served the nation as president.

WARREN BUFFETT
Investor and philanthropist

As a teenager in Washington D.C., Buffett delivered newspapers for the *Washington Post*, earning $175 a month — more than his teachers at the time. He used the savings to invest in himself and further his career. He became one of the wealthiest people in history and has pledged the vast majority of his fortune to charity.

WALT DISNEY
Entertainment mogul and visionary

Disney's father owned a newspaper distributorship in Kansas City, and Walt delivered the paper — even secretly selling extra copies on street corners for pocket money his father didn't know about. He went on to create Mickey Mouse, Disneyland, and a global entertainment empire that continues to shape culture worldwide.

RALPH BUNCHE
Diplomat and Nobel Peace Prize winner

Former newsboy who became the first African American to win the Nobel Peace Prize, awarded in 1950 for his mediation of the Arab-Israeli armistice of 1949. He later served as an under-secretary-general of the United Nations.

JOE BIDEN
46th U.S. President

Biden used his paper route to hone his people skills and combat his childhood stutter. He learned to anticipate conversations with customers, rehearsing what to say before each stop. He later served as U.S. senator for thirty-six years, vice president, and ultimately the 46th president.

RONALD REAGAN
40th U.S. President

Delivered papers in Dixon, Illinois before becoming a radio broadcaster, Hollywood actor, governor of California, and then president. He presided over the end of the Cold War and the fall of the Berlin Wall.

SAM RAYBURN
Speaker of the U.S. House of Representatives

Former newsboy who rose to serve as speaker of the house for a record seventeen years — longer than any person in American history — making him one of the most powerful legislative figures the country has ever seen.

WALTER REUTHER
Labor leader

Former newsboy who rose to lead the United Auto Workers for over two decades, becoming the most powerful labor leader in U.S. history. He was a prominent figure in the civil rights movement and a close ally of Martin Luther King Jr.

DAVID SARNOFF
Founder of RCA and pioneer of NBC

Started as a street newsboy and built RCA from the ground up, essentially inventing commercial broadcasting in America by creating NBC. He is one of the most consequential figures in the history of media and communications.

BRUCE BARTON
Advertising pioneer and congressman

Former newsboy who cofounded BBDO—one of the world's most powerful advertising agencies—and served as a U.S. congressman. His 1925 book *The Man Nobody Knows* was a number one bestseller and helped redefine modern marketing.

T. BOONE PICKENS
Energy billionaire

Pickens started his career at age 12 delivering newspapers before building BP Capital Management into a multi-billion-dollar energy empire. He became one of the most aggressive corporate raiders in American business history and later championed alternative energy.

CARDINAL FRANCIS SPELLMAN
Archbishop of New York

Former newsboy who became one of the most politically powerful Catholic leaders in American history, serving as military vicar during WWII and personally advising multiple U.S. presidents.

DR. NORMAN VINCENT PEALE
Minister and author

Delivered papers before writing *The Power of Positive Thinking*, which sold over five million copies and influenced generations of leaders. His ideas on optimism and self-belief continue to resonate in business, religion, and self-help culture.

CARL SANDBURG

Poet and Pulitzer Prize winner

Sandburg is honored in the Newspaper Carrier Hall of Fame. He won three Pulitzer Prizes—two for poetry and one for his monumental multi-volume biography of Abraham Lincoln—and became the defining poetic voice of working-class America.

JAMES MICHENER

Author and Pulitzer Prize winner

An enthusiastic paperboy from seventh through twelfth grade, working five different routes across Doylestown, Pennsylvania. He wrote in 1992: "My paper routes gave me an insight into the complexity of life in a small town that not many boys acquired." His books sold over seventy-five million copies worldwide.

ISAAC ASIMOV

Science fiction author

Former paperboy who authored over 500 books and virtually defined modern science fiction. Works like the Foundation series and *I, Robot* transformed the genre and influenced generations of scientists, engineers, and storytellers.

JOHN STEINBECK

Author and Nobel Prize in Literature

Delivered papers before writing *The Grapes of Wrath* and *Of Mice and Men*, winning both the Pulitzer Prize and the Nobel Prize in Literature. His unflinching portraits of working-class America remain essential reading.

STEPHEN KING
Author

Delivered papers before becoming the best-selling horror author of all time, with over three hundred fifty million books sold and dozens of his works adapted into major films and television series.

Entertainment Icons

BOB HOPE
Comedian, entertainer, and USO legend

Long before he became synonymous with Hollywood road comedies, Leslie Townes "Bob" Hope was helping support his family as a Cleveland paperboy. He entertained U.S. troops for over fifty years across every major conflict from WWII through the Gulf War—one of the most sustained acts of patriotic service in entertainment history.

BING CROSBY
Singer and actor

Worked a paper route before becoming one of the best-selling musical artists of the 20th century and a massive Hollywood star. His recording of *White Christmas* remains the best-selling physical single in history.

JOHN WAYNE
Actor

Honored in the Newspaper Carrier Hall of Fame, Wayne became the defining face of the American Western, received the Presidential Medal of Freedom, and remains one of the most iconic actors in cinema history.

JIMMY DURANTE

Comedian and entertainer

Delivered papers before becoming one of America's most beloved comics, with a career spanning vaudeville, radio, film, and television spanning five decades.

CARY GRANT

Actor

Delivered papers in Bristol, England before emigrating to America and becoming the gold standard of Hollywood sophistication and charm. He received an honorary Academy Award in 1970 for his body of work.

TOM CRUISE

Actor

Tossed papers as a boy before becoming one of the highest-grossing movie stars of all time, with the *Mission: Impossible* and *Top Gun* franchises cementing his status as one of cinema's last true movie stars.

BOB BARKER

Television host

Worked a paper route before hosting *The Price Is Right* for thirty-five years and winning nineteen Daytime Emmy Awards — making him one of the most enduring television personalities in American history.

CHUCK NORRIS

Actor and martial artist

Delivered papers before becoming a world champion martial artist and action film icon. His cultural footprint extends far beyond film — he has become one of the most enduring figures in internet folklore.

JIM CARREY
Actor and comedian

Delivered papers as a boy before his meteoric rise to become one of the highest-paid and most beloved comedic actors of his generation, known for *The Truman Show, Eternal Sunshine of the Spotless Mind,* and *The Mask.*

BILL MURRAY
Actor and comedian

Former paperboy who became one of the most beloved actors and comedians of his generation—a defining figure of *Saturday Night Live* and films like *Ghostbusters, Groundhog Day,* and *Lost in Translation.*

SYLVESTER STALLONE
Actor and filmmaker

Delivered papers before creating the *Rocky* and *Rambo* franchises—two of the most enduring action series in Hollywood history—and earning Academy Award nominations for both acting and writing.

Sports Legends

JACKIE ROBINSON
Baseball legend and civil rights trailblazer

Robinson delivered newspapers to help support his family, also cutting grass and running errands for extra pocket money. He went on to break Major League Baseball's color barrier in 1947—one of the most consequential moments in twentieth-century American history.

JOE DIMAGGIO
Baseball hall of famer

Former newsboy who set the all-time MLB hitting streak record at fifty-six consecutive games—a record that has stood for over eighty years and that many analysts believe may never be broken.

WAYNE GRETZKY
Hockey and "The Great One"

Delivered newspapers in his hometown of Brantford, Ontario. He holds over sixty NHL records, and his assist total alone exceeds the total point count of every other player in the history of the game—earning him the undisputed title "The Great One."

EARL "THE PEARL" MONROE
NBA champion and hall of famer

Monroe built up a profitable paper route with help from his mother, who accompanied him on deliveries. He became one of basketball's most inventive players, winning an NBA championship with the New York Knicks and inspiring a generation of guards.

PETE ROSE
Baseball and All-Time Hits leader

Delivered papers in Cincinnati before amassing 4,256 career hits—more than any player in baseball history. The record will almost certainly never be broken.

ALAN BEAN
Apollo 12 astronaut

Bean delivered papers for the *Fort Worth Star-Telegram* in his early morning rounds, pedaling through dark streets loaded with folded-up newspapers, before becoming the fourth human to walk on the moon during Apollo 12. He later became a celebrated painter of the lunar experience.

CARL SAGAN
Astronomer, author, and broadcaster

Delivered papers before becoming the world's most famous science communicator. His television series *Cosmos* reached over five-hundred million people in sixty countries, and his book *Pale Blue Dot* remains one of the most profound meditations on humanity's place in the universe.

Journalism and Broadcasting

WALTER CRONKITE
CBS News anchor and "The Most Trusted Man in America"

Delivered papers in Houston, Texas before anchoring the *CBS Evening News* for nearly two decades. His on-air announcement of President Kennedy's assassination and his editorial stance against the Vietnam War are among the most pivotal moments in broadcast journalism history.

TOM BROKAW
NBC News anchor

Brokaw won a trip to Minneapolis at age 12 because he sold so many newspaper subscriptions on his route. He anchored *NBC Nightly News* for twenty-two years, won the Presidential Medal of Freedom, and wrote *The Greatest Generation*—one of the bestselling history books of the modern era.

ED MCMAHON
Broadcaster and *The Tonight Show*

Worked a paper route and was formally inducted into the Newspaper Carrier Hall of Fame. Best known as Johnny Carson's sidekick on *The Tonight Show* for thirty years, he was one of the most recognized faces in American television.

MIKE ROWE
Television host and advocate

Delivered papers before hosting *Dirty Jobs* and becoming America's most prominent advocate for skilled trades and vocational education—a cause he continues to champion through the mikeroweWORKS Foundation.

Business Leaders and Entrepreneurs

DAVE THOMAS
Founder of Wendy's

Delivered papers before founding Wendy's in 1969. It grew into the world's third-largest hamburger chain, and Thomas became one of the most recognized faces in fast food advertising history with his warm, folksy commercials.

KATHY IRELAND
Supermodel and business mogul

Ireland became Santa Barbara's first-ever papergirl after writing a pointed letter to the editor demanding equal opportunity. By the time she retired from the route, she had made 120,000 deliveries and was voted district carrier of the year three consecutive years running. She later built a global licensing company valued at $2 billion.

Faith and Moral Leadership

BILLY GRAHAM
Evangelist

Delivered papers in Charlotte, North Carolina before becoming the most widely heard Christian preacher in history. He is estimated to have spoken to over two billion people across his career and personally counseled every U.S. president from Harry Truman to Barack Obama.

The Original

BARNEY FLAHERTY
The first paperboy in America

On September 4, 1833, 10-year-old Barney Flaherty went to *The New York Sun* inquiring about a job. While the publisher had put the ad out looking for men, he was so impressed by the boy's excitement and tenacity that he hired him on the spot. Flaherty became the first recorded paperboy in America — the founding father of an institution that would go on to shape some of the most extraordinary lives in modern history. The rest, as they say, is history.

Additional Confirmed and Widely Reported Paperboys

The following individuals are confirmed or very credibly reported as former paperboys in multiple biographical sources, press accounts, or hall of fame records.

RICHARD NIXON
37th President of the United States

GERALD FORD
38th President of the United States

MATT DAMON
Oscar-winning actor and screenwriter

CONAN O'BRIEN
Late-night legend and *Harvard Lampoon* editor

JONAH HILL
Two-time Oscar-nominated actor and filmmaker

DAN RATHER
CBS News anchor for twenty-four years

MIKE WALLACE
60 Minutes cofounder and correspondent

PAUL HARVEY
Most-listened-to radio commentator in American history

RUSH LIMBAUGH
Most-listened-to radio host in American history

CLARK HOWARD
National consumer finance radio host

JAMES BROWN
"Godfather of Soul" and most-sampled musician in history

The paper route was not merely a job. It was an apprenticeship in life—in discipline, in showing up before dawn, in serving a community one porch at a time. History's record is clear: few early jobs produced more remarkable human beings than this one.

Special thanks to my friend and General Counsel, Brian Kempner.

JOHN MORGAN

John Morgan's multi-billion-dollar legal empire was born from a profound family tragedy. While John was in college, his brother, Tim, was paralyzed in a workplace incident at Walt Disney World. Chewed up by the legal system built to protect corporate giants, the Morgan family faced devastating injustice. In response, John vowed to spend his life leveling the playing field.

In 1988, John and his wife, Ultima, founded Morgan & Morgan. Driven by the singular mission "For The People," John scaled the practice into America's largest injury law firm. Today, the firm employs over 1,100 attorneys and has recovered more than $30 billion for over 700,000 clients, routinely taking on global titans like Google, BP, and Big Pharma.

Beyond the courtroom, John is the author of *You Can't Teach Hungry and You Can't Teach Vision*, which detail his unfiltered philosophy on business, risk, and building a ubiquitous brand. He is also a fierce civic advocate who spearheaded and largely funded successful Florida ballot initiatives to legalize medical marijuana and raise the minimum wage to $15. Alongside Ultima, he directs widespread philanthropic efforts, including the Morgan & Morgan Hunger Relief Center and the Harbor House Domestic Abuse Center.

Representing a community of authors whose books have collectively sold hundreds of millions of copies, the founders of The Gray + Miller Agency launched Maison Vero, a professional publishing house that partners with rising authors to bring their thought leadership to the world. Our representation covers every aspect of thought leadership, including U.S. senators, governors, and ambassadors, billionaire founders and entrepreneurs, researchers, academics, scientists, consultants, practitioners, social influencers, C-suite leaders, adventurers, professional athletes, artists, and creators. We partner with thought leaders and world changers like you who have a story to tell. By bringing decades of professional expertise to our clients, we are charting a new path in a timeless industry that transcends publishing norms, transforming powerful thoughts into impactful books that inspire minds, ignite hearts, and open doors.

Visit maisonvero.com to view our growing list of authors, or to submit a proposal for publication consideration.

Follow Maison Vero for insight and inspiration on social media:

 MaisonVero  MaisonVero  MaisonVeroPublishing

For information about special discounts for bulk purchases, please call (949) 333-4872 or email info@graymilleragency.com.
